AMERICA ON THE VERGE

James Behr

Copyright U.S. Library of Congress • ISBN Number 978-1-365-96023-9

www.AmericaOnTheVerge.org
StarlightArtists@gmail.com

FOREWORD: A HOUSE ON FIRE

"Watch the little things; a small leak will sink a great ship." - Benjamin Franklin

America on the Verge... of what? Renewed greatness or decline? This book's purpose is to ensure the former – to provide a bipartisan plan acceptable to everyone from Liberal to Conservative, for we are a house on fire: toxic politics, federal debt approaching $20 trillion, $500-700 billion in annual trade deficits, government deficits projected above $500 billion for years to come, a shrinking middle class, ominous Chinese influence, the gradual job-killing move towards automation and robotics, record-high warming of the planet, fear that rising ocean levels may swallow cities and states (like Florida and the Carolinas), widespread anger, disturbing political divisiveness, and dishonest "news" services. The painful problems are obvious yet Washington is stuck in bitter conflict, unable to address burning issues gnawing at the heart of the republic. Indeed, *a house on fire.*

I understand what it means to face a fire. In September 2000 I woke up to the living nightmare of my living room aflame in roaring orange spigots of fire grazing the ceiling. Within minutes, fire trucks arrived and the fire was put out. When your home is on fire, firemen, EMS and police quickly come to help. *They are government.* Government does much good. It simply needs to do it *better.* This is often lost upon those who angrily attack government... and each other. It's dangerous. It's divisive. We all need to tone things down. Division can lead to terrible things. We know what happened when division reached epidemic levels in 1860. Chapters ahead address this.

This book is nonpartisan, but being nonpartisan does not mean refraining from challenging beliefs. It involves thinking out of the box. Fresh ideas. Many politicians are close-minded, refusing to hear new ideas and resorting to attacks on opponents. Kill the messenger. However, ideas presented here are for everyone, from Republican to Democrat, for we have become a nation of red and blue, we vs. them. Arguably, the last time our country encountered such extreme political division was in the 1850s prior to the Civil War. It gives pause for thought.

People hate government then overlook the good it does. This hatred – really, misunderstanding of government – is symbolized by a news report I once saw: angry people screaming, "Government, don't take away my Medicare!" It bemused me. Government *runs* Medicare! It makes a point. When it comes to government, too much is taken for granted: unemployment (in times of need), SNAP (so the poor can eat), Social Security (so the elderly can survive), courts, police, roads, water, sewage treatment, safe food and medicine, and Medicare. The list of good is large. There is too much unfair negativity. *Improving* government must be our goal.

Millions of people saw investments collapse in 2008. I sure did. Fifty percent worth. Who wants to live through *that* again? But now, politicians push to end regulations that will *prevent* future collapses. It raises themes in this book: the need for leaders to better understand complex issues and learn from the past. Insanity is doing the same thing that failed in the past and thinking next time it will succeed. There is a chapter on that.

Our inability to plan for 30 years ahead is disturbing. We must invest in the future. That is what the post-WWII generation did. They did not bleed nostalgic for the past. They did not try to save the horse and buggy industry. Then and now, good politicians embrace the future, the inevitable.

We also witness uninformed solutions by politicians. Tariffs were imposed in the early 1930s in reaction to the Great Depression. It shut down world trade and caused millions more jobs to disappear. Today there is talk of tariffs. It demonstrates why politicians need to be better informed. Franklin Roosevelt was well-versed on issues; he was an effective President. Knowledge and understanding the past lead to solving problems. There is a chapter on that.

The legacy of polarized politics is little gets done unless one party rules. President Obama, without Congressional support, signed executive orders. Executive orders can be easily changed by the next President. Only laws last. Democrats controlled all three branches in 2009 and enacted the Affordable Care Act ("Obamacare") with no Republican support. It created years of conflict. In 2017, a new President supported by a Republican House and Senate vowed to dismantle Obamacare. Only bipartisan consensus creates lasting laws. Unless parties cooperate, 180-degree swings may come every four or eight years once the minority party takes over. This is addressed in the book.

The WWII generation understood the need for experimentation, innovation and *cooperation*. It is why our economy flourished for decades. It is why laws were *not* repealed after the minority party won the next election. We need the can-do attitude of that era. Politicians clashed yet put differences aside for the country's good. FDR and JFK had bold ideas. Congress listened and acted. Modern leaders should better understand political predecessors. It might shake things up.

This is where *America on the Verge* steps in. It provides a sensible bipartisan plan for the future with a focus on issues that don't get enough attention – *hidden diseases*. It offers solid analysis with historical insights – an imaginative plan of depth. Foresighted solutions are offered in chapters about the banking system, trade, fusion power, shrinking middle class, outsourcing, nuclear terrorism, drug abuse, population growth, poisonous politics, troubled schools, vanishing arts, solar energy, electric cars, huge federal debt, oil addiction, the warming planet, and scarily rising oceans.

This book presents a path from solar energy to economic investment to political reforms like publically funded elections. Breathtaking change is envisioned with a no-nonsense approach to stubborn problems. America needs courageous leadership of the likes of Franklin Roosevelt and a foresighted 21st Century agenda. And here it is: solutions to put us back on track as an economic superpower and beacon of democracy.

There is an adage our leaders should heed: a friend is not one who tells you what you *want* to hear, but what you *need* to hear. Leaders throughout the 50 states will change the status quo once they choose to speak the truth and patriotically act for the common good. *Change the status quo and the rest will flow.*

We need to plan for 30 years down the road. It will require cooperation and fresh ideas. The WWII generation demonstrated that. We must return to that constructive way of thinking. We achieve great things when leaders embrace giant ideas. After reading this book you will see light at the end of tunnel *for it's time to save a house on fire.*

Chapter 1

THE SLEEPING GIANT
Lessons from the Past

The Sleeping Giant is oblivious to all around him. He goes about life in a daze, slumbering, without direction, plan or goal. He drifts. His mind is elsewhere. His vitality wanes. His dreams evaporate and he seems not to notice or care. He is mocked by enemies who taunt him and laugh at his fading powers, but he is seen admiringly by others who ask, "When will he rise and fight?" But he never does. He heartbreakingly stumbles, numbly staring into the empty distance as time and life pass him by. He becomes more lethargic, a steadily vanishing giant in stupor who once knew towering majesty. He tragically wastes his great potential. He slowly crumbles. He is America...

*   *   *   *   *

The 2008 election of Barack Obama was viewed by many as a signal of resurgent hope. Hope was a dormant quantity in the prior years defined by 9/11, wars in Afghanistan and Iraq, and the Wall Street meltdown and Great Recession. Years have since passed. The economy improved and the stock market recovered, but stubborn problems remained. Division in Washington, if anything, is worse. The middle class languishes and the two percent grow richer. *The giant still sleeps.*

The sleeping giant metaphor is often used in describing America on that sleepy December 7, 1941 Sunday morning in Hawaii when Japan, in what was then history's most brazen sneak attack, bombed Pearl Harbor, killing over 2,400 sailors, sinking 19 navy ships and forcing a nation to enter the raging war ravaging the world. The country rebuilt the antiquated military and decimated navy, and a nation on its knees transformed an economy reeling from years of economic depression into the *Arsenal of Democracy* that saved the world from fascism. It happened within two years.

That generation understood, as Franklin Delano Roosevelt said, its "rendezvous with destiny." They offer us a message, perhaps a gift, that wonderful change can come quickly when the nation's leaders have giant goals and work together. This is lost upon us in downcast modern times.

The brazenness of 9/11 is reminiscent of Pearl Harbor. Three years and nine months after Pearl Harbor, the war was won and Nazi and Japanese fascism was defeated. For us, years passed since 9/11 yet problems linger. We encountered something quite different from the World War II generation. Then, government tackled problems. Politics was put aside. FDR and a bi-partisan Congress enacted numerous laws, regulations and federal agencies to manage an economy and Wall Street ravaged by the 1929 crash and unemployment peaking at 25 percent. They did the same when war came. They overcame disagreement and managed to solve problems... or tried and experimented.

Many modern leaders refuse to accept these ways of governing. Gridlock has taken over. Compromise is a dirty word. Some even seem *proud* of gridlock. Cooperation is defeat. Things are different from the depression and World War II era when Republicans, Democrats and the southern Dixiecrat wing supporting segregation put differences aside. A war was won and economic crises were managed. Somehow leaders ran a country competently. Can we say the same?

During the 1960s, similar political factions managed to pump out important change such as civil rights legislation, Medicare and anti-poverty programs. Lyndon Johnson notoriously led the country into Vietnam, overshadowing his successes domestically. As a former Senate majority leader, he knew how to interact with Senators and Congressmen to get things done. LBJ's better aspects ought to be studied more by modern leaders. Much was accomplished despite political sparring. As in the FDR era, some initiatives had disappointing results, but one senses *something* was being done. Innovation and experimentation were in the air. Now, sharp divisiveness defines the times.

Washington was humorously called in past times *first in war, last in the American League*, a reference to the perennially bad Washington Senators baseball team and a time when people understood that Washington was capable of taking action. Today, who could trumpet such a quip? Malaise now plagues the nation. Frustration manifested into intransigent Republican and Democrat camps. Politicians in the post-WWII era bickered yet managed to build a national road system, confront segregation, and create an inspiring space program. We do not have such bold, inspiring plans today.

A term coined since FDR's early days in office in 1933 emerged: *the first hundred days.* It signifies a President's window for enacting policies offered during the campaign. Today the term implies little can be done after the first year of the President's term. The following three years are tough. By year two, the opposition seems to focus on the next election. In the FDR era, even after year one Congress enacted important legislation and sought innovative change. They were not limited to 100 days. Money, political fundraising and lobbyists now seem to dominate Washington more so than in the past. Infrastructure built during the FDR, Eisenhower and JFK eras, from sewers to bridges, deteriorates. *The giant sleeps.*

Annually we see huge trade and federal deficits and the importing of hundreds of billions of dollars of foreign oil – money that goes to unsavory governments working against our interests. Oil imports (especially in Europe) make ruthless foes like Russia powerful. Seething anger that Wall Street got its way dominates the country. *Wall Street vs. Main Street.* Should they be enemies? We need banks... just ethically run banks.

While unemployment is down and the stock markets that crashed in 2008-9 recovered, the middle class has not recovered. Demands that the minimum wage be raised are derided by many leaders – people oblivious to just how hard it is to live on $15-17,000 per year. The wealthy emote a lack of compassion for millions struggling to survive. The term "Wall Street" implies selfishness and a government apathetic to the needs of the middle class and poor.

After Pearl Harbor, a generation understood its "rendezvous with destiny." Do we understand ours? We hurt ourselves in ways our enemies could not. Terrorists did not unglue Wall Street nor create a real estate bubble nor did terrorists force banks to create twisted financial schemes that brought down banking behemoths Bear Stearns and Lehman Brothers nor did terrorism cause banks to sell shady mortgages. Terrorism is not the reason why car executives turned their industry to dust by 2009 (and fortunately recovered thanks to the TARP act and...

government!). They are not the reason why business leaders outsourced millions of jobs nor the reason why we have poor schools, crumbling infrastructure or millions of teenagers getting high on drugs from Mexico and Afghanistan nor why corporate-hired lobbyists in Washington dominate leaders. No, our problems are of our own making and while thousands of soldiers fought or died in Iraq and Afghanistan, something dark brought on by our own government overwhelmed us on the home front.

Like the WWII generation, we need to embrace problems. We must fear our problems as surely as they feared Hitler. But armies will not destroy us this time. Apathy will, and in this modern war, our cities may be occupied not by armies, but the 21st Century enemy – the rising ocean. The World War II generation did not have TV. They read newspapers, a troubled medium in our times. Dishonest news reporting, the Internet and fake news did not define their era. The WWII generation was more likely to read a newspaper, be informed and listen to radio news programs and political speeches.

Millions recycled anything from bubble gum wrappers to cooking oil. Ask someone today to recycle a plastic bag... oh come on. You sense our generation lacks the dedication to a common cause that defined the WWII generation. We need that same dedication. John F. Kennedy, a World War II PT boat commander who fought in the Pacific (and was gravely injured) was a product of his generation. People understood him when he said years later, *"Ask not what your country can do for you, but what you can do for your country."*

Their experience is a reminder that each generation must confront problems and expect government to help. They teach us that a sleeping giant can rise again. Politicians now exclaim America is no longer great. When did we stop being great? Were we ever that great in the first place? I hardly thought so when I grew up seeing film clips of southerners blasting water on innocent people asking for dignity and a chance to vote.

Said New York Governor Andrew Cuomo, "Somewhere along the way we lost that energy of 1962, somewhere along the way we lost that confidence of 1962 – at least in terms of government ... The problem is, if you don't build and grow, someone else will."[1]

A year after 1962, JFK was assassinated. Soon after came the killing of Martin Luther King, Jr., Robert F. Kennedy, and the disaster of Vietnam. A part of the nation's soul from the WWII era vanished. We have not been the same since. We are not the economic superpower and world-respected leader we once were. We want to restore this. We need to examine the WWII generation, how their spirit was lost, and learn from them. We lost something important that they had.

If anything made us great, it was the desire to rid us of injustice alongside a Congress that cooperated and enacted laws to make things better. Have we lost greatness or have we just lost the will to innovate... or at least try? So goes the adage from the cartoon *Pogo*, read daily in newspapers from the World War II era: *for we have seen the enemy, and he is us.*

Chapter 2

GOVERNING CREATIVELY
Thinking Out of the Box

Presidents, Senators and Congressmen enter office with the promise of change. Presidents run into a wall called Congress. Congressmen run into a wall called gridlock. Everyone runs into the walls of lobbyists and endless fundraising. The old election ended, yet raising money for the next election becomes a nearly full-time effort, a drain on time and energy... time that should be devoted to studying issues and new legislation. True change requires comprehensive legislation, fresh ideas, long-term planning, and thinking out of the box. That is how FDR viewed problems during the Depression. Innovation and experimentation were in the air. Vision may not always succeed, but lack of it always fails. Poisonous division defines the present. Experimentation and innovation are lacking in modern Washington. From lobbyist domination to the pressure to raise millions for elections, it must change if we are to see a better future and a restoration of trust in government. At the end of the chapter, powerful proposals are presented to promote innovation and better-informed leaders who think out of the box.

*   *   *   *   *

General Motors in 2008 symbolized the status quo and problems plaguing our nation – and still plaguing us. What happened to GM, an icon of American industrial might that entered bankruptcy in 2009, portends future decline when corporate and government leaders refuse to innovate. GM's demise threatened tens of thousands of jobs. GM had lost over $72 billion over the previous four years and thousands of jobs teetered on oblivion."[2] GM is a warning: terrible things happen when leaders refuse to innovate.

Oil is another example of the refusal to innovate. Oil reserves will not last forever. Some act as if it will. How long can the earth's environment withstand the daily billions of cars, millions of factories, and thousands of airplanes spitting out oil's poisonous fumes playing havoc with the environment? Oklahomans should not have to withstand man-made earthquakes brought on by oil production practices of pumping enormous amounts of wastewater into the bowels of earth without understanding the consequences. Ask Oklahomans who faced 907 earthquakes in 2015,[3] up from 21 in 2005 and 2006.[4]

This is why government must step in to help. Government needs to balance the needs of industry with the needs of a safe environment. From Oklahoma earthquakes to the warming oceans and rising ocean levels, we need balanced, innovative government policies. Government as well needs to innovate and not be captive to the past, campaign donors and lobbyists, otherwise we all collectively sweep problems under the rug.

Good government prevents disaster. The Great Recession and bank industry falling prey to greed could have been avoided had firm regulations been in place, yet years later politicians still yearn for bank deregulation. Lax regulation caused the 2008 disaster! It's easier to campaign by berating government than offer ways to make it work better. It's easier to trumpet clichés than study issues. There will be more fiascos if we attack government instead of making it work better.

Our leaders spend vast time raising money rather than studying complex issues. Their priorities become those of their donors, often corporations, and this is not what is in the best interest of the nation. If Oklahoman politicians get money from oil firms pumping wastewater into the earth (causing a geometric increase in Oklahoma earthquakes), how likely are they to address the problem? This is the tip of the iceberg. Donors make leaders unable to address serious problems because of the risk of losing money needed for elections.

Fresh ideas need to be discussed – thinking out of the box – like ending politicians being captive to moneyed interests (see Chapter 11). Instead we witnessed presidential candidates in 2016 talking about penis size, hands and hair. Instead of seeking enlightened ideas for progress – planning out a long-term future – politicians often surrender to lobbyists and money. In the meantime, federal debt increased $100,000 in the time it took for you to read this sentence (check the debt counter online). Poor leadership and dated ways take us to a dangerous place.

THINKING CREATIVELY:
CONSERVATION & MODERN TRANSPORTATION

Seemingly unrelated issues are an interrelated "soup" that must be addressed simultaneously without the pressure of donors. Decreasing oil imports requires addressing many matters from conservation to clean energy. Has Congress considered a fifteen-year "Apollo" effort to encourage industries to convert to electric cars, or mandate utilities to more efficiently deliver electricity, or create an "800" green hotline to explain government conservation programs? *That* is thinking out of the box. That is how entrepreneurs created new technologies. Think about anyone from Thomas Edison to Apple's Steve Jobs who changed the landscape of life. Government must catch up to the 21st Century by becoming innovative and experimental. *Would corporate donors allow that to happen?*

Government inaction discourages progress. Only 32% of potential electricity produced by utilities ever reaches its destination.[5-6] Such stunning waste! There is so much more lawmakers can do, but for some reason they don't. Massive electricity waste – just the tip of the iceberg.

Eliminating oil imports means dealing with utility inefficiency and little-discussed matters. How about promoting conservation? It means encouraging MBA programs to teach the next generation to care about it. It means lower speed limits on national highways to decrease oil consumption. It means the FCC requiring TV and Internet sites to advance conservation ideas through public service announcements. It means government coordinating many efforts among many industries, *but would corporate donors allow that to happen?*

How about a quantum leap forward like manufacturing, on a large scale, cars that get up to 300 mpg with reasonable range? They exist. Apteras had a car that got 300 mpg with a 120-mile range.[7] It went out of business in 2011. The technology for highly efficient engines exists. The largest American auto companies are just not promoting it. The EPA, with Congressional approval, could promote this fuel-stingy technology.

How about the auto industry mass-producing pure-electric cars that use no gas at all? Tesla's *Roadster*, purely electric, has a 245-mile range per charge and goes 0 to 60 mph in four seconds, but it starts at prices way out of range for most people. Price is the problem, not technology. Make these affordable and within 10 years, oil imports ballooning trade deficits could vanish. With mass production and government tax subsidies and credits, it could be done. We need to reduce carbon emissions. Automakers could move away from gas-guzzling SUV's. What's holding us back? Vision. *Would auto and energy campaign donors allow that to happen?*

Google ultra-efficient cars, read, then ask why GM, Ford, Chrysler and Washington are slow to change. How about policies encouraging the merging of innovative companies like Tesla so that GM, Ford and Chrysler more quickly innovate? It means the EPA enforcing quantum leaps in mileage standards − not 30-ish mpg, but 70-ish. It means helping the auto industry improve battery technology and electric car range by coordinating engineers and research.

It means building a network of "electric" pumps to service the millions of new electric cars on national highways. It means tax subsidies for electric cars to keep the price affordable. It means having government work closely with the auto industry not unlike what government did during World War II when GM, Ford and Chrysler converted from cars to airplanes and tanks. We have precedents.

How about alternatives to airplanes? How about infrastructure projects like we had in the 1950s. Build 300 mph trains connecting all American cities. Google the Beijing-Shanghai HSR that goes 300 mph.[8] The technology is a reality. China has it. We have clunky Amtrak: slow, constantly late, rickety tracks, poor service. Other nations surpass us. It has been a long time since NASA dazzled the world in sending men to the moon. We need that same can-do spirit now. We stand by watching others innovate... like China. So much can be done, but it means *thinking out of the box... and investing in the future.*

THINKING CREATIVELY: INDUSTRY/EDUCATION ZONES

A well-known problem is the lack of skilled workers trained for the needs of emerging industries. This need for skills ranges from knowledge of emerging technologies to robotics to new factories. In the spirit of thinking out of the box, how about creating a system for close collaboration among industry, local government and schools?

This concept involves emerging industries in need of labor collaborating with local governments in terms of creating school programs that train young students or the unemployed for jobs that will soon be required. It means industries committing to building factories and offices in communities willing to commit to such training programs. It means federal programs designed to promote such collaboration between industry and local government. It means providing high school and community college students with alternative schools that train them for industries in their neighborhood (or industries agreeing to soon build facilities in that region).

It means granting students not interested in college to instead attend special high schools or community colleges with programs that train them to man emerging industries in that region. It means allowing industry to collaborate with community colleges and specialty high schools for purposes of explaining their employment needs.

It means local governments, through an economic/education zone, arranging for emerging industries to open factories in a region, be given tax and other incentives and provided with trained labor in return for firm commitments. It means industry investing in such schools so that they have skin in the project and keep commitments to open new factories and, therefore, new employment opportunities. It means new concepts like free education/training in return for a commitment to work for a company for a guaranteed period and livable wages.

It means granting community colleges the option of collaborating with local industries to create courses specifically designed for those industries. It means creating government-approved schools and colleges that ensure certification and guarantee scam schools are pushed out of the picture. It means creating low-tuition or tuition free-education in regions especially hard-hit by economic setbacks. It means a whole new way of thinking about education and industry working together to fill the needs of people who need work.

THINKING CREATIVELY: EDUCATION

No Child Left Behind fell short of its goals. Many problems were not considered. Learning cannot shut down once children leave school. If they do not study, what's the good of hiring more teachers? Comprehensive legislation means addressing what kids do *after* school. They watch TV, play video games, Facebook or Tweet (or do the next fad), or text for the rest of their waking hours… or use drugs or hang out with violent gangs. Comprehensive legislation means addressing everything.

It means addressing drug abuse – 20% of 8th graders have smoked marijuana, and 52.8% of 12th graders have used drugs.[9] Addressing these means creating adequately funded programs that send tutors to a troubled student's home or adding drug enforcement and rehab to schools.

It means a sugar tax on soda to create funds to hire tutors who help struggling students in their homes while at the same time putting a break on the mass consumption of sugar. Politicians need not reflexively say no to healthy new programs alongside ways to pay for them. Saving teenagers from drug abuse or preventing them from going down the path of crime will save government revenue. It costs less for afterschool programs and tutors than it does to pay for them in prison years later because government did not help them when they were vulnerable. It's a smart investment worth being studied – and keeping an open mind! That's thinking out of the box.

How about mandatory nationwide testing for dyslexia to ensure that vision and perception conditions causing students to have trouble reading or concentrating are addressed by trained personnel? How about studying the Ukrainian approach to education where one teacher monitors a student's progress for years and becomes a mentor? How about funding more community centers that offer tutors and sports activities to poor families? How about inner city school "playgrounds" (little more than harsh parking lots with basketball hoops) being replaced with grass so that children can play on something even little bit resembling nature? How about clamping down on truancy then offering truants the choice of school or taking a job cleaning parks and streets so that they learn responsibility and not drift to drugs and gangs. How asking labor unions to be flexible about this idea or requiring teachers to help parents learn how to get their children to study more?

Comprehensive legislation means offering music, theater and dance classes so that teenagers have something positive to experience during or after school. It means offering grants to schools so that children can get musical instruments or dance shoes. It means providing money so that fine musicians can teach kids about all the things they are missing (and rarely see on TV). It means addressing obsessive video game-playing so that kids study and parents can program devices to not work during certain times of the day. It means requiring device-makers to install easy-to-use shut-off apps.

It means making kids shut off smartphones so that they do not obsessively text during school hours and that they pay attention to teachers. It means confiscating phones when kids do not follow rules. It means nutritious food in school cafeterias, not junk food, and removing soda and candy vending machines so that kids don't get sugar highs and become hyperactive. It means ensuring they get a decent breakfast so that they can concentrate all morning, or permanently removing drug peddlers and violent juveniles from schools then providing programs, run by mental health experts, to help them find a healthy path.

Everything is interrelated. If government is serious about improving education, legislation must creatively address many problems simultaneously. It means *thinking out of the box.*

THINKING CREATIVELY:
FROM AFGHANISTAN TO DRUGS

Many foreign threats get little attention. Afghan Taliban forces endlessly oppose the west. One troubling fact getting little attention is that Afghan warlords fighting our way of life actually help ruin it. They reap huge sums of money selling opium. About 90 percent of opium worldwide is believed to come from Afghanistan. Their wealth flows in the blood of millions of American children who unwittingly fund our enemies each time they buy drugs for a high. How about a new approach to Afghanistan to focus on destroying opium crops or emboldened domestic programs discouraging teenage drug use?

How about subsidizing Afghan farmers so that they stop growing poppy and instead grow much-needed food or redirecting our military to rid Afghanistan of opium? Starve our enemies of drug money they use to buy arms. How about drones dumping chemicals on opium crops? The same can be said of Mexican drug suppliers. It is time to think out of the box and revisit foreign policy goals. From the Afghan war to teenagers buying drugs to the international crime gangs: everything is interrelated. Afghan and Mexican drug profits flow in the blood of millions of teenagers. Act firmly with those drug criminals.

GOVERNING CREATIVELY: CONCLUSIONS

Innovation and thinking out of the box require leaders who are open-minded and have time to study complex problems. Time lacks when legislators spend countless hours raising money for elections. It has nothing to do with legislating, yet it's a permanent drag on schedules. This must change if the public wants better results from leaders. Here are two proposals addressing such hidden diseases.

1. *Studying Complex Issues.* Many professions require ongoing training and education. Doctors, computer programmers, you name it: they keep up to date on new developments. Elected officials must be held to the same standard. Instead, they devote huge amounts of time to raise money for campaigns. It has become a nearly full-time occupation. According to a MSNBC report, winning Congressional candidates in 2012 raised on average $1.69 million and Senators raised $10.78 million – $2,315/day for Congressmen and $14,351/day for Senators.[10]

They spend time daily raising that money! They regularly fly to their districts to raise money at public expense. According to the CBS *Sixty Minutes* episode "Dialing for Dollars", many Congressmen spend up to 30 hours per week (30!) making phone calls in small rooms reserved for them.[11] They make cold calls daily, reading scripts like telemarketers. It has nothing to do with legislating. Leaders may not have adequate time and energy to study complicated issues in legislation.

The pressure to raise money behooves revolutionary change: public financing of elections. The benefits would be breathtaking. Leaders would be freed from pressures from donors. Let them focus on studying complex issues instead of fundraising (as addressed in Chapter 11). *It is time to change the status quo.*

2. *Improved Leadership.* Better leadership skills will help. Dysfunction and gridlock we witness in government demonstrate the need for better professionalism. There is little leadership training in Washington. Being a Congressman or Senator is one of the most important jobs a person could have. Everyone would benefit by seminars, required by statute (yet to be enacted), teaching methods for cooperation, negotiation skills and respectful behavior. Legislators have obligations of professionalism just as you and I have in the workplace. When I was a law school student, I took seminars on mediation: showing respect, encouraging others to hear new points of view, problem-solving, and encouraging discussion between opposing parties. Skills I learned *as a student* are violated regularly by our leaders. They often lack important skills necessary for conflict resolution, let alone enacting major legislation. Break gridlock by breaking patterns.

Most politicians are well-meaning people, but the status quo must change if we want a better future. They fall short in not meeting public expectations. It's hardly a wonder when so many leaders spend 30-plus hours a week fundraising (or telemarketing!). This must be addressed if we are to end negative patterns and gridlock. The potential for revolutionizing government through public financing of elections (discussed in a later chapter) has breathtaking implications.

Free our leaders of the burden of fundraising. Let them focus on becoming savvy on issues. Require better leadership skills as opposed to the tendency to bicker, play to microphones or insult those who disagree. Only revolutionary change and obligatory standards will truly change the status quo.

It is time to think out of the box.

Chapter 3

TAKING ON FREE TRADE
& OUTSOURCING
Ethics & Fair Play Matter

An adage: Put a frog in a pot of boiling water and he jumps out, but put a frog in cool water slowly heated to a boil and he slowly boils to death.

Is America that slowly boiling frog? When it comes to vanishing industries, outsourcing, decreasing middle-class quality of life, and problems faced by millions of Americans, America probably is that slowly boiling frog. The idea behind this slowly-boiling-to-death metaphor is that over the past decades bad things happened and ultimately destroyed the American Dream for millions of hard-working people.

Over the decades America has developed, shall we say, some bad habits – habits that turned into one debilitating crisis after another. It has eroded the quality of life for millions of Americans. The kinder world they once knew is a distant memory, and current trends threaten the collective hope for a better future.

We watched as free trade eroded our manufacturing base. Politicians stood by as industries left our shores and left rusting, crumbling factories where there once stood a pillar of so many communities. The rich became richer, the poor became poorer, the middle class became angrier... and the decline continues. The pot of water gets hotter and hotter for the majority of hard-working Americans.

Refusing to make changes, government looked the other way for decades. The shocking 2016 election resulted. People seek solutions but look in the wrong place. They probe the past, not the future. This almost always is a mistake when it comes to economics, for the past is increasingly distant. Many leaders fail to see this.

Our economy reflects free trade, but, unlike the frog boiling to death, we can still spare our country a bleak future. Change starts with *thinking-out-of-the-box* trade policies, for up until now free trade for millions of Americans has had dismal results. Some leaders look to the past for answers as if coal or high tariffs were our salvation. We cannot bring the horse and buggy era back or watch old movies and say, "I want that again." This is not how life works. *The disease was brought on by foreign countries whose people are paid a small fraction of what Americans earn.*

It is time to revise the way we view free trade. Change the ways things are done abroad. Complex as trade is, it boils down to this: future trade policy must firmly and patiently pressure trade partners to raise wages, improve labor rights, and enforce environmental standards approximating American standards *within 10 years*. This is the underlying premise of this chapter. The *other* threat to American jobs is the steady transition to automation and robotics. Millions of Americans face this mounting threat. *That* will be addressed in the following chapter.

A FRESH APPROACH: RAISE FOREIGN STANDARDS

The goal of returning prosperity to America – "make America great again" (as some say) – will take years to accomplish. It means pressuring trade partners to dramatically raise labor wages and environmental standards. It will require firm commitment to these goals. Such change will not come quickly or easily, but it is the only realistic path forward. The alternative – reckless tariffs, protectionism and trade wars – spells doom to our economy. All that was accomplished since World War II in creating worldwide prosperity would be lost. What was started was the correct approach. We now need to do it in concordance with 21st-century needs.

The fiercely nationalistic steps of tariffs and protectionism taken during the 1930s failed miserably. They caused severe unemployment, historic economic stress and, ultimately, a terrible world war. This is not to say history will repeat itself, but it is a stark reminder of failed trade policies. Approaching international trade with catchy promises that stir millions of people won't get the job done. This is a complex problem requiring meticulous planning, expertise, and carefully considered solutions. Tweets won't cut it.

It took decades to get us where we are. It will take years to get things right. Our leaders must be honest with the country. FDR honestly told the country during the dreariest days of 1933 that it would take years to restore the life they knew. He then led Washington to a flurry of action that helped improve the economy. Today we need the same: innovation, honesty, intensity of action, *and patience*.

There is a clear need for a new philosophical view of trade that achieves our goals while continuing to promote ideals 1940s leaders sought. We must not brazenly ruin what they began. We need a modern concept of international trade that improves the quality of life for millions of Americans. We need a new economic paradigm: *make free trade work for us*.

DECLINING WAGES & QUALITY OF LIFE

The problem with free trade, as it currently is, is that it failed to work for the majority of Americans. The widespread diminished quality of life for middle-class America is the result of a confluence of trends poisoning the well that was decades in the making. It's why the chapter opens with the boiling frog adage. The majority of Americans – people earning less and less – are that boiling frog.

Yes, the frog could have jumped out of the pot, but the reality for millions of Americans is that there was nowhere to jump. They watched well-paying jobs vanish as free trade and outsourcing vanquished once-thriving industries. People started to work, symbolically, at the Walmarts and Home Depots for a fraction of the pay their parents earned in past times. This, for them, is the reality of free trade.

Raising wages in America is part of the solution. It's never been easy for those living on minimum wage, but it's much harder now than it was in 1970. The national minimum wage rose from $1.60/hour in 1970 to $7.15 in 2017, yet millions of people fell behind in terms of paying for basics. Minimum wage is a bellwether of what happened to Americans – falling behind even as you move forward.

According to studies, people now earn less in real terms than they did in the 1970s. Let's coin a new term: *struggle level*. People work hard yet face greater financial stress than in the past. The 1970 federal minimum wage rose 353% by 2012. That sounds wonderful, but the reality is people in 1970 fared better.[12] Wages fell behind relative to the cost of living. The cost of education is a perfect example. According to one study, someone working in 1970 at minimum wage could pay for a year of college tuition by working for 755 hours. By 2010 that person worked 1,823 hours to cover a year of tuition. Analogous rises in the cost of living run across the board from rent to food to buying a house.[13]

According to various studies, if the minimum wage today were equal in spending power to that of the late 1960s, workers would earn anywhere from $12 to $21/hour.[14-15-16] It's hardly a wonder why people struggle. It is not easy to calculate spending power when comparing 1968 to the present. TVs and clothing may be cheaper, but rent and college tuition may be much higher. Overall, it's harder to survive. Wages, in real terms, are much lower than they were decades ago. The boiling frog metaphor fits. Let's not get caught up in whether the minimum wage should be $12 or $15 or $21. The message is that wages would have to be much higher for people to merely *maintain* the same standard of living they had in 1970. This must change as a matter of fairness and smart economics.

This is where free trade policy kicks in. As long as Chinese, Mexican or Pakistani workers earn a tiny fraction of what Americans earn, we must expect jobs to leave our shores. Until this reality changes, economic realities will pressure American companies to manufacture products abroad. We must accept this reality and let this guide trade policy: a key goal is to raise wages abroad.

THREAT OF WINDOW DRESSING VS. REAL CHANGE

The *struggle level* partly explains the stunning 2016 election of Donald Trump. Hillary Clinton symbolized the old guard. Her husband, Bill Clinton, oversaw the signing of NAFTA, which is seen by millions, rightly or not, as a disaster. People resent free trade, but, when it comes to outsourcing, the reality is far more complex than the 2016 electioneering would suggest. People want quick, easy solutions. Politicians provide them. The problem is this: quick, easy solutions are fiction. Promises to end outsourcing created a swell of support among understandably angry voters, but those promises will almost certainly not create real change.

Free trade and outsourcing are at the top of the political agenda. The real threat now is window dressing – the appearance of change but no actual change. We must not be lulled into thinking the problem has been solved just because we see a small handful of success stories.

We risk seeing isolated instances of small victories and being seduced into thinking things are really changing. Carrier, for example, kept 700 or so jobs in America after intense pressure, but 700 is barely a drop in the bucket in a country of 300 million people. It was heart-warming publicity, but it marked no change in the underlying cause of the problem: the very low cost of foreign labor. Until *that* is addressed, we may see little more than isolated "Carrier" stories.

Simple solutions are like swimming upstream against fast rapids. We cannot change the economic laws of physics. For all the complexity of free trade and outsourcing, it boils down to this: our trade partners' workforces earn terribly little and it is pulling American wages and employment down. American industries, under intense price pressure, can only survive in competitive markets by keeping prices low. They have little choice other than to build factories abroad, where labor and costs are much lower. The alternative is business failure and bankruptcy. What can you do when foreign competitors undercut your prices?

So what's the solution? For starters, it won't be a quick fix. Anyone who suggests otherwise is being dishonest or naïve. A sophisticated and long-term view is needed. Post-WWII leaders led in vastly different times. Late 1940s concepts of trade focused on helping poor or war-raged nations enter the world economy – and those nations have done exactly that! China, Japan, Vietnam, Mexico – you name it. Once-rural countries now have vibrant economies. They sell clothing, refrigerators, sneakers, steel, tires, and almost anything you can think of – products that _had_ been manufactured in the U.S in an era long lost. That world of the 1970s (or the 1950s?), where America still manufactured TVs, shoes and clothing, vanished. What was left for millions of workers? Inadequate and low-paying jobs.

So here we are. In a way, the 2016 election made a statement: do something! Exactly what that "something" is becomes the center of future trade policy debate. Acting in haste or anger or with irrational expectations is cutting off your nose to spite your face. Answers won't come in tweets. Answers will come with sophisticated new trade policies... _and patience._

TURNING ANGER INTO EFFECTIVE TRADE POLICY

Anger has spread among millions of Americans. Millions in the more Democratic coastal regions seem to be, shall we say, a bit removed from the harsh employment realities of red states. Bitter feelings are the status quo. That could change with bipartisan, effective and innovative change in trade policy. Smart solutions cross party lines. Good solutions involve viewing the world economy as it is _now,_ not for what it was in 1960 when China had a rural farming economy and people bought sneakers or TVs made in America. _A new world needs new ideas._

The solution is to change key trade partners' characteristics that have not changed: foreign workers are paid very poorly; minimum wages are (by American standards) a disgrace; environmental protections are shameful (Amazon and Africa regions); water and air are filthy (China); labor rights are often nonexistent (Bangladesh); forests are chopped down (Brazil); and labor has little in terms of pensions, healthcare and widely accepted protections in the U.S. (anywhere).

Shortcuts like paying people horribly and wreaking havoc on the environment will lower manufacturing costs. In a way, it's cheating by playing by foul rules that impair our prosperity. One solution is slashing American wages to lower production costs yet destroy our way of life. That's a really bad solution. The better solution is pressuring trade partners to improve as a condition of Most Favorable Nation Status (MFN) with the U.S.

American companies move factories abroad because labor costs and standards are lower – and perhaps a bribe here or there will grease the way. There is a reason why made-in-America becomes a relic of the past. There are reasons why Americans earn less, adjusted for inflation, than they did in 1970. Until such realities are addressed in future trade pacts, the likelihood is that little will change.

Once our leaders envision trade in terms of labor standards, we may see real change... over time. When our trade partners start to treat _their_ environments and labor with the same high standards with which we treat ours, _their_ costs will rise and the playing fields will level. It must be a condition for trade. Their people will also live better. It's a win-win policy in terms of trade and social justice worldwide.

This is the right path for future trade agreements. If implemented over a period of several years, jobs may realistically return to the U.S. and trade deficits could be balanced or even show a surplus. *Surplus!* Imagine that. Our country last had a trade surplus in the 1970s. Some $9.2 billion in 1975. *1975.* Hmm, did you vote for Gerald Ford or Jimmy Carter in the coming election? Long time ago, eh?

Higher labor costs abroad may mean that American industries once again find America is a good place to build factories. This marks a clear policy goal of this chapter. We need sophisticated trade agreements that pressure trade partners to improve wages and environmental standards. We should do this not because it is the right thing to do (though it is) but rather because it is the only realistic path. As long as foreign labor is half the cost (or less), companies will send jobs abroad.

TRADE PACTS: *STICKS & CARROTS* & 10-YEAR DEADLINE

In the field of political science, the expression *sticks and carrots* is used to outline foreign policy and economic options. In a word, punish those who do not give us what we want and reward those who give us what we want. This expression is likely borne of the notion of a pet rabbit (go figure). *Sticks beating the bad rabbit, carrots feeding the good rabbit.* Good luck training a rabbit, but, when it comes to "training" trade partners, we have the ability to reward or punish.

Incorporate *sticks and carrots* in trade pacts within a ten-year period. It involves requirements to raise labor wages and environmental standards. If trade partners comply, we will welcome trade with them and provide the prized *Most Favorable Nation Status* (MFN). After the ten-year transition period, countries refusing to satisfy labor and environmental standards will be denied MFN and will face increasingly harsh tariffs until such time that they remedy concerns. It will make it hard to sell products in the U.S and elsewhere. They must improve standards and not pull the rest of the world down to their shabby standards.

Because it's done over time, it's a fair warning – a shot over the bow. It is a foreign policy of *sticks and carrots.* It means acting with strength. It worked in the past. Teddy Roosevelt termed it as "speak softly and carry a big stick." Being tentative has not gotten us what we want. Former baseball shortstop and manager Leo Durocher once famously said *nice guys finish last.*

This approach should apply to future treaties. It gives countries a ten-year window to adjust. It gives fair notice. It will give us what we need without withering threats, bullying or wrong-headed imposition of tariffs. It will be a transition that is tough but fair. It is a philosophy for free trade that will ultimately create fairness, level playing fields, and a better future for American workers.

The remainder of this chapter goes into specifics with examples of trade violations and examples of shabby treatment of foreign workers. It presents obstacles we face and must overcome. It will not be an easy or quick fix. A complex problem requires patience and sophistication. It requires leaders who are honest and explain the truth. It requires major changes in tax laws. It requires leaders who do not resort to tweets and, rather, provide a realistic path forward. We cannot turn things around in a year or two. Let's make that clear from the start.

Translating our objectives into results means lengthy trade agreements of such dizzying complexity that it would turn your head. The now-defunct Trans-Pacific Trade Pact (TPP) was like that. As a result few truly understood it. Perhaps it did not go far enough in protecting our interests. Trade experts will need to translate our 10-year labor and environmental goals into treaties that get the job done.

We need *sticks and carrots*. It may sound folksy (rabbits and all), but the premise is solid. Negotiate from strength, be firm, and be fair. Let trade partners know that they will have ample time to remedy violations, but set a firm time deadline. Reward those that comply. Heavily punish those that don't, but give them 10 years notice. That's fair. Remain confident that we are on the right side of history. In sum, the policy is this: *firm quality standards for labor rights, wages and environment; a 10-year window for phasing them in; and timely demand that steps are met in the interim in order to maintain MFN status with the U.S.*

From ethics to outsourcing to livable wages, our government must ride the course in terms of achieving noble goals as we move forward in creating a 21st-century free trade approach that protects our people and interests.

GLOBALIZATION WITH DISRESPECT OF DECENCY

Free trade is a stepchild of the culture of greed. It lowered prices of foreign goods but harmed American workers. It eroded our industrial base while allowing foreign labor to work at poverty wages, in miserable conditions, and in decrepit factories or sweatshops contracted or owned by U.S. multinationals.

> *ChinaLaborWatch.org on Walmart: "One factory manufactures stationery, such as notebooks and holiday cards. The other produces toys, such as battery-operated trucks. In both factories workers receive dismal wages, are cramped into hot dormitories and work exhausting hours at an unbelievably fast pace. Workers are working up to thirteen hours a day, six to seven days a week. Workers are denied health insurance, maternity leave, paid holiday leave, marital leave or leave to bury family members. In both factories workers are told exactly what to say to inspectors."*[17]

A painful era throughout the "rustbelt" is symbolized by the signing of the North American Free Trade Agreement (NAFTA), the hallmark of the Clinton era. NAFTA opened up trade with Canada and Mexico especially. December 8, 1993, the day NAFTA was signed into law, was a glorious day for proponents of free trade and globalization. It paved the way for a hated word: *outsourcing.* By one estimate, nearly 900,000 jobs could have been lost due to NAFTA.[18] According to the Department of Energy, each $1 billion in trade deficit costs America 27,000 jobs.[19] Free traders believe globalization is good for America. Ask the millions who lost well-paying jobs. They see things differently.

It goes beyond NAFTA. According to *The Economic Policy Institute,* trade with China accounted for nearly 2.8 million lost jobs by 2006.[20] By other estimates, some 3.2 million jobs (or one in six manufacturing jobs) disappeared since 2000. Princeton economist Alan Blinder, Federal Reserve vice chairman during the Clinton administration, predicted that up to 40 million jobs would be at risk over the next 20 years.[21] This is the legacy of free trade and globalization.

> *ChinaLaborWatch.org, The Story of Li Chun Mei: "The 19-year-old had collapsed and died last November at the end of a 16-hour shift. Like many of*

the staff, she often had to work past midnight, especially in the run-up to Christmas. The girls who shared her dormitory found her lying on the bathroom floor with blood pouring from her nose and mouth. The bosses, who were Korean, did not deny that Li had died on their premises. They blamed the death not on overwork but on earlier injuries Li suffered when she was hit by a motorcycle." [22]

As foreign investment conditions improved, CEOs saw benefits to outsourcing and shutting American factories. That middle-class families suffered was of little consequence. Only profits were on the radar screen. Corporate earnings rose and stock prices increased. Affluent stockholders win, workers lose. Multinationals profited while millions of jobs evaporated. Patriotism and concern for fellow Americans are not part of the equation.

The two disturbing stories above (with more to come) send a message about the nature of our trade partners. Inclusion of human rights and livable wages/benefits in trade pacts would lead to higher foreign labor costs. Foreign products would be costlier, and American-made products in turn would become more competitive. It's a win-win: *promoting human rights while improving U.S. trade prospects.*

PROTECTIONISM IS NOT THE ANSWER

Foreign wages are a fraction of American labor costs, as are construction costs and labor benefits (often nonexistent in many countries). It's hardly a wonder that American companies move factories abroad. If they kept such factories on America soil, they would soon go out of business. Foreign-made products sell at lower prices. Some politicians lobby for protectionism and tariffs perhaps as high as 35 percent. That was tried during the 1930s. The results were disastrous. It deepened the depression worldwide and caused economic contraction. We don't want that or the resulting inflation from dramatically costlier foreign imports.

If politicians want to hear the roar of crowds, bash free trade agreements. In truth, how do you get the result you want? Tariffs and protectionism may intrigue frustrated voters at campaign rallies, but it's like scratching a mosquito bite. It feels good at first but makes things worse. Protectionism would make things worse: economic contraction, rising unemployment, inflation. Hey, if you like protectionism, study 1930s economics. There's a name for it: *The Great Depression.* Well, let's not go down that path again.

There's a better way, but it's too complicated to explain in tweets or news sound bites. Bashing trade agreements gets votes, but the smart approach requires sophisticated input from trade specialists, changing arcane tax codes that encourage multinationals to move factories or headquarters abroad (like *inversions*), and incorporating ethics and higher labor standards in trade pacts. More on this later.

OUTSOURCING TO SWEATSHOPS: ETHICS MATTER!

Labor is cheaper abroad. Environmental regulations are lax. IRS tax codes and loopholes, thanks to corporate lobbyists, encourage outsourcing. Profits rose as labor costs dropped but at the stiff price of eliminating millions of good jobs.

Newint.org on Mexico: "Each shift is from 8.30 am until 8.30 pm, but if *workers do not complete the number of clothes they have been told to make that day, they must work longer without any pay; on Saturdays, people must work from 8 am until 5 pm without a lunch break; workers are paid between $30 and $50 per week; girls as young as 12 and 13 work in the factory.*"[23]

Globalization added to the problem. According to a *Business Week* report, there are thousands of sweatshops throughout Asia and Latin America. People work 16-hour days and are paid poorly. Such "factories" are contracted by American multinationals. In a report, Baruch College Professor S. Prakash Sethi said, "It would be extremely generous to say that even 10% [of Western companies] have done anything meaningful about labor conditions." The report interviewed garment industry consultant Robert Antoshak, who said, "American retailers are driving down prices, which ends up squeezing labor."[24]

This is the dark face of free trade. It must not be what purists had in mind in 1947 when the General Agreement on Tariffs and Trade (GATT) was signed. There are positives to globalization: cheaper goods and efficiency. On balance, it is not worth the benefit of lower prices if millions abroad are treated shabbily and millions of Americans lose jobs. It was encouraged each time politicians acquiesced to corporate lobbyists.

There is something to be said about the notion that corporations should act honorably and not support poor labor conditions. CEOs must make ethical decisions. In the past, corporations made money and also provided Americans with jobs – jobs that treated people with dignity. The stock markets of today do not reflect the loss of jobs; corporate earnings rise nonetheless. Middle-class America got lost in the shuffle, and, while millions of well-paying industrial jobs disappeared, the word *Rustbelt* established itself as a new noun in the dictionary.

Newint.org on Sweatshops in Mexico: "[W]hen women are hired, they are tested to see if they are pregnant. If they are pregnant, they are fired. If you arrive 15 minutes late, you must work for 3 days without pay. When one man was sick for a day, he lost a whole week's pay... Women have no protective goggles to wear when they are sewing at their machines. Sometimes the needles break and fly up into their faces." [25]

Ford, the ultimate in "apple pie" American companies, has factories in Mexico. Many American multinationals moved factories abroad. More recently in 2016, Carrier elected to shut down its Indiana factory; 1,400 would lose well-paying jobs, $23/hour. Carrier would open a factory in Mexico where workers could earn a quarter of that amount.[26] It was avoided somewhat, but more "Carriers" loom.

The trend will continue until trade pacts and tax codes are amended. Displaced blue-collar workers increasingly take on lower-paying jobs of the likes of Walmart. According to the U.S. Dept. of Labor, over 3.8 million workers were displaced between Jan. 2003 and Dec. 2005 with 49% of it due to factories closing or moving.[27] Think of the hemorrhaging that will come if the automobile makers moved all their factories abroad. By some estimates, one in ten jobs in America is believed to be car-related.

While economists point out that globalization brought on inevitable problems, is there any good reason for our own government to *promote* globalization that means millions more Americans may lose their jobs? It is the duty of government to help Americans and soften the blows of free trade. Government need not always acquiesce to corporate America and its putsch for ever-greater profits. Said FDR, "Our greatest primary task is to put people to work. This is no unsolvable problem if we face it wisely and courageously."[28]

> *The Telegraph, UK, India, The Gap: "Police have rescued 14 children from a New Delhi sweatshop at the centre [sic] of a scandal involving US clothing giant Gap... Indian police did not raid the address until the Daily Telegraph produced photographs of the children still at work... The Telegraph was shown to a series of 12 dingy rooms where both adults and children squatted on the floor performing delicate embroidery and stitching. Photographs of the children, many of whom appeared shockingly young, were shown to the child rights charity Global March Against Child Labour [sic], who immediately contacted police. Authorities raided the building a few hours later."[29]*

GATT & THE ORIGINAL SPIRIT OF FREE TRADE

Free trade theories are noble, but that which happened is sad. Free trade idealists did not anticipate $500-700 billion trade deficits annually. It's time to reassess theories. Trade theorists never intended to impoverish people. The opposite was the intention. The 1947 General Agreement on Tariffs and Trade (GATT), since revised by the WTO in the 1990s, was intended to promote economic recovery after World War II, not the outsourcing and epidemic of factory closings we witness nowadays.

In 1947, when GATT was agreed to by 27 nations, America, its cities untouched by war devastation unlike those in Europe and Japan, dominated the world and ran trade surpluses. We manufactured shoes, clothing, washing machines and televisions... domestic industries that have since vanished. In 1947 Harry Truman was President, people watched Milton Berle on clunky black-and-white TVs, Jackie Robinson broke the color barrier in the major leagues, *Brigadoon* opened on Broadway, and the Brooklyn Dodgers played in the World Series (losing to the Yankees in seven games, what else?). Yeah, it's time to revisit free trade.

> *The Telegraph (UK) on India: "The boys, some as young as eight, looked utterly terrified as a police inspector explained that they were working illegally and would shortly be returned to their families. There were chaotic scenes as the children, many dressed in little more than their underwear, were given a few minutes to dress and gather their few belongings before being ushered from the premises... said Bhuwan Ribhu, a Delhi lawyer and activist with the Indian branch of Global March Against Child Labour. [sic] 'The children are aged eight to 15 and at least three of them have told me already that they were working for no pay at all.'"[30]*

In 1947, American foreign policy focused on rebuilding war-shattered Europe through the Marshall Plan and helping poor third world countries. We did our job well... perhaps too well. Japan, then in ruins, and those poor third-world nations now compete with us. China, a closed communist society with a rural economy, was not even in the picture. Trade policies still flow within philosophies from the 1940s when post-war reconstruction was the agenda. GATT and WTO intended to reduce tariff barriers and subsidies. Nowadays nations cheat in subtle ways. The situation has deteriorated for us since the onset of GATT. Free trade meant something very different in 1947.

NTBs: NON-TARIFF BARRIERS TO TRADE

Non-Tariff Barriers – this relatively arcane term is at the center of our problem. GATT and (after 1993) WTO were supposed to end tariffs and barriers. In reality, we still face tariffs but by names like "countervailing duties" and "government subsidies". These are in effect tariffs, tactics used by trade partners (and China in particular). The U.S. trade deficit in 2015 was $531 billion.[31] Chinese imports ($365.7 billion[32]) accounted for nearly 70 percent of the deficit.

Technically, NTBs may not violate WTO agreements. It's iffy, though NTBs do violate the spirit of free trade. Some might call this "cheating." We pay a steep price for it. NTBs are valid when used to protect health, safety or the environment, but that's not what happens in the real world. Think of NTBs as loopholes creating unfair trade practices minus the technical term "tariff". When the Chinese government pours money into industries, it subsidizes industries, lowers prices and violates the spirit of free trade and GATT/WTO understandings.

The U.S. government does not subsidize industry. If China does not play fairly, why should we? It boils down to this: China (and other countries not in compliance) must end NTBs; else we will impose similar NTBs on China (et al) until China cleans things up. Play by the same rules. In the long run, it is better that those rules be fair and healthy. Make it so though in the short term it may require harsh actions against China before sensible compromise prevails.

TAX LOOPHOLES & INVERSIONS EXACERBATE PROBLEMS

Free trade allows developing nations to pay and treat workers poorly while dictating terms (low prices) that lead to our economic setbacks. We must stop our own multinationals from taking advantage of this by imposing harsh tax penalties and shutting down loopholes and inversions. Imposing labor decency standards upon trade partners is the next step. It is unethical to sell goods cheaply by treating workers miserably. Each time we buy a low-cost foreign-made product, we may be supporting ugly practices. We save money, but look at the results. Multinationals sell products without giving Americans jobs. What makes them American if their factories are not here? Tax codes don't obligate them to pay full income tax to the IRS if their headquarters are located abroad. This concept is called *inversion.*

According to *Investpedia,* "Corporate inversion refers to re-incorporating a company overseas in order to reduce the tax burden on income earned abroad... Companies undertaking this strategy are likely to select a country that has lower tax rates and less stringent corporate governance requirements."[33]

A more recent example is drug-maker Pfizer's proposed merger with Allergan, based in Ireland. The inversion would lower Pfizer's taxes. The merger would let Pfizer move its headquarters to Ireland, where corporate tax rates are 12.5%.

American tax rates are as high as 39%. Revised tax codes could eliminate inversions. Tax codes can be amended by Congress to make it painful for corporations to move headquarters or close factories. Why won't Congress do it? Refer to Chapters 2 and 11, noting how leaders rely on donors to fund elections. Pfizer and other large corporations give money to Senators and Congressmen for upcoming campaigns. Money buys influence, but what's good for companies is not always good for American workers.

The Pfizer-Allergan deal failed. An inversion was thwarted. Amended tax codes could shut down inversions. Change lies with the IRS and arcane tax codes.

10 YEARS TO END POOR WAGES & POLLUTION

Educatingforjustice.org on Nike: "Workers Receive 15% of Legal Minimum Wage. On April 6th, 2005, one week prior to the release of Nike's 2004 Corporate Responsibility Report, a respected labor rights group in Indonesia reported that workers at a Nike contract factory were paid wages that were extremely far below the legal minimum wage, violating both Indonesian labor law and Nike's own Code of Conduct. FNPBI reported that workers at the factory, Didachi Makmur Abadi, owned by South Korean investors, had gone on strike to protest the starvation wages. The workers were producing 40 pairs of shoes per hour for the Nike and Puma corporations. Although the minimum wage is $72/month, the workers at Didachi were paid $47/month." [34]

Foreign companies sell goods cheaply by paying people horribly. Chinese government-subsidized industries dump, uh, sell cheap goods. ("Dumping" is a NTB in violation of GATT/WTO understandings.) How can private companies compete? Dumping, polluting, near-slave wages: these are realities of free trade. They are linked together, and trade pacts must address it all. Firm U.S. positions in trade negotiations are essential if we are to promote social justice and avoid more job losses. China has much to lose if America imposes NTBs that threaten China's massive export industry. It would be a temporary tactic to force fair play.

Dealing with bullies in real life means being firm. China would be motivated to compromise. China relies too much upon trade with America to risk a major economic downturn. It would destabilize their economy, threaten the massive export industry, and challenge China's one-party authoritarian grip on the country as the one-billion-plus population grows restless during a potentially severe recession. Effective negotiation means recognizing leverage and using it to obtain your goals – *sticks and carrots*. Teddy Roosevelt aptly said over a century ago: "Speak softly and carry a big stick, and you will go far."

An estimated half of the products we buy are manufactured abroad. Money we spend leaves America. Foreign workers have a right to make a living but not at the expense of Americans losing jobs.

Educatingforjustice.org on Nike: "Workers only received $11/month or 15% of the legal minimum wage. To put this into perspective, 15% of the legal minimum wage would mean ... 77 cents per hour or $6.16 for an 8-hour day [in the U.S.]. Unfortunately, this is not a rare case. One week after this information was publicized, Nike's Corporate Responsibility Report stated that *in 25% to 50% of Nike's partner factories (between 175 and 300 factories), workers are paid less than the legal minimum wage."[35]*

Indeed, there are reasons why foreign products are cheaper. Disturbingly, every time each of us buys clothing or sneakers, we may be abetting labor travesties. Equally disturbing is that many American companies display no sense of conscience and our government, thus far, has done little to address this.

Meeting U.S. standards must be a condition for selling products in the U.S. There is something to be said about ethics and decency in business and trade policy. If foreign companies or American firms manufacturing products abroad sell goods in the U.S., foreign factories must treat employees the same as the American government requires workers here to be treated. Close corporate tax loopholes and require other countries to vastly improve pollution standards and wages. Trade pacts would phase it in over 10 years to give ample notice and time to adjust.

It is right to expect foreign labor be treated properly as a condition of trade with the U.S. Ethics and morality are nonpartisan issues. Exploitation must not be supported. No businesses should be complicit to unjust labor practices.

DEMAND PUBLIC DUTY FROM CORPORATIONS

The concept that government can ask corporate America to think about the common good is something that has evaporated in recent decades. A bit of history often overlooked in our times is John F. Kennedy's decision to stand up for the public and face down big business. He did this during the 1962 Steel Crisis in publicly attacking the steel industry (we had a large one in those days) for behavior that he felt was unpatriotic.[36] In 1962, Kennedy said this during a press conference:

"United States Steel and other leading steel corporations, increasing steel prices by some 6 dollars a ton, constitute a wholly unjustifiable and irresponsible defiance of the public interest. In this serious hour in our nation's history, when we are confronted with grave crises in Berlin and Southeast Asia, when we are devoting our energies to economic recovery and stability... servicemen to risk their lives – and four were killed in the last two days in Vietnam – and asking union members to hold down their wage requests, at a time when restraint and sacrifice are being asked of every citizen, the American people will find it hard, as I do, to accept a situation in which a tiny handful of steel executives whose pursuit of private power and profit exceeds their sense of public responsibility can show such utter contempt for the interests of 185 million Americans... the American people have a right to expect in return for that freedom, a higher sense of business responsibility for the welfare of their country."[37]

He stood up to big business! One wonders if JFK would have put up with outsourcing. FDR also challenged business practices in his 1933 inaugural address:

"The moneychangers have fled from their high seats in the temple of our civilization. We may now restore that temple to the ancient truths. The measure of the restoration lies in the extent to which we apply social values more noble

than mere monetary profit. Happiness lies not in the mere possession of money; it lies in the joy of achievement, in the thrill of creative effort. The joy and moral stimulation of work no longer must be forgotten in the mad chase of evanescent profits. "[38]

We need this today. Presidents have the bully pulpit. They can use it far more effectively. Corporations owe something to their country and workers. Some call this civic duty or public responsibility. Some call it *patriotism*. FDR and JFK demanded it. So should we.

A 10-YEAR PLAN OF ACTION

It is time to think out of the box. From ethics to providing all nations with livable wages, our government must take firmer stands. Here below are parameters that should drive future trade negotiations, bearing in mind *sticks and carrots* while being fair and patient. That which will be asked of trade partners, from improving environmental standards to paying labor properly, will take time. We must give them that time, but we must also make it clear that our patience is not infinite. Let 10 years be our goal – and their deadline. Fair is fair, but enough is enough.

Protect U.S. Jobs. We must firmly protect our interests. Ending the practice of outsourcing must be central to all future trade agreements.

China. China grows; do not let it come at our expense. It's time to take a stand. An improved, far more potent version of the currently-defunct TPP is needed – an agreement that addresses conditions raised in this chapter including vastly improved wages, labor rights, environmental standards, and NTB violations.

Labor. Emerging nations must be obligated in trade pacts to pay and treat labor well in order to receive MFN status. This will make labor more expensive and remove U.S. corporate incentives to move factories abroad. Free trade idealists never intended labor and environmental travesties.

Pollution. All trade pacts must require industries to maintain high environmental standards and low carbon emissions.

NTBs. The U.S. may have to dangle NTBs to press trade partners to compromise and end NTBs. Free trade is about bringing the entire world up to a higher standard *without cheating*.

Tax Codes. Congress must amend corporate tax codes: 1) prohibit inversions, 2) close loopholes to encourage jobs/factories/investment here, 3) allow companies to repatriate foreign earnings at reduced rates, thus bringing billions in tax revenue,[39] 4) lowering the corporate tax rate, as high as 39%, to compete with countries with lower rates, and 5) ban or heavily punish offshore tax havens (like the Caribbean). Tax codes must encourage industry growth on American soil.

Livable Wages. Egregiously low-paying trade partners must vastly raise wages over a 10-year period. Violating, stubborn nations must be denied MFN status and access to American markets. If we do not impose such change, nations with intense disrespect for labor rights, livable wages and environmental standards will forever drive down American wages and pull down the entire world. It must stop. Change must be ushered in within 10 years. We need to impose clear deadlines.

Comprehensive Ethics & Fairness. Incorporate fairness and decency in trade agreements and require this of companies doing business in America. Far more must be part of the equation: government subsidizing, dumping of goods, treatment of workers, lack of pensions or health benefits, pathetic pollution standards, and carbon emissions.

International Unity. Getting all developed nations (Europe, Australia, Japan, etc.) to enforce high standards in emerging/developing nations is crucial to success. For example, if Vietnam refuses to comply and France buys cheap Vietnamese products anyway, the ugly practices will continue. All nations must agree to punish countries that do an end run. _A small leak will sink a great ship._

The time has come for nations clinging to poor standards to change and rise to standards held in the western world. A rising tide lifts all boats.

HITHER PLUTOCRACY?

Being an economic superpower is a privilege each generation must preserve. It means granting dignity to the common man. The people who work in our factories are the foundation of wealth. It is these workers who suffer due to free trade. When Washington turns a blind eye, it betrays the nation. Corporate America, while having valid rights, must not monopolize government. Our constitution mandates a duty to _"insure domestic Tranquility [and] promote the General Welfare."_ When government abandons this mandate, it evolves into _plutocracy:_ rule by the wealthy. When a tiny minority dominates, democracy is endangered.

Free trade is more than an economic principle. It reflects a state of mind altering the balance of power. When Democracy caters to the narrow interests of the two percent, it becomes democracy in name only. This cannot be what our founders envisioned. It is time to think about such matters, for more is at stake than jobs. The republic and democracy are at stake. Ethics and fair play matter.

Chapter 3

AUTOMATION &
THE "GIG" ECONOMY
The Real Job & Income Killers

Self-driving taxis. Driverless trucks. Cashier-less stores. Artificial Intelligence (AI) in banks and on Wall Street. Automation is coming. About 38% of American jobs are vulnerable, according to a *PricewaterhouseCoopers* study.[40] An article in *The Economist* predicts 47% of jobs are at risk.[41] When it comes to jobs, both trade *and* automation matter. The previous chapter proposed a ten-year deadline for raising foreign salaries and environmental standards. Let's not fool ourselves. Automation may eliminate millions more jobs over the next 20 years than free trade ever did. *We'll need a plan.*

Do a Google search and you'll read that millions of jobs are at risk. Nearly a million taxi drivers alone could be put out of work if trends continue. Over three million truck-drivers are vulnerable if self-driving trucks take over. Scanning technology could kill countless retail jobs. Even the legal, stocks and banking sectors seek to lower costs by replacing people with AI. What will those people do?

The economy may create new opportunities, but will it mean millions of people will move from well paying jobs to near-minimum wage? Is government planning for schools and colleges that train people? This chapter does more than restate what we already know. It provides a plan should things get as bad as experts predict. We enter a period of change analogous to the 1900-30 era when new technologies crystallized. America moved from horses to cars, trains and electricity. Government was passive. Everything collapsed in 1929. We witness similar passivity from leaders today. *Indeed, we'll need a plan.*

Not to be overlooked is another impact of automation: the so-called "gig" economy. This entails people having a job (statistically a "job" for unemployment rate purposes) yet struggling to earn enough to get by. Many national chains offer work, but hours weekly salaries vary. Do people work 25 hours/week or 39? How do they manage? Companies *game* the system by providing part-time work and avoiding healthcare. Automation encourages this. It eliminates jobs or makes full-time work less necessary as businesses benefit from automation.

Nearly 40 percent of Americans are expected to be "gig" workers within the next 10 years. It leads to a paradox: work full time yet face poverty.[42-43] Large franchises too often abuse this "gig" business model. Millions of people (and likely millions more in the coming years) work at firms like McDonald's (or any large firm) at near-minimum or mediocre wages knowing hours will change from week to week. It is hard to make a living this way. Income can plummet any given week if assigned hours are low. Without unionization or caring government leaders addressing the "gig" economy, workers have little recourse. National chains game the system, doing an end run around healthcare. Laws encourage this.

Laws need to change if we are to avoid growth in poverty. Minimum wages (and perhaps minimum hours) need to increase to compensate for the "gig" economy. As you can see, automation means more than putting people out of work.

It also means placing them in "gig" jobs that pay poorly, provide insecure hours and ever-changing weekly salaries, and trap people into de facto part time work that makes a middle class life impossible. *Indeed, we need a plan.*

SKILLS TRAINING & VOCATIONAL SCHOOLS

The emerging automation economy will provide new jobs to replace those that are lost. Those new jobs will require training, education, and special schools to train people for new vocations. Train people for new vocations and have government encourage industries to build facilities in areas hardest hit.

The new economic paradigm requires an innovative education system where people are given needed skills years in advance. The public school approach in Germany is a model: vocational schools. It gives students at the high school level training that prepares them. Students graduate from high school with marketable skills in industries where such skills are in demand. A similar concept is also needed in American community colleges so that displaced adults can train for new vocations. It must be free of charge. Industries should be fully involved so that courses are designed for those industries. Give people skills that are in demand.

Given well-documented problems in public education – like dropouts and "social promotion" where students are sent to the next grade without meeting basic reading, math, science and writing skills – a new approach to education is warranted. Vocational schools make sense. Training high school students for jobs in demand is smart policy. If 18-25 year-olds were provided with vocational schools that put them to work, think of the implications: lower crime and unemployment, crushing gangs and drug networks, and less need for costly prisons.

Germany provides opportunity as early as 10th grade to choose a vocational school providing skills for industry as it is *now*. Students graduate with professions. The German system provides training in up to 350 vocations. Over half of German students elect to attend such vocational schools. We can learn so much from our European ally. Community colleges must provide similar vocational training for adults *free of charge*. It requires a new vision for education.

PROFIT SHARING & A "NATIONAL DIVIDEND"

If widespread unemployment and poverty occur, there will be ugly repercussions. The implications of 20 then 30 million people in dire straits are mind-boggling. Where will politics head if that happens? Let's not fool ourselves. Extremism permeated America during the Depression. Google Father Coughlin, the IWW and Huey Long. America withstood the unrest and fascism that plagued Germany, Italy and Eastern Europe. All fell prey to events. Indeed, widespread unemployment has consequences. Further, the U.S. population is growing. Experts say it will reach 400 million within decades. If so, 50 to 60 million jobs may be needed. Automation occurs alongside this.

The wiser path is to accept the coming realities and embrace two principals: 1) redesign our public education system (as discussed above) and 2) embrace the notion that everyone should benefit from efficiency and increased wealth gained from automation. This requires a new way of thinking about wealth. Corporations become increasingly profitable once automation and AI take hold. Everyone, not just stockholders, must benefit. If things get bad, we will need *a national dividend.*

The idea has been discussed in Washington. Called Universal Basic Income (UBI), it involves payments, so to speak, just for being born. This is going too far.[44] The proposal here, quite different, is to help those who suffer due to automation. It would be need-based and temporary, and would have strong incentives to get better work. UBI concepts exist in Canada and Finland. We are not *there* yet. The plan should only kick in if unemployment surges and becomes stubborn year after year.

In principal, just as stockholders are paid dividends and benefit when companies grow and become more profitable, we as a nation should accept the notion that *everyone* deserves to share the benefits of automation. The problem we face is not shrinking wealth and income. Rather, it is *how we share wealth.*

If poverty and unemployment eventually surge due to automation, the solution may require a break from centuries-old concepts of business ownership. If predictions made (stubborn and high unemployment, profitable corporations) come to be, government may eventually need to tax windfall profits and pay a \$100 to \$1,000 dividend monthly to individuals or families working part time or at near-minimum wage. This program would have to kick in if unemployment reaches 10%-plus year after year and U6 (those working part time seeking full time work) closes in on 20%.

The *dividend* need not be permanent. It would only be available to those at the bottom of the economic ladder until such time as they get jobs that pay enough to live comfortably. The *dividend* will keep millions of people out of poverty and provide political stability. *The program must not create a welfare state.* This is discussed later.

This economic paradigm would require a new government agency similar to Social Security. The agency would be funded through targeted taxes of revenues generated by thousands of companies benefiting from automation and efficiencies drawn from it. This new agency – let's call it *The Public Dividend Administration or "PDA"* – would help people who suffer the most due to unemployment and automation. It means a person may work 15 to 20 hours a week and the remaining 20 hours of salary would be subsidized by the "PDA."

Society must transition to this new way of thinking just as successful businesses adjust to changed circumstances. IBM understood that 1940s-era punch cards and typewriters would not be in use generations forward. IBM survives to this day because it embraced change, transitioning to computers then data storage and business services. Similar things can be said about ATT, which evolved from telephone landlines to cell phones, Internet and cable TV. Who talks about Westinghouse or Kodak? They were once giants. Heard of Blockbuster? It was once huge. When was the last time you rented a VCR tape?

It is similar when it comes to how we view wealth. Times are changing.

EVERYONE MUST BENEFIT FROM AUTOMATION

The needed economic paradigm change is how we view national wealth. It involves Wall Street profits and windfall taxes. Conservatives and tax-cutting advocates may find proposals presented here unappetizing. Think twice. Leaders were passive during the 1920s. They thought laissez faire was working. Then came *1929*. Their economic approach brought on collapse, depression and a world war. Let no one today feel so secure with his or her cherished beliefs.

One thing we can be sure of is this: as automation improves efficiency, hundreds of large corporations will see profits rise. Are we only going to allow corporations and stockholders to become richer, or are we going to allow everyone to benefit from automation? In time the Dow Jones may reach 30,000, perhaps 40,000, but without change few will share the benefits of growth. It begs for widespread anger, poverty and political instability. No one benefits from that.

It boils down to this: let S&P 500 corporations become richer as stocks rise and profits grow while poverty mounts or commence a profit sharing system.

One way or another, sharing of national wealth will happen. Will it happen through violent spasms or wise leadership? We should not be so arrogant as to think what happened in Russia in 1917 and Germany in 1933 cannot happen to us. Given enough poverty, people become desperate.

How soon will automation kick in and start to peel away millions of jobs? As soon as self-driving trucks are perfected. The trucking industry would jump at such savings. That alone could slash 3.5 million jobs. It's probably coming. If GDP grows by 50% yet 90% of growth goes into the hands of the rich, we're going to witness historic resentment and anger. It is not good for democracy... or business.

Profit sharing must be part of the new economic paradigm. This is an economic paradigm whose time may eventually come. Money earned by companies sowing profits from automation and efficiencies must be shared even with those who don't own stock. It's kind of like Wall Street paying dividends to everyone. We should all take some ownership of the benefits of automation. If things get bad, it may well be the only solution that keeps the republic and democracy functioning.

This would understandably offend Conservatives, but the alternative to widespread anger and poverty has scary implications for future politics. The alternative is watching millions of people fall into poverty and desperation. **Brace for unpleasant change.** We must not emulate what the 1920s laissez faire generation "accomplished." Their passivity brought on economic collapse and pandemic unemployment. We must do better. *We can avoid a 1929-like disaster.*

The wealthy and powerful stand to lose if they cling to old ways – like disregard for the needs of millions of their countrymen struggling to get by. Our democracy and economic system may be at risk. Conservatives who embrace 50-year-old concepts of economics need to question just how government will manage the automation economy. We need to prepare. Ominous change approaches.

MOTIVATING PEOPLE TO GET BETTER JOBS

One concern with a national *dividend* is the effect it could have upon motivation to get a better job. Put bluntly, if I work 20 hours/week and earn $25,000 ($15,000 for the job plus a $10,000 *dividend*), what incentive would I have to get a better job? Suppose I got a better job – 40 hours/week for $30,000 instead of 20 hours/week for $25,000 (untaxed). "I work longer hours and come home exhausted yet earn the same salary? No way! I'll keep the part time job."

We must make sure this does not happen.

A good program anticipates results and human nature. Provide incentives. No one should work harder yet get the same salary. If someone gets a better job, he/she should receive a *bonus*: $5,000 and/or a year of tax-free income. Give people a benefit to moving up the economic ladder. Do not create a permanent welfare class.

10 FACTS & TRENDS TO CONSIDER

The changes we will face are of similar enormity to the transition from horse to train or punch card to computer. Here are concepts and questions to think about:

1. Self-driving cars and (eventually) trucks alone threaten 4.5 million jobs, and competition abroad will encourage lower wages as a means for competing against foreign nations with low taxes, poor environmental standards and low labor-costs.

2. Politicians talk of taking action, but steps proposed (changed trade and import/corporate tax policies) will likely have little effect on employment.

3. According to studies, the creation of at least 50,000 jobs per month is needed just to keep up with population growth. Thus, 600,000 new jobs must be created annually just to stand still.

4. As automation mounts, greater efficiency will benefit corporations. Profits will grow. We face the conflict of increased wealth for a few and increased unemployment and low income for the majority.

5. It is likely that new jobs created to service automation and AI will not keep up with population growth and millions of people will steadily be put out of work. The likelihood is that government or Federal Reserve intervention cannot stop this.

6. As stocks grow in value, the majority of the country will be left out. Only a small percentage of the country owns stocks.

7. A comfortable middle class life will be shut to millions. Low-paying jobs (Office Depot, McDonald's, Walmart, etc.) replace well paying jobs. Businesses avoid hiring full time to avoid health insurance.

8. We already see a trend towards political extremism. We saw the consequences of anger in the 2016 election.

9. As near-minimum wage jobs mount, the only way for millions to survive will be increased reliance on SNAP (food stamps) and entitlements. What are the implications in terms of government debt alongside the obsession to cut taxes?

10. Experts predict that if proposed tax cuts are enacted (like lowering corporate rates to 15%), government debt will soar $4 to $7 *trillion*. Annual deficits would balloon $400-700 billion and could reach *$1 trillion* annually. Tax cuts are based upon vague assurances of economic growth. What are the odds it will work out?

A TIME TO QUESTION CONVENTIONAL BELIEFS

If things get as bad as many experts predict, widespread anger will force things upon us. Democracy is threatened when the majority is at arms. The risk of becoming a two-class rich/poor nation is huge. Our leaders must be realistic and answer this question: could you survive on $400/week? That is what millions more people may face as automation kicks in. Just how do you suppose they will react? Let's hope the automation talk will be a false alarm and enough jobs will be created. But if the jobs are not created, *we will need a plan*.

Chapter 5

DEREGULATION &
THE BROKEN BANKS
The Hidden Diseases

greed *(greed) n.* an <u>excessive</u> desire for food or wealth.

self•ish *(self-fish) adj.* acting or done according to one's own interest and needs without regard for those of others, keeping good things for oneself.[45]

If you could choose just two words to define Wall Street over the past years, greed and self•ish would get a lot of nods. What bankers did leading up to 2008 is accurately summed up in those two words. A new term has evolved to describe Wall Street: culture of greed. Don't get this wrong. It's not about class warfare or being anti-business. It's about *honesty* and *ethics* in business.

We need stocks to invest in and banks to lend money to homebuyers or businesses that build factories providing jobs and products we need. Wall Street and Main Street need each other. We just need a vibrant banking system that is run *honestly*. We don't want conflict. We just want things done ethically. Only government can ensure this.

While nobody wants socialism, on the other hand, expecting unregulated businesses to self-impose high ethical standards and *never* do anything to harm people... well, let's be realistic. We live in an imperfect world where some people are simply mean and readily do things that hurt others (let alone millions of people). Let no one be naïve. Government sometimes has to step in to ensure that reasonable standards of decency and honesty in business are followed. No reasonable politician wants to deal with thousands of angry constituents who were cheated by unethical businessmen.

The 2008 banking collapse reflected what happens when government stands by and lets "market forces" go unregulated. It pushed Wall Street to a disturbing place. Americans observed smug CEOs who for years defied any duty to act in the country's best interests and showed little remorse for decisions that harmed millions of people. They moved factories abroad. They built cars that were inferior to competitors'. Their executives arrogantly flaunted corporate jets even as their companies lost billions of dollars or accepted government bailouts. They gave shady loans and mortgages to millions of unsuspecting, financially unprepared people and just as quickly foreclosed on homes as soon as opportunity arose. They embraced poisonous banking schemes that led to the 2008 sub-prime disaster, millions of foreclosures, a 50% plunge in the stock market, and a terrible recession. And now people push for deregulation? It just makes no sense.

People indifferent to the suffering of others; executives obsessed with self-enrichment: right or wrong, this accurately defines the widespread perception of Wall Street, bankers and S&P 500 CEOs. Concepts like "executive bonuses" became a lightning rod for anger at smug executives who run companies into the ground (but earn millions), outsource jobs (but see stocks soar), and live good lives (but seem unsympathetic to millions of Americans struggling to survive).

Indeed the hidden diseases of greed and self•ish accurately reflect Wall Street, banking and corporate practices over the past two decades. Leading up to 2008, greed especially permeated and corrupted a previously conservative and well-run banking industry in ways not witnessed since the onset of 1930s-era banking reforms and regulations. The 1933 Glass-Steagall Act, amidst the catastrophic 1930s banking crisis, created regulatory agencies that competently monitored Wall Street for nearly 70 years. Its repeal in 1999 unleashed terrible decisions by modern-day Wall Street executives. It brought on the 2008 sub-prime crisis and years of a deep recession and avoidable suffering.

We again hear talk of deregulation, creating the specter of a return to the laissez-faire-like 2000-08 period leading up to the disastrous sub-prime crisis. The Wild West era of banking. We don't want that... or maybe you want to see your stock portfolio drop by 50% again. We need reasonable regulation, not to interfere with free market principals but to prevent reckless schemes that hurt millions of people. The hidden diseases of greed, selfishness and ill-conceived deregulation must forever be contained – "2008" must remain a lesson to everyone.

"WALL STREET" IS A STATE OF MIND

Greed defines Wall Street. Executives are paid millions of dollars whether the company succeeds or not. Merrill Lynch, leading up to the 2008 banking crisis, paid up to $6 billion in bonuses in 2006.[46] Some 100 employees received about $1 million in bonuses (with an average of $5 million), and 1,900 had an average of $700,000. One executive pocketed $35 million. The company went bankrupt and only survived via a government-arranged merger with Bank of America. Bailout funds from TARP (taxpayer money) helped Bank of America avoid bankruptcy.

This was the tip of the iceberg, for similar things permeated Wall Street. All told, in 2008, despite Wall Street's implosion and TARP giving $700 billion in bailout funds, bankers still paid themselves over $18 billion in bonuses. Then-President Obama reflected the country's outrage in calling this "the height of irresponsibility, it's disgraceful." Has the situation really changed?

Wall Street has become a glaring symbol of what is wrong with the corporate world. Unapologetic for shady practices that brought the country to its knees, Government prior to 2008 supported the Wall Street crowd that brought on the Great Recession. Was the meltdown a harbinger of future practices? It is doubtful that FDR or JFK would have found recent Wall Street practices acceptable. They lashed out against business greed. The political ideologies from the 1980s demonizing government and the abandonment of regulation (of banks especially) failed us. An economy, still recovering, imploded because of an industry's poisoned values and lack of government oversight. Lessons must be learned by all leaders, from Democrat to Republican, from Liberal to Conservative.

WHAT NEXT TO PROTECT THE BANKING SYSTEM?

There has been progress since the sub-prime crisis after new regulations like the 2010 Dodd-Frank Act were enacted, but the hidden diseases that brought on the 2008 economic collapse still lurk. Essentially, the same state of mind that created the crisis remains in place. Let's not fool ourselves: now-profitable banks and a rising stock market do not hide the fact that mean-spirited schemers still lurk and bank lobbyists are still powerful – and "government is the problem" politicians are still pushing for banking deregulation. They unwittingly want to take us right back to the era of unregulated banks that led to the 2008 disaster. Will they ever acknowledge the harmful impact of deregulation?

Human nature forces upon us its fair share of selfish, conniving people who will ruthlessly do anything to enrich themselves. We cannot abolish that small but influential clique of bad apples who obsessively relish wealth no matter how many people are harmed, but we can at least control them. This is what government can do well. This is what regulation is about. It is not about interfering with markets or free enterprise but about making sure business is conducted ethically. When politicians obsess over vague promises to deregulate across the board, they fall prey to the adage of throwing the baby out with the dirty bathwater.

In the coming pages, we will explore bank deregulation, the reasons why regulatory agencies were created, why we desperately need firm banking oversight, and how regulations can be modernized to address 21st-century needs. A list of "cures" is offered afterwards, but first we must diagnose the disease.

DIAGNOSIS: THE UNWISE RUSH TO DEREGULATE

In dealing with life-threatening diseases, cures are often painful. It reminds me of a quip I heard from Florida retirees about getting old: the alternative is worse. When we are sick, we see doctors. Good doctors listen to you before diagnosing. They need to know your medical history. Our economy, like disease, requires this. The 2008-9 collapse of Wall Street exemplifies *treating the symptoms but not the disease*. When Congress passed the 2008 Troubled Assets Relief Program (TARP) providing $700 billion to bail out collapsing banks, it threw money at the symptoms. It left in place the roots of the disease.

Henry Paulson, Treasury Secretary at the time, said TARP was necessary for the banking system was a blink away from meltdown. He was right. Economic conditions would have been worse but for the TARP intervention, but problems persist: toxic derivatives and too-big-to-fail still plague the banking industry. The possibility of reverting to weak regulation of the industry is pervasive in Washington, to the amazement of many economists. Banking practices suggest disaster could happen again if the industry is not properly regulated in the coming years. A political movement to deregulate the industry ignores the reality that this type of deregulation brought on the 2008 disaster.

Frankly, many people rallying for widespread deregulation barely understand the nature of banking, its history, or the reasons why the SEC, FDIC and banking regulators were created in the first place back in the 1930s. Many chanting for deregulation sound as if they have never taken Economics 101 yet think they know better. Vote-seeking politicians cater to ignorance instead of using leadership and intellect to explain basic banking principles. It is likely that many politicians don't understand fundamental banking principals. It's dangerous. *The hidden diseases.*

If our leaders do not address hidden diseases plaguing us, our recent crises may mark an era of permanent decline. Centuries ago Portugal was a superpower. So was Spain. That sure changed. Utterly incompetent kings made it so. If we do not govern intelligently, terrible things will happen. Portugal and Spain learned. *Hidden diseases can destroy mighty empires.*

THE DISEASED MAPLE TREE

dis•ease *(di-zeez) n.* an unhealthy condition caused by infection or diet or conditions of life, or inherited.[47]

This definition well defines the state of our economy. We have:

an unhealthy condition... *(diminished middle class, income inequality)*
caused by infection... *(the Great Recession, outsourcing, millions of lost jobs)*
or diet... *(poisonous political division, 1% control 35.6% of private wealth[48])*
or conditions of life... *(rust belt, growing poverty, unlivable wages)*
or inherited. *(nearly $20 trillion government debt & growing, bottom 40% of population has a __negative__ net worth[49])*

Indeed, dis•ease defines our situation. Our national disease is not unlike a diseased tree. When deadly fungus infects the trunk of a majestic maple tree, rot spreads all over. Soon, the branches are diseased. Soon leaves turn brown, fall, and deprive the tree of energy from the sun. It happens gradually. The stumbling economy and government are that rotting maple tree.

The Fed, Treasury Dept. and SEC – *bank regulators* – could have prevented the 2008 disaster with reasonable monitoring and regulation. Those who think *government is the problem* should honestly revisit the wisdom of deregulation. If they want another banking meltdown, dismantling regulatory agencies will do the job. If they want their net worth to be cut in half again (like 2008), deregulation is the way to go. Okay, who wants that? Perhaps some regulations stymie progress and growth. If so, address problematic regulations one by one, but don't attack regulation as a whole. It's throwing the baby out with the dirty bathwater.

Whether Republican, Conservative, Libertarian, or Democrat, we all need intelligent regulation to protect us and our wealth. We need to be protected from bad things, for bad things happen. Or do you want to go through *2008* again?

FDR *NEW DEAL* REFORMS REMAIN ESSENTIAL

The Glass-Steagall Act of 1933 commenced the modern banking era. It created a foundation for stability of the banking sector that powered steady 20th-century economic growth. Glass-Steagall began firm regulation of the banking industry following disastrous nationwide banking failures in the 1930s. It led to the creation of various new government agencies including, most notably, the Securities and Exchange Commission (SEC) and FDIC, insuring money in bank accounts.

Glass-Steagall placed restrictions on banks recklessly investing in volatile stocks and placed requirements that banks keep sufficient money on hand for depositors. It limited the amount of money people, investment banks and businesses can borrow to buy stocks – margin limits. It put an end to hideous stock market practices that brought on the 1929 crash. It kept banks stable and healthy for decades and ensured that millions of people would never again fear losing their life savings in bank runs, which were so common during the laissez-faire era.

Glass-Steagall was repealed in 1999 in the Gramm–Leach–Bliley Act. It set the table for the 2008 collapse. Some regulations were restored in the 2010 Dodd-Frank Act, but many experts doubt it was sufficient to properly monitor the banking system or prevent future disasters. The 1933 Glass-Steagall Act separated banks from "investment" banks. Its repeal in 1999 paved the way for the 2008 disaster. Had Glass-Steagall been in place, the 2008 collapse may have been prevented. Full separation of traditional banking and investment banks is wise policy.

We need smart government that carefully plans with long-term vision and takes into consideration the darker aspects of human nature. That is why regulation, from banking dishonesty to shady stock market practices, is needed. By demonizing government, a generation's *government is the problem* philosophy harmed reasonable efforts to prevent reckless business practices that harm us all.

Government is the problem policies gained steam for decades. The movement grew. Trashing government became a way of life in Washington. By the late 1990s, then Republican House Speaker Newt Gingrich (serving from 1995 to 1999) oversaw the *Contract with America* promoting "government is the problem" policies. Republican House Majority Leader Tom DeLay, disgraced following indictment for money laundering, also played a key role. The banking system collapsed in 2008. *This* was the legacy of deregulation.

There are reasonable limits to any ideology. Government oversight (or, really, lack of it) is of utmost importance to the health of our economy. Regulatory agencies police the banking system, equity markets and lending policies of banks — the gears that make our economic engine run.

Who would have imagined that a topic as Saharan-dry as 1930s banking regulations, a subject taught in an economics class, would become the focal point of a systemic banking collapse? Depleted 401K accounts and collective pain were brought on by deregulation. Why were so many politicians eager to deregulate considering the tragic lessons learned from the Great Depression? A review of the New Deal would do everyone some good, for forceful oversight was created for good reason. There are still many lawmakers who do not respect the reasons why strict regulation is needed. Until they accept this, our banking system will be in peril, hence a "hidden" disease.

Forceful banking regulation began after FDR took office in 1933. The banking system nationwide was in shambles, bank runs were epidemic, and nearly 25% of the country was unemployed. Millions survived through soup kitchens. Foreclosures were pandemic. Countless thousands of people roamed the country in search of farm work. It was the basis for Steinbeck's classic *The Grapes of Wrath*. The stock market was in the fourth year of a swoon. Rampant margin calls left many with crushing debt – all this in addition to bank runs that bankrupted scores of banks and wiped out savings accounts of millions of people. FDR came from a laissez-faire culture that believed government should not be involved. FDR changed that. The depression forced it. Good leaders embrace reality.

The 1990s deregulation obsession undid what the New Deal accomplished and thereby returned our country to aspects of sickly 1920s laissez-faire economics. An era notoriously lacking in government oversight of Wall Street culminated in the disastrous 1929 stock market crash, the collapse of banks nationwide, and decade-long depression with unemployment peaking at 25 percent. Modern deregulation proponents overlook these historical events. It makes little sense. Our leaders must better understand economics history and principals.

Soon after taking office, FDR oversaw an unprecedented flurry of legislation creating new programs that would never again allow the insanity leading to the 1929 crash and depression (or so we thought). The "alphabet soup" of programs emerged: SEC, NRA, TVA, FDIC, SSA (Social Security), CCC, and WPA (the admired Civilian Conservation Corps and Works Progress Administration, providing thousands of jobs in public projects).

New Deal programs became household names that helped steady the nation's course as it faced pandemic poverty, unemployment and bank failures. (Google "Hoovervilles" to see the result of inaction before FDR.) Government was deservedly seen as a force for good. Vast numbers among of the unemployed soon went to work building bridges, roads and parks. Government was seen as a friend, not the problem. Government helped millions in countless ways.

The changes FDR promoted addressed ills of the laissez-faire era. Among them was the 1933 Glass-Steagall Act creating agencies policing reckless banking practices and risky investments. FDIC was created to insure bank savings. In a single swoop, disastrous bank runs ended. In recent times, FDIC was spared in the rush to deregulate. We were spared the most painful aspects of the depression: the wiping out of life savings in bank runs.

Another building block was the Securities and Exchange Commission (the SEC, first run by Joseph Kennedy, father of our slain 35th President), which commenced regulation of fraud and toxic practices in financial markets. Glass-Steagall ensured banks would not foolishly risk assets in speculative investments. Regulations also addressed excessive margin buying, which was out of control and magnified the 1929 crash.

THE REPEAL OF GLASS-STEAGALL

The repeal of depression-era banking regulations, which stabilized the banking and stock industries for decades, was a key goal of the "government is the problem" movement. The decades of hacking away at depression-era regulations climaxed in 1999 when the final barriers to banks were removed; thus commenced the notorious "Shadow Banking" system functioning outside the scope of intelligently crafted regulations. November 12, 1999 was a giant day for the "government is the problem" movement, for it was on this day when the Gramm-Leach-Bliley Act removed the last barriers to investment banks. It set banks free to invest in speculative and highly risky investments. The vote was strictly along party lines in the Senate: Republicans in favor and Democrats against.

It was ironically considered a hopeful day (at the time) as Treasury Secretary Paul Rubin and Federal Reserve chairman Alan Greenspan triumphantly watched President Clinton sign that infamous legislation removing the final barriers to risky practices – the same practices that brought on the Great Depression. The legacy has been a disaster. Almost immediately upon repeal of remaining Glass-Steagall regulations, a shadow banking system emerged. Banks steadily invested hundreds of billions of dollars in risky mortgages derived from real estate values, hence *derivatives* (as bankers called it). The rest, as they say, is history.

Once the real estate bubble burst a few years later, trillions of dollars vanished because of scandalous schemes concocted by, supposedly, the greatest minds in the banking industry. They went about their schemes with virtually no government oversight. Many legislators did not understand what was happening – many of whom had voted over the years to repeal regulations that were meant to protect the financial system from these kinds of abuse. Notorious terms sum up the legacy: toxic derivatives, SWAPS, MBSs, CDOs. Renowned MIT professor and Nobel Prize-winning economist Paul Samuelson described these creations as "Frankenstein" and "monster-like."[50]

Many politicians have forgotten why regulations were important, and we see the consequences. Regulations protected us by creating a floor, and, literally, you do not want to be standing on that floor if it collapses. We can breathe more easily knowing that the "government is the problem" movement did not eliminate FDIC (insuring bank accounts) or margin limits for investors. However, this was not the case for the Wall Street investment banks, as will be demonstrated up ahead.

LAX OVERSIGHT & DEREGULATION FUELED
A REAL ESTATE BUBBLE & SUB-PRIME CRISIS

The mounting real estate bubble and sub-prime crisis after 2000 may have been avoided had oversight been in place – and therein lie the tragedy. Low Fed interest rates and lax lending requirements fueled the crisis. Housing prices doubled or tripled in a few years because. Millions of buyers who could not afford such mortgages emerged. It only became affordable when lax oversight allowed banks to lend money to virtually anyone who applied for a loan. Deregulation allowed it.

Imagine a $500,000 mortgage with no money down, no income verification of cash assets, or a $30,000 income. Stuck with costly monthly payments, borrowers were overwhelmed as adjustable mortgages raised payments due to terms they had not understood. Soon came a horrible recession, and hundreds of thousands lost their jobs; they fell behind in mortgage payments, and soon came the bank warnings of delinquency. Next came the realization that they could not sell their homes because the market collapsed and their homes were worth less than the mortgage.

The poison spread to giant New York investment banks, which foolishly gobbled up thousands of these risky mortgages and created derivatives (Mortgage-Backed Securities – *MBS*), bundled them into packages and sold them to other banks (the infamous Collateral Debt Obligations – *CDO*), which in turn bundled them yet again and resold them. As housing prices tumbled, many of those risky derivatives lost up to 50% of their value. Total global losses were nearly $15 trillion.[51] The International Monetary Fund estimated that global banking losses reached $1.5 trillion.[52]

Government let it happen. For years, bank lobbyists pressed lawmakers to chip away at banking regulations. The 1999 repeal of Glass-Steagall was merely the last nail in the coffin. Banking behemoths took advantage of lax margin limits. Banks recklessly invested in risky MBS-CDO "investments." As if that were not enough, the highly leveraged banks bought inaccurately-rated derivatives at very high margin ratios. The ratio was nearly 32 to 1 for Lehman Brothers.[53] Government allowed it.[54] Sure enough, the floor collapsed. Soon came the panic and *redemptions*. Bear Stearns and 153-year-old Lehman Brothers perished virtually overnight – essentially a modern-day bank run! What were the politicians thinking back in 1999 when they so proudly repealed Glass-Steagall?

The house of cards collapsed. Merrill Lynch, Citigroup, Goldman Sachs, Morgan Stanley, Wachovia, Bank of America, WaMu, and others faced an unprecedented crisis threatening a complete collapse of the American banking system. Contagion spread worldwide among foreign banks. Insurance giant AIG, which insured those derivatives, collapsed and was saved only by nearly $100 billion from the bailout. Investment banking giants left standing live on though in diminished capacity. "Government-is-the-problem" gave us this. Modern-day politicians promoting banking deregulation must acknowledge the tragic result of deregulation efforts leading to 2008... or will they? That hidden disease remains.

THE FAULT LIES NOT IN THE STARS BUT IN OURSELVES

Who let mortgage firms lend so irresponsibly? Who allowed investment banks to bundle up thousands of risky mortgages into toxic CDOs? Who let everyone make such colossal errors? Government deregulators. *Et tu, Brute.* A nation paid dearly for years of poor judgment and deregulation obsession.

Bank lobbyists and Wall Street executives were at fault, but the bottom line is that lack of government oversight led to the collapse. Compliments of lobbyists pushing for deregulation, government allowed the shadow banking system to go on for years virtually unregulated. The key lessons to be learned remain ignored by many politicians. The deregulation movement doomed the banking system by trusting the marketplace. That's letting the inmates run the asylum. We must resist such urges today, for the 1990s generation of politicians created a dangerous modern-day-laissez-faire.

Debacles were brought on by greed and government abandonment of its duty to regulate the dark aspects of human nature. Leaders believed the seven deadly vices had mystically vanished. They have not. The deadly vices must forever be contained through *regulation, oversight and enforcement.* This is not a Republican or Democratic party concern. It's a concern to anyone who borrows or invests. There were many lobbyists casting influence from 1999 (when sensible Glass-Steagall regulations were repealed) to 2008 (when all hell broke loose). Many of us thought laissez-faire was behind us. We were wrong. It merely took on new names: MBS, CDO, SWAPs, derivatives, bundling. The chemists concocting these reckless schemes betrayed their duty to responsible banking – and a nation.

It all could have been prevented had firm oversight been in place. The smartest people in the land, numbed, did not see it coming. Indeed, everyone would have benefited from paying attention to the lessons from the Great Depression. Unless we put the reckless genies back in their bottles, we may encounter more shenanigans. The 1920s marked the zenith of laissez-faire: astronomical margin buying of stocks, a stock market crash, banks wiped out, plummeting real estate prices... hold on – are we talking about 1929 or 2008? Sadly, *both.* And that's the point: to forever remind us that regulation is essential.

TOO-BIG-TO-FAIL IS TOO RISKY

Reforms now in place through Dodd-Frank are helpful yet inadequate. This spells trouble for future stability of the banking sector and reinforces the need to enact stronger legislation that firmly and permanently protects our country's economy and banks. Pivotal issues continue to haunt the banking sector.

Enactment of legislation addressing the three proposals below will be a huge step forward in terms of preventing future banking disasters.[55]

1. *Too-Big-To Fail*. Some major American banks are so large that the collapse of any one of them could have a terribly disproportionate effect on the American economy. That which happened to the stock markets and banking sector in 2008, when Bear Stearns and Lehman Brothers collapsed, cannot be allowed to happen again. Preventing such future disasters will require the Fed and banking regulatory agencies to break behemoth banks into smaller ones. Were this done, the economy would be protected from the collapse of any one bank. Its effect would be limited and manageable by FDIC and the Federal Reserve. The policy of severing huge banks into smaller ones will understandably trouble free market proponents who prefer that government allow markets to function freely, but, when we all think about it, is it really in our best interests to allow the banking sector (and country) to be so vulnerable to the collapse of a single bank? We know what happened in 2008 when Bear Stearns, Lehman Brothers and AIG collapsed. It brought on the Great Recession, nearly 10% unemployment (closer to 20% if one includes other statistics), pandemic foreclosures, devastating bank failures, and, of course, a 50% stock market plunge. Is protecting behemoth banks worth risking future disaster?

2. *The Federal Reserve*. The Fed should be empowered to address the too-big-to-fail problem. Congress must pass legislation that will empower the Fed and banking regulatory agencies to address the ticking time bomb of too-big-to-fail. Congress must act and not risk potential disasters, such as the collapse of a behemoth bank, that could lead to panic and a future collapse of the banking sector and stock markets similar to what we tragically witnessed back in 2008-09. Simply put, we must not risk a future Great Recession… or something worse.

3. *Support Smaller Banks*. In addressing the too-big-to-fail problem, policies could better support small and community banks. Let them grow. Address banking regulations and requirements that limit their growth while providing huge national banks with unfair competitive advantages. Favoring large banks is unwise. It will only harm the health of the overall banking sector. Small banks need not follow rules envisioned for large national banks. Banking requirements and regulations must be revised. *One-size-fits-all* regulations make no sense. Government must let smaller banks grow. Small and community banks are unfairly burdened by current regulations. Banking regulations should support their growth.

These three important proposals should be included in future banking legislation (or deregulation). We don't want a new "2008" down the road.

FUTURE THREAT REMAINS

Declawed regulatory agencies (especially the SEC) must be modernized and empowered with authority beyond what they had before repeal of Glass-Steagall, given the possibility that bankers may concoct new poisonous schemes. The traditional 12-to-1 ratio of deposits to bank cash-on-hand must be permanently applied to everything including the so-called "shadow" banking sector. There must never again be a shadow industry outside the scope of SEC, FDIC and Federal Reserve oversight. Nothing should be exempted when it comes to modern banking, for we saw the results of "exceptions" back in 2008.

While the Dodd-Frank Act restored some regulation of the banking sector, many reliable experts believe it was not sufficient in terms of ensuring the prevention of future banking and stock market meltdowns. Improvements are needed for monitoring a long list of modern practices that did not exist in the 1930s. They must address modern mortgage lending practices, derivatives, MBSs, CDOs, untrustworthy stock/bond/equity rating services, credit default swaps, hedge funds, reckless buying on margin, and commodities futures. Newly-created consumer fraud agencies that thankfully protect Americans from unethical practices must be supported and allowed to grow in order to address new problems that emerge.

As you sense, things are far more complicated than they were back in 1933 when the regulatory agencies were first created. We need to firmly monitor margin limits, bank funds ratios, insurance firms, and foreign banks doing business in the U.S. Banking is now international, far more complex, and interconnected. Stock market practices require deeper probing into practices in order to ensure that markets are run ethically and honestly.

Mortgage-lending also was corrupted in the early 2000s. As noted above, all kinds of shady practices became commonplace. Countless thousands of people lost their homes due to such practices. So much avoidable suffering! It should never be allowed to happen again. Lending requirements must be monitored. Margin ratios (in the 30s during the crisis) must never again be so loose. Credit card debt must be included in the equation. In sum, a more comprehensive and global system of regulation is needed and it must be designed to react quickly to changing conditions. There must be greater collaboration and planning among regulatory agencies including the Fed, Treasury, SEC, FDIC, commodities futures and consumer protection agencies, and foreign banks. Are regulatory agencies up to the task?

The time to start preventing the next crisis is now. Government foolishly entrusted the banking sector to police itself. Will modern regulators act firmly, or will they become lax again if wrongheaded leaders take the helm in Washington? The specter of future problems lurks. Among the hidden diseases: politicians who do not respect the need for oversight despite everything that happened. Deregulation remains a mainstay of many leaders. Past lawmakers ceded control to lobbyists hired by the likes of Lehman and Bear Stearns. Those giants are gone forever. Take a hint. For the sake of ill-conceived concepts that the marketplace is best equipped to decide our fate, the American people got punched in the nose. It could happen again. *Remember the rotting maple tree.*

As FDR wisely said during his March 12, 1933 Fireside Chat:

> *"Some of our bankers had shown themselves either incompetent or dishonest in their handling of the people's funds. They had used the money entrusted to them in speculations and unwise loans... It was the government's job to straighten out this situation and do it as quickly as possible − and the job is being performed."[56]*

Indeed, let us now make sure "the job is being performed."

SUMMARY: CURES FOR THE SICK MAPLE TREE

Let us not lose perspective. Our goal is not burdensome regulation. It is intelligent regulation to prevent 2008-like collapses and maintain ethical business practices, for glaring problems still afflict us. Let's not lull ourselves into thinking all is well because the Dow Jones rose. Here are policies for consideration.

➤ Regulatory Agencies. All agencies must be firmed up as powerful regulators. They allowed the shadow banking system to thrive. The Federal Reserve, Treasure Dept. and SEC must firmly regulate all emerging financial practices and quick thwart future schemes with resolve.

➤ Too Big To Fail. Bank size is crucial in preventing a future banking sector crisis. Note what happened in 2008 when Lehman Brothers and Bear Stearns collapsed. Breaking up huge banks (thereby increasing the number of banks and healthy competition) will decrease the chance of future systematic failure. No bank should be so large that it can wreck the banking sector. It means breaking up banks that are dangerously large. Behemoth banks control the industry. We remain scarily vulnerable and should help, not burden, community and smaller banks.

➤ A Modern Glass-Steagall. Glass-Steagall separated traditional banking from investment banks. Its 1999 repeal paved the way for unregulated "shadow" banks that brought on the 2008 disaster. Separation of investment banks must be firmed up by a modernized, more sophisticated version of Glass-Steagall.

➤ Global Regulation. The spread of the 2008 sub-prime crisis globally makes it clear that we are vulnerable to foreign crisis. We can only control what banks do here. As activities abroad can harm us due to globalization, global regulation is required.[57] This will require treaties and better communication among nations and their respective equivalent of our Federal Reserve.

➤ Short-Term Debt. One significant portion of bank loans left largely unregulated is short-term debt (or "runnables"). Short-term refers to loans due within a year.[58] These types of loans are largely unprotected and uninsured by government. They should be. Congress must grant agencies authority to monitor this. We are vulnerable to this important oversight. A devastating bank run could destabilize the banking sector. A dam with a gap is useless.

➤ Ratings. During the 2000 era of CDOs and derivatives bundling mortgage holdings, ratings firms gave good opinions of dubious investments. Had ratings been honest and accurate, banks and investors may have shied away from offerings that collapsed once real estate prices plummeted. Regulation of these ratings agencies is needed to ensure that ratings are accurate and truthful.

➢ SEC. Fraud prosecution became lax due to weak enforcement and SEC staff cuts. The New York Times called the SEC "a paper tiger."[59] Prosecutions dropped from 513 cases in 2002 to 133 in 2008. The Justice Dept. handled nine cases in 2007, down from 69 in 2000 (an 87% drop). In 1933, Ferdinand Pecora, a N.Y. Asst. District Attorney, gained fame as chief counsel for the Senate Banking and Currency Committee in his muckraking crusade to expose fraud.[60] We need a modern-day Ferdinand Pecora. The SEC also needs a much larger staff.

➢ Lobbyists. Influence through campaign donations plagues Washington. Banking lobbyists will continue to oppose regulation. Reforms must be imposed to contain lobbying corruption and domination (the focus of Chapter 11).

➢ Abolish The "Shadow" Banking System. Government must police new schemes and impose regulations that will never again allow a "shadow" banking system to function outside the scope of oversight. Regulatory agencies must police risky investments, margin, credit card lending, insurance firms, mortgage lending practices, and down-payment requirements.

➢ Mortgages. Thousands ill-prepared to buy homes got mortgages anyway. Lending must be regulated including down payments, income requirements and adjustable-rate mortgages. Option ARMS lenders offered low rates that ballooned and affected two million homeowners. It led to waves of foreclosures.[61] It must be addressed.[62] Further, the 1997 Taxpayer Relief Act should be repealed. It exempted sellers from capital gains taxes for the first $500,000 and turned purchases into investor havens. The Fed estimates 17% more homes sold due to this law.

➢ Blue-Ribbon Commissions. As Wall Street is run by clever but often unwise financiers, government must keep pace with new ventures, some of which may be risky. Biannual commissions must revisit regulations as problems emerge.

DENOUEMENT: THE DISEASED MAPLE TREE

We see politicians who resort to cheerleading: tell voters what they like to hear, not what they *need* to hear. Power derives from industrial might and planning. If we are to avoid becoming a paper tiger, we had better walk the walk. Will lawmakers in need of campaign donations cave in to lobbyists then campaign for deregulation that sets the table for future economic collapse? This mindset will fail us again and again. *This hidden disease is still in place.*

What has also not changed is the tendency to fight government instead of leaving good practices in place. This hidden disease also remains. Government is like a ship. The ship must be steady, not a political pendulum swinging opposite every four or eight years. If we are to continue to lead the free world, we must treat the rotting maple tree and make it healthy and strong again. Wall Street and the banking system are our maple tree. Make both strong. Make both work ethically.

We must not deceive ourselves. We need government to protect us from corruption and greed. The 2008 sub-prime debacle demonstrated this clearly. *Like a maple tree, banks only stand strong upon roots of integrity.*

Chapter 6

RISING OCEANS & TEMPERATURE
Just The Facts

This chapter is fact-driven and presents scientific reports by trusted government agencies and scientists *in their own words*. It focuses on the effect warmer air and ocean temperatures have on the northern hemisphere Arctic Icecap, Greenland glaciers and (most importantly) southern hemisphere Antarctica, a continent 50% larger than the U.S. covered by miles-high glaciers. There is enough water inside that frozen continent to raise ocean levels anywhere from 217 to 260 feet.[63-64-65-66-67]

Antarctica is truly the end game. For skeptics of global warming, your feelings are understandable. You are unconvinced global warming is the result of man-made carbon emissions. You are unmoved by predictions of weather changes in coming decades, but what about ocean level? Now that's a different ballgame. The ocean has risen about eight inches since the onset of the 20th Century, and there is one indisputable fact we all agree on: the warmer air and water are, the faster ice melts... and fills the ocean.

The warming of air and water in polar regions is well documented. Melting will continue as the air and ocean get warmer. A catastrophic 200-plus foot ocean rise is way off in the future.[68] It could take 1,000 years for all of Antarctica to melt and raise the ocean over 200 feet, but as for the ocean rising 2 to 5 feet, that's a different story. That could happen within 50 to 80 years according to the best scientific minds in the world.

How soon could that happen? Scientists are not clairvoyants who know the future. All they can do is sift through data and come up with plausible theories, but scientists are smart, fact-driven and nonpolitical. Whether Republican or Democrat, we must heed what the majority of scientists say and not cherry pick, for if we pick favored opinions that turn out wrong, we all are threatened by the effects of a rising ocean, from Florida to Louisiana to California. Too much is at stake to take the position *let's wait and see*. Read the below facts, footnoted so you can check sources.

- *The ocean has risen eight inches since 1900 and the rate of ocean rise is faster now than it was two decades ago.[69]*

- *Average ocean temperatures rose 1.5 degrees over the last century.[70]*

- *Increased flooding plagues North and South Carolina.*

- *Florida is especially vulnerable as huge swaths are five feet above sea level.*

- *Glaciers from Alaska to the Himalayas are melting worldwide.[71-72]*

- *"The Arctic is losing about 30,000 square miles (78,000 square kilometers) — an area roughly equivalent to the state of Maine — of sea ice each year, NASA scientists say."[73]*

- *Historically ice-packed Arctic shores are now clear and the Arctic icecap is much smaller than it was a century ago, exposing more dark ocean water to sunlight heating it up.*

- *Coastal flooding has increased and sea life is affected by warming waters.*[74]

- *NASA has expressed concern. Its facilities encounter flooding. NASA's Climate Adaptation Science Investigators working group predicted a "sea level rise from five inches to two feet by 2050" that endangers coastal launch pads.*[75 76]

- *NASA's Goddard Institute for Space Studies reports average global temperature increased by about 1.4° Fahrenheit since 1880, with two-thirds of the warming occurring since 1975.*[77]

- *Carbon Dioxide (CO2) levels increased 25% since 1958.*[78]

- *Antarctica ice/glaciers are, on average, 1.6 miles deep and cover almost all of the continent. It contains about 70% percent of the planet's fresh water.*[79]

- *"Science" and "National Geographic" report ocean temperatures rose 15 times faster in the past six decades than the previous 10,000 years.*[80 81 82]

Facts support the argument that warming is mostly caused by man, not nature. It boils down to this: if you believe warming is due to nature, do nothing; if you believe warming is due to human activities, we must act. There is a tendency to feel we can wait until warming trends are irrefutable. There is a problem with this logic. Scientists agree that once key events occur in the glaciers of Antarctica, it will be impossible to reverse ice melt draining into the ocean. We don't know when we reach that point of no return, but once we do it may be impossible to stop catastrophic melting of Antarctica's continent-wide glaciers.

If changes scientists expect are true, our future is dire. The risk is that if we do too little now, action in 50 years may come too late. The continent of Antarctica is covered by miles-high glaciers and huge underground lakes locked within. Scientists report a complete melting will raise ocean levels 217 to 260 feet.[83-84-85-86] Entire countries would be submerged. Florida and Georgia would disappear. See what the U.S. map would look like if the Antarctic glaciers melted. It is chilling to see: *https://m.youtube.com/watch?v=VbiRNT_gWUQ*

The southern shore of America could be a line from South Carolina to Missouri. It could take 1,000 years for Antarctica to melt, but even a three-foot rise, foreseeable in our lifetime, would be catastrophic. Below are quotes by top scientists and government agencies. Read then decide how real the threat is.

BY THE NUMBERS:

21 million	metric tons of coal used daily worldwide (2013)[87]
2.7 million	gallons of gas burned each minute in the U.S.[88]
1.2 billion	tons of coal consumed in U.S. in 2008[89]

1.2 billion	*number of cars worldwide[90]*
2 billion	*projected number of cars worldwide in 2035[91]*
20,000	*estimated pollution-causing airplanes worldwide (2013)[92]*
35,000	*estimated airplanes expected by 2035[93]*
400	*carbon dioxide parts per million (ppm) (NASA, 2013)[94]*
100	*ppm increase above ppm in previous one million years[95]*
24	*percent carbon dioxide ppm increased since 1958[96]*
1700	*U.S. manufacturing & generating facilities using coal[97]*
50	*percent of energy in U.S. derived from coal[98]*
32	*total energy production in U.S. using coal[99]*
3.7	*tons of coal consumed annually per each American[100]*

U.S. DEPT. OF COMMERCE:[101]

• *[S]ea level has been rising at the rate of about 0.6 inches per decade since 1900. Since 1992, satellite altimeters indicate that the rate of rise has increased to 1.2 inches per decade – a significantly larger rate than at any other time over the last 2000 years.*

• *In the next several decades, continued sea level rise and land subsidence will cause tidal flood frequencies to rapidly increase due to typical storm surges and high tides in many coastal regions.*

• *In the United States, almost 40% of the population lives in relatively high-population-density coastal areas, where sea level plays a role in flooding, shoreline erosion, and hazards from storms. Globally, eight of the world's 10 largest cities are near a coast, according to the U.N. Atlas of the Oceans.*

• *Higher sea levels mean that deadly and destructive storm surges push farther inland than they once did, which also means more frequent nuisance flooding. Disruptive and expensive, nuisance flooding is estimated to be from 300 percent to 900 percent more frequent within U.S. coastal communities than it was just 50 years ago.*

NASA.GOV, NOAA & NASA/NOAA SCIENTISTS:[102]

• *Scientific evidence for warming of the climate system is unequivocal ... The current warming trend is of particular significance because most of it is very likely human-induced and proceeding at a rate that is unprecedented in the past 1,300 years.*

• *The heat-trapping nature of carbon dioxide and other gases was demonstrated in the mid-20th Century.[103] Their ability to affect the transfer of infrared energy through the atmosphere is the scientific basis of many instruments flown by NASA. There is no question that increased levels of greenhouse gases must cause the Earth to warm.*

• *The global concentration of carbon dioxide in the atmosphere – the primary driver of recent climate change – has reached 400 parts per million (ppm) for the first time in recorded history, according to data from the Mauna Loa Observatory in Hawaii.*

• *Since 1958, the Mauna Loa Observatory has been gathering data on how much carbon dioxide is in the atmosphere. Carbon dioxide [CO2] has increased by about 24 percent since the beginning of this record.[104]*

- *CO2 concentrations haven't been this high in millions of years. Even more alarming is the rate of increase in the last five decades and the fact that CO2 stays in the atmosphere for hundreds or thousands of years. This milestone is a wake up call that our actions in response to climate change need to match the persistent rise in CO2. Climate change is a threat to life on Earth and we can no longer afford to be spectators. – Dr. Erika Podest, Carbon and water cycle research scientist.[105]*
- *The world is quickening the rate of accumulation of CO2, and has shown no signs of slowing this down. It should be a psychological tripwire for everyone. – Dr. Michael Gunson, Global Change & Energy Program Manager; Project Scientist, Orbiting Carbon Observatory-2 satellite mission - NASA Jet Propulsion Laboratory[106]*
- *Ice cores drawn from Greenland, Antarctica, and tropical mountain glaciers show that the Earth's climate responds to changes in greenhouse gas levels. They also show that in the past, large changes in climate have happened very quickly, geologically-speaking: in tens of years, not in millions or even thousands.[107]*
- *Global sea level rose about 17 centimeters (6.7 inches) in the last century. The rate in the last decade, however, is nearly double that of the last century.[108]*
- *Both the extent and thickness of Arctic sea ice has declined rapidly over the last several decades.[109]*
- *Glaciers are retreating almost everywhere around the world — including in the Alps, Himalayas, Andes, Rockies, Alaska and Africa.[110]*
- *The number of record high temperature events in the United States has been increasing, while the number of record low temperature events has been decreasing, since 1950. The U.S. has also witnessed increasing numbers of intense rainfall events.[111]*
- *Since the beginning of the Industrial Revolution, the acidity of surface ocean waters has increased by about 30 percent.[112] [113] This increase is the result of humans emitting more carbon dioxide into the atmosphere and hence more being absorbed into the oceans.*
- *The amount of carbon dioxide absorbed by the upper layer of the oceans is increasing by about 2 billion tons per year.[114] [115]*

UNIVERSE TODAY, SPACE AND ASTRONOMY NEWS:[116]
- *[C]arbon dioxide is a greenhouse gas. Various wavelengths can pass through this invisible gas, but it's very effective at trapping heat. Light from the Sun strikes the ground of Venus, and warms it up. The ground tries to radiate heat back into space but the carbon dioxide traps much of it around the planet keeping it so warm. This is the same thing that happens when you keep your car windows closed on a hot day.*

- *Scientists think that Venus used to be more similar to Earth, with lower temperatures and even liquid water on the surface of the planet. At some point, billions of years ago, the planet started to heat up. At some point, all the water on the surface evaporated into the atmosphere. Water vapor is an even more powerful greenhouse gas than carbon dioxide and this caused temperatures to rise even more. Then the surface of Venus got so hot that the carbon trapped in rocks sublimated into the atmosphere and mixed with oxygen to form even more carbon dioxide. And so today we have a carbon dioxide atmosphere on Venus, which is 92 times more dense than Earth's atmosphere at the surface.*

• *Could this happen on Earth? Scientists think that if the same process happened on Earth, we would have temperatures with several hundred degrees C, and an atmosphere 100 times as dense as we have right now.*

NOAA NATIONAL CLIMATE DATA CENTER, U.S. DEPT. OF COMMERCE:[117]

• *The 20th Century has been like no other ... carbon dioxide concentrations in the atmosphere have risen from 290 parts per million (ppm) to 369 ppm [Author: and 400 ppm since article publication], with strong evidence pointing to the burning of fossil fuels as a primary cause of these increases ... Many climate researchers and policy makers are concerned that increases in population and rising standards of living will lead to ever higher levels of carbon dioxide and other greenhouse gases.*

• *The last time there was this much carbon dioxide (CO2) in the Earth's atmosphere, modern humans didn't exist. Mega toothed sharks prowled the oceans, the world's seas were up to 100 feet higher than they are today, and the global average surface temperature was up to 11°F warmer than it is now.*

CLIMATECENTRAL.ORG:[118]

• *CO2 levels are far higher now than they have been for anytime during the past 800,000 years.*

• *Carbon dioxide is the most important long-lived global warming gas, and once it is emitted by burning fossil fuels such as coal and oil, a single CO2 molecule can remain in the atmosphere for hundreds of years.*

• *Global CO2 emissions reached a record high of 35.6 billion tonnes [sic] in 2012, up 2.6 percent from 2011. Carbon dioxide and other greenhouse gases warm the planet by absorbing the sun's energy and preventing heat from escaping back into space.*

• *[W]hen was the last time that CO2 levels were this high, and what was the climate like back then? ... studies show a wide date range from between 800,000 to 15 million years ago. The most direct evidence comes from tiny bubbles of ancient air trapped in the vast ice sheets of Antarctica. By drilling for ice cores and analyzing the air bubbles, scientists have found that, at no point during at least the past 800,000 years have atmospheric CO2 levels been as high as they are now.*

• *That means that in the entire history of human civilization, CO2 levels have never been this high. The Keeling Curve, showing CO2 concentrations increasing to near 400 ppm in 2013. Credit: NOAA.*

• *For a 2009 study, published in the journal Science, scientists analyzed shells in deep sea sediments to estimate past CO2 levels, and found that CO2 levels have not been as high as they are now for at least the past 10 to 15 million years, during the Miocene epoch.*

• *"This was a time when global temperatures were substantially warmer than today, and there was very little ice around anywhere on the planet. And so sea level was considerably higher — around 100 feet higher — than it is today," said Pennsylvania State University climate scientist Michael Mann, in an email conversation. "It is for this reason that some climate scientists, like James Hansen, have argued that even current-day CO2 levels are too high. There is the possibility that we've already breached the threshold of truly dangerous human influence on our climate and planet."*

• *Sea levels are increasing today in response to the warming climate, as ice sheets melt and seas expand due to rising temperatures. Scientists are projecting up to 3 feet or more of global sea level rise by 2100, which would put some coastal cities in peril.*

UNIVERSITY OF ARIZONA (Planet Venus & Greenhouse effect):[119]

• *CO_2 absorbs the infrared radiation and it does not all escape into space, but much of it is trapped.*

• *[T]he [Venus] surface heats to 730K*

• *Carbon dioxide (and water) have absorptions near 7 and 15 microns that produce a greenhouse effect that warms the earth to a comfortable temperature for life as we know it. The difference from Venus is that carbon dioxide is only 0.03% of the atmosphere of the earth, whereas it is 96.5% of the atmosphere of Venus.*

NASA-SUPPORTED NATIONAL SNOW AND ICE DATA CENTER (NSIDC) ON SHRINKING ARCTIC:[120] [121] [122]

• *Arctic sea ice appears to have reached a record low wintertime maximum extent for the second year in a row ... Through 2016, the linear rate of decline for October is 66,400 square kilometers or (25,600 square miles) per year, or 7.4 percent per decade.*

• *Since the late 1970s, the Arctic has lost an average of 20,800 square miles (53,900 square kilometers) of ice a year.*

• *2016 Arctic Sea Ice Wintertime Extent Hits Another Record Low. Arctic sea ice appears to have reached a record low wintertime maximum extent for the second year in a row.*

• *The atmospheric warmth probably contributed to this lowest maximum extent, with air temperatures up to 10 degrees Fahrenheit above average at the edges of the ice pack where sea ice is thin, said Walt Meier, a sea ice scientist at NASA's Goddard Space Flight Center in Greenbelt, Maryland.*

• *Since 1979, that trend has led to a loss of 620,000 square miles of winter sea ice cover, an area more than twice the size of Texas.*

• *Arctic sea ice plays an important role in maintaining Earth's temperature—its bright white surface reflects solar energy that the ocean would otherwise absorb.*

• *"In places where sea ice has been lost, those areas of open water will put more heat into the atmosphere because the air is much colder than unfrozen sea water," Francis said. "As winter sea ice disappears, areas of unusually warm air temperatures in the Arctic will expand. These are also areas of increased evaporation, and the resulting water vapor will contribute to increased cloudiness, which in winter, further warms the surface."*

LIVESCIENCE.COM:[123]

• *The Arctic is losing about 30,000 square miles (78,000 square kilometers) — an area roughly equivalent to the state of Maine — of sea ice each year, NASA scientists say. And while ice cover at the North Pole has rebounded from last year's record-setting lows, Arctic sea ice continues to retreat and* thin *at an alarming pace.*

• *In 2012, the ice cap over the Arctic Ocean shrank to its lowest extent ever recorded.*

• *Since 1980, the Arctic has lost approximately 40 percent of its sea ice cover, Meier said.   "In the 1980s, the Arctic sea ice at the end of the summer was about the size of the lower 48 U.S. states," he explained. "If you imagine taking a road trip across the sea ice — say you want to go from Los Angeles to New York — you could have driven on the sea ice the whole way. Now, you'd reach the ice edge at around the middle of Nebraska, so we've lost everything east of the Mississippi [River]."*

• *If current melting trends continue, the Arctic region will see completely ice-free summers in the future, he said.   "At this point, we're looking at 'when' as opposed to 'if,'" Meier said ...Ten years ago, researchers predicted the Arctic could experience ice-free summers by the end of the century. "Now, it's really looking pretty likely that it could come mid-century at the latest, and perhaps even within the next couple of decades," Meier said.*

• *With ice cover shrinking in the Arctic during the summer months, less sunlight is reflected off the icy surface, which means the ocean absorbs the sunlight instead. This heats up the ocean and surrounding area, and this effect has the potential to change global weather patterns.*

• *"The Arctic also has massive stores of methane in the permafrost and sea bed,"
Wagner said. "As we lose the sea ice, we have more heat going into the ocean,
causing more permafrost to die, which can destabilize the sea bed and trip the
release of this methane, which could cause spikes in temperature."*

REALCLIMATE.ORG:[124]

• *According to this reconstruction, 20th-century sea-level rise on the U.S. Atlantic
coast is faster than at any time in the past two millennia.*

NCAR/UCAR ATMOSNEWS: (Univ. of North Carolina)[125]

• *Averaged over all land and ocean surfaces, temperatures warmed roughly 1.53
degrees Fahrenheit (0.85 degrees Celsius) from 1880 to 2012, according to the
Intergovernmental Panel on Climate Change ... In the Northern Hemisphere,
where most of Earth's land mass is located, the three decades from 1983 to
2012 were likely the warmest 30-year period of the last 1,400 years.*

SMITHSONIAN MUSEUM-OCEAN PORTAL:[126]

• *[S]ea level is 6 to 8 inches (15-20 centimeters) higher on average than it was in
1900... for the previous 2,000 years, sea level hadn't changed much at all.*

• *Sea level started rising in the late 1800s, soon after we started burning coal, gas
and other fossil fuels for energy. When burned, these high-energy fuel sources
send carbon dioxide up into the atmosphere.*

• *Carbon dioxide absorbs heat from the sun and traps it, warming the atmosphere
and the planet.*

• *Warmer temperatures cause ice on land like glaciers and ice sheets to melt, and
the meltwater flows into the ocean to increase sea level. Second, warm water
expands and takes up more space than colder water, increasing the volume of
water in the sea.*

• *Land that is today home to between 470 and 760 million coastal residents will be
inundated by sea level rise associated with a 4 degree Celsius warming that
will occur if we fail to curb the amount of carbon dioxide in the atmosphere.*

• *[T]he climate stabilized and sea level rise slowed, holding largely steady for most
of the last 2,000 years, based on records from corals and sediment cores. Now,
however, sea level is on the rise again, rising faster now than it has in the past
6,000 years.*

• *Ice shelves support ice sheets and glaciers by holding the ice on land. But as
ocean temperatures increase, warm water laps at the ice shelves, weakening
them and causing them to cave glaciers into the sea... This destabilization and*

acceleration has already been observed at some Greenland glaciers like Jakobshavn Isbrae.

- *Warming has already caused major changes in the ice sheets, continental masses of ice which hold a greater volume of ice than glaciers and ice caps combined.*

- *These changes are irreversible in the short term, says NASA's Eric Rignot, and it would take centuries to reverse the trail of ice retreat.*

- *In addition to polar ice, the melting of mountain glaciers, like those in the Andes and Himalayas, has caused an equal amount of sea level rise to date. However, because mountain glaciers include only one percent of all land ice, polar ice will eventually greatly surpass their contributions to global sea-level rise.*

GLOBALCHANGE.GOV:[127]

- *Global sea level has risen by about 8 inches since reliable record keeping began in 1880. It is projected to rise another 1 to 4 feet by 2100.*

- *Models suggest a range of additional sea level rise from about 2 feet to as much as 6 feet by 2100, depending on emissions scenario.*

- *Since 1992, the rate of global sea level rise measured by satellites has been roughly twice the rate observed over the last century, providing evidence of additional acceleration.*

- *The oceans are absorbing over 90% of the increased atmospheric heat associated with emissions from human activity.*

TEN HOTTEST YEARS SINCE 1880:[128] [129]

YEAR(s)	RANK
2016	1
2015	2
2014	3
2010	4
2013	5
2005	6
1998/2009	7 (tie)
2012	8
2003/06/07	10 (tie)

ANTARCTICGLACIERS.ORG:[130]

- *Global sea levels are predicted to rise by 20-60 mm by 2100, and possibly up to 1 metre. This is mostly from glacier melt and thermal expansion of the oceans.*

BUSINESSINSIDER.COM:[131]

• As the rising sea crawls farther and farther up the shore, in many places it will seep into the freshwater sources in the ground that many coastal areas rely on for their drinking water. These underground water sources, called aquifers, are crucial springs of freshwater

• Those same freshwater sources we use for drinking also supply the water we use for irrigation ... Saltwater can stunt or even kill crops, but creating freshwater from saltwater is a costly and unsustainable practice.

• The tourism and real estate industries in coastal areas are likely to take a hit as prime beachfront properties and recreational areas are washed away by rising waters.

• As rising ocean water seeps into the ground, the soil near the coast will become saltier. Some plants will simply be unable to cope ... According to Climate Central, a nonprofit organization dedicated to communicating climate science to the public, trees will have an especially difficult time.

• As the rising ocean erodes the shoreline and floods the areas in which coastal animals live, animals like shorebirds and sea turtles will suffer... Their habitats may be so damaged by flooding or changes in the surrounding plant life that they can no longer survive in the environment. It will hurt the economy.

THE REAL DEAL: SOUTH FLORIDA REAL ESTATE NEWS:[132]

• Miami Beach property values may fall as sea levels rise: experts - The ocean could rise two feet by 2060, putting western half of Miami Beach under water. Parts of Miami Beach could be inundated with flood waters in as little as 15 years, and property values may slide amid the rising tide, according to nearly two dozen university heads and climate change experts who were on hand to answer questions on the effects of sea-level rise on South Florida during a Miami Beach Chamber of Commerce event.

• Already, media around the globe are publicizing the fact that South Florida is "ground zero" for the adverse economic impact of sea-level rise, Pathman argued. Unfortunately, the region is still behind in preparing its infrastructure for the future.

• Thanks to a slowing gulfstream, warming oceans, and ice flows submerging beneath the ocean from Greenland and Antarctica, the oceans are rising faster than ever, said Keren Bolter, research coordinator for Florida Atlantic University Center for the Environmental Studies.

• By 2100, the oceans are projected to increase by seven feet, Bolter added. At that level, The Keys, along with large chunks of Miami-Dade and Broward counties, will be inundated with sea water at high tide.

CHARLESTON CITY PAPER:[133]
- *If the worldwide average high tide rises two feet above current levels, Colonial Lake could spill over into the surrounding neighborhood streets every day at high tide. At four feet above current high tide levels, beachgoers face standing water while driving on Folly Road. At five feet, the northern end of Park Circle becomes waterfront property.*

- *"More than 800 square miles of land lie less than four feet above the high tide line in South Carolina," Strauss and other researchers write in a report accompanying the map. "Some $24 billion in property value and 54,000 homes."*

- *NOAA has made broad-ranging predictions on how much the global average sea level will rise in the next 100 years, from 1 foot (if the level only continues to change at its current rate) to 7 feet.*

- *The change will likely be noticeable even within 50 years, with the most dire prediction by NOAA putting high tide 2.28 feet above 2012 levels in 2062.*

- *In what could be a glimpse of the future as ocean levels continue to rise, water can sometimes be seen gurgling up through manholes and storm drains.*

- *Massive drainage tunnels and pump stations are currently being installed under the City Market and the intersection of Spring and Fishburne streets.*

NPR.ORG:[134]
- *"You hear predictions of up to 3 or 4 feet over the next century," said Chris Bergh, of The Nature Conservancy's Florida Keys program.*

- *With an average elevation of just 3 or 4 feet, there are few places in America where the rising sea level is a bigger threat than in the Keys.*

- *On Big Pine Key, one of the chain's largest and most environmentally diverse islands, you can already see changes brought on by the accelerating sea level rise.*

- *A spot not far from the island's coast used to be a pine forest. Now, it's tidal wetlands — home to a few salt-tolerant plant species and the desiccated remnants of the old forest. Bergh described some of the changes brought on by the rising sea level.*

- *[S]aid Frank Ackerman, a senior economist at the Stockholm Environment Institute, who has studied what impact climate change – and sea level rise – will have on Florida. His model calls for a sea level rise of just over 2 feet by 2060 ... Florida stands to lose almost 10 percent of its land area and the homes of 1.5 million people ... "There's residential real estate worth $130 billion in*

54

that, half of Florida's beaches, two nuclear reactors, three prisons, 37 nursing homes, and on and on."

- Ackerman has added up the impact that more powerful hurricanes, higher average temperatures and declining tourism will have on Florida. He says the cost of inaction — doing nothing to slow climate change and sea level rise — would add up to $345 billion, or 5 percent of Florida's total income, by 2100.

- The concerns are not just in South Florida. The Army Corps of Engineers recently published guidance for its staff members, directing them to consider the impact a rise in sea level will have on all corps projects nationwide.

MAP OF U.S. CITIES IF OCEAN RISES 5, 12 & 25 FEET:[135]
Interactive website showing what ocean rise will do to New York, Baltimore, Northern California, Charleston, Boston, Houston, Los Angeles, Miami, Mobile, San Diego, Washington, D.C., New Orleans, and many other cities:
http://www.nytimes.com/interactive/2012/11/24/opinion/sunday/what-could-disappear.html?_r=0

CLIMATECENTRAL.ORG:[136]
More than half of the area of 40 large cities (over 50,000) is less than 10 feet above high tide line. Cities affected by a 10-foot ocean rise:

City / Population
New York City: 703,000
New Orleans: 342,000
Miami: 275,000
Hialeah, FL: 224,000
Virginia Beach: 195,000
Fort Lauderdale: 160,000
Norfolk: 157,000
Metairie, LA: 138,000

MAP OF U.S. IF ENTIRE ANTARCTICA ICE/GLACIERS MELT:[137]
- Virtually all of Florida, Georgia and Alabama would be submerged. Charleston and enormous chunks of Texas, Louisiana and Missouri would vanish. The southern border of the U.S. would be a line from South Carolina to Tennessee:
http://www.climatecentral.org/news/us-with-10-feet-of-sea-level-rise-17428

NATIONAL SNOW AND ICE DATA CENTER:[138]
- Together, the Antarctic and Greenland ice sheets contain more than 99 percent of the freshwater ice on Earth. The Antarctic Ice Sheet extends almost 14 million square kilometers (5.4 million square miles), roughly the area of the contiguous United States and Mexico combined. The Antarctic Ice Sheet contains 30 million cubic kilometers (7.2 million cubic miles) of ice. The Greenland Ice Sheet extends about 1.7 million square kilometers (656,000

square miles), covering most of the island of Greenland, three times the size of Texas.

- *Ice sheets contain enormous quantities of frozen water. If the Greenland Ice Sheet melted, scientists estimate that sea level would rise about 6 meters (20 feet). If the Antarctic Ice Sheet melted, sea level would rise by about 60 meters (200 feet).*

- *The mass of ice in the Greenland Ice Sheet has begun to decline. From 1979 to 2006, summer melt on the ice sheet increased by 30 percent, reaching a new record in 2007.*

- *Most of Antarctica has yet to see dramatic warming. However, the Antarctic Peninsula, which juts out into warmer waters north of Antarctica, has warmed 2.5 degrees Celsius (4.5 degrees Fahrenheit) since 1950. A large area of the West Antarctic Ice Sheet is also losing mass, probably because of warmer water deep in the ocean near the Antarctic coast. In East Antarctica, no clear trend has emerged, although some stations appear to be cooling slightly. Overall, scientists believe that Antarctica is starting to lose ice.*

OCEANITES.ORG:[139]

- *Antarctica's proportions are enormous ... approximately the size of the United States and Mexico combined.*

- *Ninety-nine percent of Antarctica is covered by a permanent ice sheet, which averages over a mile in thickness, and in some places is almost three miles thick.*

- *Ninety percent of the world's ice and 70 percent of the world's fresh water is locked in this ice pack.*

- *[I]f the trend is not reversed, even Antarctica will be consumed by our never-ending, sometimes wrong-headed search for food and fuel.*

CLIMATECENTRAL.ORG:[140]

- *A portion of the West Antarctic Ice Sheet that is home to some of the fastest-flowing glaciers on the continent appears to have entered a state of retreat and melt that is "unstoppable," two new studies have found.*

- *"It has passed the point of no return," said Eric Rignot, lead author on one of the studies and a glaciologist at the University of California, Irvine, and NASA's Jet Propulsion Laboratory.*

- *The West Antarctic Ice Sheet has been of concern to climate scientists because it contains enough ice to add 10 to 13 feet to global sea level rise.*

- *"The retreat of ice in that sector is unstoppable," Rignot said.*

• The collapse of the ASE alone could contribute about 4 feet of sea level rise, and its demise would leave more inland portions of the ice sheet vulnerable to melt and collapse.

NATIONAL GEOGRAPHIC:[141]

• A massive glacier system in West Antarctica has started collapsing because of global warming and will contribute to significant worldwide sea-level rise, two teams of scientists warn in a pair of major studies released Monday.

• Scientists had previously thought the two-mile-thick (3.2 kilometers) glacier system would remain stable for thousands of years, but new research suggests a faster time frame for melting.

• A rapidly melting section of the West Antarctic Ice Sheet appears to be in irreversible decline and will sink into the sea, scientists at the University of California, Irvine and NASA reported.

• "This retreat will have major implications for sea-level rise worldwide," said Eric Rignot, a UC-Irvine Earth science professor and lead author of a study to be published in a journal of the American Geophysical Union ... The study presents evidence, based on 40 years of observations, that six big glaciers in the Amundsen Sea "have passed the point of no return," Rignot said.

• The glaciers contain enough ice to raise global sea level by 4 feet (1.2 meters) and are melting faster than most scientists had expected.

• Rignot says that once the six glaciers near the coast melt, it is possible that the rest of the ice in West Antarctica could eventually follow ... If the entire West Antarctic Ice Sheet did melt, sea level would rise 11 feet (3.3 meters), according to previous research.

LIVESCIENCE.COM:[142]

• Summer high tides are getting higher in the eastern Gulf of Mexico, boosting the destructive power of hurricanes, a new study finds ... The trend is strongest in Florida, such as in Key West, where tidal flooding regularly inundates low-lying city streets. Summer sea levels are now 1.8 inches (4.5 centimeters) higher than before 1993.

NATURE.COM:[143]

• Average global flood losses in 2005 are estimated to be approximately US$6billion per year, increasing to US$52 billion by 2050 with projected socio-economic change alone ... With climate change and subsidence, present protection will need to be upgraded to avoid unacceptable losses of US$1trillion of more per year.

EPA REGARDING ALASKAN TEMPERATURES: [144] [145] [146]

• Over the past 60 years, the average temperature across Alaska has increased by *approximately 3°F. This increase is more than twice the warming seen in the rest of the United States. Warming in the winter has increased by an average of 6°F and has led to changes in ecosystems, such as earlier breakup of river ice in the spring. As the climate continues to warm, average annual temperatures in Alaska are projected to increase an additional 2 to 4°F by the middle of this century.*

NEW YORK TIMES REGARDING ALASKA[147]

• *A New York Times report about Alaska noted that many towns in Alaska are suffering due to warming temperatures and the rising ocean. Temperatures in Alaska have risen nearly twice as fast as the lower 48 states and 31 towns and cities face serious risk or destruction due to the rising ocean.*

CONCLUSION

For those who remain unmoved after reading the above reports, consider this: 1) scientists believe that within a few decades trends may become irreversible and, once Antarctic glaciers cave into the ocean and melt, nothing can be done to stop it; 2) the processes eroding the gigantic Antarctic storehouse of water may start to unleash catastrophic melting even before a huge deluge starts; 3) all we need is 3-5 feet of ocean rise to face disaster, let alone the 200-plus feet of ocean water locked within Antarctica; 4) what if you are wrong? Is burning fossil fuels more rational than the risk of disasters unfolding?

Our destiny is still in our control. Yes, some industries may be harmed, but their CEOs are smart and will convert to emerging clean-energy industries that will be equally lucrative... and perhaps even more lucrative. The cost of losing huge portions of the U.S. to the ocean will be astronomically greater, by trillions of dollars, than the cost of converting to a clean-energy economy. If we wait – assume it is a hoax – we take an enormous risk. The upside of doing too little is small compared to the downside of the worst-case scenarios. It is a dangerous Pascalian Wager not worth risking.

American success has always been about embracing the future. Clinging to the past is neither smart nor logical. Though it cannot be proven without doubt that human activities cause rising sea levels, common sense dictates that, if we continue to pollute the environment, there will be a negative impact. The risk of doing too little outweighs the benefit. Logic dictates that immediate action is the safest option.

Be fact-driven. Be logical. Decide.

Chapter 7

FROM OIL TO A GREEN ECONOMY
A Wartime Urgency

Oil. It moves our cars, heats our homes and powers our giant economy. It provides electricity and food from California as trains and trucks move about. It is also the focus of potential environmental disaster (as noted in the previous chapter). Oil also enriches enemies, using oil revenues to make international mischief. It goes to countries like Iran sponsoring terror groups like Hezbollah (destabilizing Lebanon) and Hamas (launching rockets into Israel daily). Saudi money subsidized Lashkar-e-Taiba, responsible for the 2008 India massacre.[148] Syrian oil fields funded murderous ISIS. Think of it this way: each time you pump gas into your tank, part of a penny per gallon is a Terrorist Tax funding barbaric criminals.

This author respects the oil industry, its dedicated workers and the products they provide (the author owns oil stock), but it's a matter of gravitas shared by *all of us.* We all need to cooperate on matters crucial to our very existence, for more is at stake than cities being inundated by the ocean. We read increasingly of decreasing rain, growing deserts and droughts from Africa to California.[149]

WE NEED A WARTIME EFFORT

The problems need to be treated with the urgency of war, for we are threatened on many levels. We need a long-term plan to end our dependence on imported oil, amounting to hundreds of billions annually. It has been this way for decades. The danger is not that Washington will act. It will, but most likely it will go about things casually and reluctantly. Half-measures. Anything less than wartime urgency will leave us complaining about the same-old-same-old 20 years from now, and by then, we will have given away yet more trillions of dollars paying for oil imports. How much longer can we survive this bleeding? How much longer do we risk catastrophic warming of the planet and oceans?

It is not enough to raise EPA standards a bit. Doing it correctly means an all-out effort and declaring a national urgency. Our leaders must see the big picture and not kick the can down the road. Government must act now, not when panic arrives. JFK's famous "moon" speech offers a warning: *"If we are to go only half way, or reduce our sights in the face of difficulty, in my judgment it would be better not to go at all."*

The way politicians avoid issues will fail us again and again. Let's not fool ourselves; we have no plan. We need a national goal similar to the 1960s Apollo moon program started so eloquently by JFK in 1961 in a speech before Congress. Half steps won't work; only a bold plan will. If government treats the crisis with urgency, supported by programs with teeth, people will be impressed.

Millions of Americans would love to buy a $20,000 car that gets 100+ mpg (or uses no gas!). They exist. The Tesla Roadster is electric, accelerates 1 to 60 mph in four seconds and has a range of about 245 miles without a charge.[150] If anything, technology only improved for this (and everything) since publication of this book. Apteras (sadly out of business) had an affordable car that got 300 mpg with a 120-

mile range.[151] The problem is people are apathetic. Price can do that. The Tesla Roadster is expensive.

Government can change all that. It happened during World War II. It can happen again. After Pearl Harbor, resolve filled the air: government and industry worked together as a team. It took about a year of furious industry transition. We will benefit by studying their successful approach. Industry has much to gain from an ambitious plan. Giant goals are needed. JFK demonstrated this in 1961 when he said before Congress, *"I believe that this nation should commit itself to achieving the goal, before this decade is out, of landing a man on the moon and returning him safely to the Earth."* [152] Eight years later, a captivated world watched Neil Armstrong walk on the moon.

Soon after Pearl Harbor was attacked, FDR practically took the country's breath away when he announced the goal of building 60,000 airplanes, 45,000 tanks, 20,000 antiaircraft guns, and 8,000,000 tons of shipping for 1942.[153] This was in the context of industries gutted by years of depression, empty factories, or car factories converting quickly. Skeptics said it was impossible, but a determined government pressed on. Acting with resolve, agencies were created to accomplish that task. Factories were quickly retooled. By the time Japan and Germany surrendered some three years later, America produced 88,410 tanks and self-propelled guns, 257,390 artillery weapons, 105,055 mortars, 2,679,840 machine guns, 2,382,311 military trucks, 97,810 bombers, and 324,750 military aircraft.[154]

America went from depression to this in three years. Unemployment was under 2%. We can do the same, only we need to produce electric and ultra fuel-efficient hybrid cars, and energy-clean products (batteries, solar panels). The World War II generation had something we do not yet have. *Resolve. Boldness. Vision.*

The world is changing and coming to accept the mounting climate changes. Industry may well agree with a bold program to convert. Even oil-giant ExxonMobil made the below statement regarding the Paris Climate Agreement:

"ExxonMobil supports the work of the Paris signatories, acknowledges the ambitious goals of this agreement and believes the company has a constructive role to play in developing solutions. We have been working for many years to reduce emissions in our operations and provide products that help consumers reduce their emissions. ExxonMobil continues to pursue technology solutions with leading scientists in industry, academia and nongovernmental institutions."

Indeed, the world is changing. We may find more powerful allies in such a bold green energy program than we realize. A bold plan must not resonate solely with idealists. It must have practical relevance. The civil rights movement meant something powerful for those who were oppressed. The atom bomb program of the 1940s was about survival and winning a war against a truly evil enemy. The moon program was about a challenge mankind dreamed about since earliest days of history.

Bold plans for a non-oil green economy, as outlined ahead in this chapter, will resonate with the American people for several reasons: 1) polls indicate Americans widely accept that global warming is real and must be addressed; 2) people are upset by petro dollars flowing to vulgar countries, terrorist-supporting regimes and "frenemies;" 3) the economic and jobs potential of carbon-free cars and solar energy is enormous; 4) conservation of oil and energy will save people significant money; 5) solar power will eventually drop utility costs to a relatively small amount; 6) people genuinely fear the enormous damage we will face as ocean levels rise; and 7) air pollution would vanish.

RESOLVE: 100 MILLION GREEN CARS IN 15 YEARS

Much attention is placed lately on the emerging technology of self-driving cars (which is intriguing), but it is important that we, as a country, keep our eye on the ball and what is more important: making cars clean, electric and carbon free. The President must challenge Congress and the nation to the goal of complete independence from foreign oil within 15 years and, supported by an emboldened Congress, establish a national program for the American car industry to annually manufacture up to 10 million electric/hybrid cars that average 100+ mpg. Government can commit us to the goal of having *every car owner* convert to a "green" electric car within 15 years through subsidies, tax credits and no-interest loans. Imagine the historic economic turnaround our country would enjoy. To inspire is to commit to a bold goal.

If the White House proclaimed such a goal, it would take the nation's breath away. Even if we fell behind schedule, we would still be making progress. JFK and FDR had vision. Their generation met challenges. Our generation is ready. If Congress ended its bickering like Congress did during the Great Depression and World War II, we could succeed. We are ready. People are fed up with stagnation. A generation waiting for light at the end of the tunnel will finally see that light.

The WWII government effort spawned a spectacular economic boom. We can study their approach to help create programs that will work now. Government and private sector cooperation would lead to technological breakthroughs. The Apollo program and Manhattan Project (during World War II, which rapidly invented the atomic bomb) show what can be accomplished. Such titanic efforts have not been tried in recent times. Talent has not vanished; only vision has vanished.

Skeptics note that the WWII generation was different. We lack their urgency. Today's consumer-oriented people have gone soft. To answer this, how will we know until we have tried? Is our generation to surrender? As FDR said: *"This great war effort must be carried through to its victorious conclusion by the indomitable will and determination of the people as one great whole. It must not be impeded by the faint of heart."*[155]

No bombs or warships threaten our existence as much as the reality that we will run out of oil someday. We are vulnerable to blackmail. Imagine what would happen if oil imports plummeted. It happened already in the 1970s during the Arab oil embargo. If we faced a similar crisis today (given our huge dependence), the economy would collapse. Note what happened in 2009 when Ukraine squabbled with Russia. The gas pipelines were shut and parts of Europe went dry. People shivered in the cold. We are all hostage and our oil exporting "friends" know it. Consider this:[156]

• 97% of U.S. transportation is oil-based (car, truck, train, air, ship).

- A 22% increase in U.S. oil demand is expected from 2005-30.

- Only 6% of U.S. energy used is supplied by renewable sources.

- Over $1.16 trillion was transferred to oil-producing countries over the past 30 years, accounting for over a third of our trade deficit.

- According to DOE, 27,000 jobs are lost for each $1 billion in trade deficits.[157]

- America's hot tubs alone use $200 million in energy each year.[158]

RESOLVE: ALL BUILDINGS
SOLAR-POWERED WITHIN 10 YEARS

What a goal! The implications are revolutionary. If the goal is to make America far wealthier, forever energy independent, green, clean, provide millions of good-paying jobs to unemployed millions, vastly reduce carbon emissions, and potentially end warming and rising oceans, the goal of making every building in America solar-powered is a game changer. It would create industries and factories throughout the country, especially in suffering rust belt states like Pennsylvania and Ohio, cities like Detroit, and regions like West Virginia and Appalachia suffering due to the collapse of coal and other industries. It would create powerful new markets abroad that would reduce, if not eliminate, trade deficits. It would place America on the cutting edge.

The notion of solar panels and batteries on the roofs of every structure in the country is doable. This "real estate" over our heads is the most wasted space in the country. Roofs are devoid of value, empty, unseen, and therefore a perfect solution for improving our prospects on every level: creation of millions of good-paying jobs, new industries for trade, elimination of carbon emissions, a clean environment, and ending the warming and rising of oceans. The argument (and plan) for quickly "solarizing" the country is presented in more detail in the upcoming chapter on solar power.

A 15-YEAR "GRAND PLAN"

There is huge upside to going green. The plan below offers a comprehensive plan with the goal of making America oil-import-free within 15 years, and virtually oil/coal-free within 30 years. Once America entered World War II, it took about a year to convert to a wartime economy. In other words, change can come quickly, but comprehensive planning is needed. The time has come for a *grand plan* inspired by the visionary WWII model free of lobbyist meddling. Below is a comprehensive six-part grand plan for quickly converting the country to solar energy, electric cars and clean, safe energy powering homes, offices and factories.

1. Administration of Ongoing Projects

> *Government Programs*. The plan requires new agencies overseeing tasks: electric and ultra fuel-efficient cars (research, production, factory conversion, tax credits), energy conservation, renewable energy (solar, wind, tidal, geothermal, etc.), consumer subsidies, R&D (government/industry cooperation), state/federal

conflict resolution, and an energy information center (providing nation-wide information services through TV, radio, the Internet, and an "800" telephone hotline answering questions about new programs ranging from conservation to solar panel and electric car subsidies).

➢ *An Apollo-Era Goal To End Reliance on Oil*. The White House needs to give the nation a goal similar to the 1960s moon effort. We lack urgency (especially with low oil prices). Congress can support such urgency through "a declaration of war against oil."

➢ *Nature*. Plants absorb carbon dioxide: nature is our best ally yet forests are under attack worldwide due to development. A policy of nationwide reforestation is essential; government must lead efforts to help nature *help us* and promote worldwide efforts. We enhance that goal by being a role model.

➢ *Conservation*. Electricity production accounts for 37 percent of U.S. carbon dioxide emissions.[159] Conservation and efficiency will dramatically help to limit emissions. Government agencies must actively encourage utilities, industries and households to embrace conservation programs.

2. Production of Solar Panels, Batteries, Electric Cars & Clean Fuels

➢ *Solar Panels On All Buildings*. Converting the country to clean solar energy must be a high priority for government, which must use its influence and resources to encourage industries and the public to use endless sunlight to power homes, offices and factories. Through widespread education on the green and cost-saving benefits of solar energy, plus targeted tax credits/incentives for emerging industries and converting to solar power, this can be done over a 10-year period. It offers wonderful implications for the goal of eliminating annual 400-600-billion-dollar trade deficits, improved employment prospects in emerging solar/auto/battery industries targeted for rustbelt states and coal mining regions where job loss is epidemic, and ending the processes that warm oceans and dangerously raise sea levels.

➢ *Subsidize Purchasing 100 Million "Green" Cars*. This plan, backed by subsidies and no-interest loans, will have *every* car owner in the country purchase electric or ultra fuel-efficient hybrid cars within 15 years. Government will help auto industries retool. The goal is to permanently end oil imports. Government will require carmakers to manufacture electric and fuel-efficient hybrid cars that average 100+ mpg. (A later chapter elaborates on this plan.)

➢ *Green Cars*. Cars that get 100+ mpg are a reality. Google the Tesla Motors website, where you will read about electric cars (0 to 60 mph in 3.9 seconds, burns no oil, 245 miles per charge, pennies per mile).[160] Apteras had cars that got 300 mpg. Also Google Chevy Volt, advertised as being able to "move more than 75% of daily commuters without a single drop of gas."[161][162][163]

➢ *A $15,000 Electric Car.* Cars must be affordable. Government subsidies alongside efficient mass production by the car industry will help; we need $15,000 entry-level green cars. Programs to help poor families must be a priority so as to speed up converting the country to electric cars.

➢ *Car Batteries.* As many people drive up to 100 miles per day, electric cars must have a large range per charge to make such cars practical. Mass production of low-cost batteries is needed.

> *Electric Pumps*. We must create a national network of "volt stations" in every gas station. Within two years, we must see an "electric pump" everywhere. These "pumps" will let cars charge within 15 minutes. We need improved technology to make this possible. Within 30 years, let gas stations be relics of the past.

> *Batteries*. Battery range is not the problem, price is. The Tesla Roadster goes 245 miles on a charge. New technologies must speed up charging times. One option would be a national network of "volt stations" where drivers can quickly switch to fully charged batteries and leave spent batteries, all at a modest cost. To promote this, all cars should use one of three types of batteries (just like gas).

> *Government/Industry Cooperation*. Government must aid rapid industry-wide conversion. Give industry (especially oil) a blank check and tax incentives to convert.

> *Oil Industry*. Some oil firms may resist. Some, like ExxonMobil, may be supportive. Either way, we need them in this effort as *allies* that benefit by capitalizing on the huge emerging industries. Government must encourage the oil industry to convert to new energy products and *plan beyond oil.* Oil reserves will run dry in time and they know it. Energy companies must benefit from new industries like solar, wind and other products. It will be a challenge to get them aboard; we must appeal to their patriotism and find solutions to encourage fast conversion and profitability. They must research synthetic fuels that are carbon-free. Incentivize the oil industry to sell "green" electricity, batteries, solar panels, etc. Give them mind-boggling incentives. Oil is temporary; energy is permanent. Everyone must *think out of the box.*

> *Wind and Solar Industries.* Wind energy requires huge amounts of land. By some estimates, it would take a plot the size of Connecticut to power New York City. But solar panels on roofs can power individual buildings, especially in sunny regions in the South. All buildings must be required to install solar panels on roofs. Batteries must be installed. These two industries will therefore become enormous within a few years, as every structure will be refitted to have solar panels on roofs and batteries to store energy for nights and cloudy days. Let the oil firms invest in lucrative new solar panel industries as incentive for full cooperation. They deserve this since oil revenue will decline.

> *Airplanes and Trucks*. The same goals apply to trucks. As for airplanes, government must encourage research on synthetic fuels that do not produce hydrocarbons. Greater air dynamics efficiency and use of electricity must be researched.

> *Heating Fuel*. Home/building/apartment boilers are expensive to replace. It will take a generation to make it happen. A 30-year transition is more realistic. As homes/buildings replace boilers with new ones using solar power and emerging technologies, owners will be given huge incentives to convert.

3. Government & Politics

> *Politics*. Politicians must lead the way and not cater to lobbyists.

> *Auto Industry*. Encourage innovators who will lead the way, not block it; 1) produce only electric and ultra fuel-efficient cars that average 75 mpg or better; 2) replace old executives with executives from companies like Tesla, which have a

proven record of commitment to electric cars; 3) build SUVs that are electric; 4) Promote cars that get up to 300 mpg, as Apteras did.

➤ _Solar Industry_. Federal and state governments must do everything possible to encourage the solar and battery industries. This includes tax credits to encourage consumers to purchase and install solar electric panels for homes, offices and factories; programs to help industries more quickly train personnel on the details of installing and monitoring the new technology; and tax incentives to industries to encourage the building of new factories in the U.S. and conduct R&D to improve the technology and, especially, battery storage technology. There must also be a clear understanding that not every company and initiative will succeed. Critics too easily attack programs when something goes wrong. Well, something always goes wrong when huge initiatives begin. Imagine how WWII would have ended if such leaders constantly faced such negativity every time something went wrong. There must be articulated, from the start, the need for patience and an understanding that things won't always go smoothly and according to plan.

➤ _Harmed Industries Get Huge Incentives._ Industries harmed by conversion should get huge incentives to join the effort. Oil companies, for example, are aware that trends over the coming decades indicate oil consumption will drop as the world converts to clean energy. This plan must present the most lucrative tax-free and interest-free incentives government can offer to encourage conversion to new industries.

➤ _American Jobs._ One of the key points of this initiative is the creation hundreds of thousands of jobs _for Americans_. This means government must enact laws that will severely punish companies attempting to outsource or build factories abroad. Tax codes and trade policy must be enacted immediately in order to ensure the new industries will be largely built on American soil. While money will be made by industry, industry must be required to reward American workers. A key aspect of the initiative is to create jobs for Americans that pay well. Efforts should be made to encourage industries to build factories in areas hardest hit in the past by outsourcing and free trade.

➤ _"Rust Belt" & Hard-Hit Regions._ Regions with higher unemployment or lower wages, like the Rust Belt and coal-mining regions, should be given highest priority. Government cannot lecture industry on where to build factories, but federal and state tax policy can certainly reward industries that choose to invest in specific states and regions. All Americans, especially those hardest hit by economic trends of the past decades, should benefit from the emerging new industries.

➤ _Public Transportation_. Public transportation must be promoted and fares must be subsidized to encourage ridership. Europe has a superb infrastructure of trams and intercity trains. Our cities can do better. Amtrak can be promoted to provide intercity alternatives. In many cities, trams and "green" buses can be put into service (which will also decrease traffic congestion and air pollution).[164]

➤ _Federal/State Cooperation_. Federal regulations often prevent progress. An example is a 2008 initiative in New York requiring 13,000 gas-guzzling taxis to convert from 12-14 mpg to hybrid cars getting 25 mpg. Blocked in federal court, it failed due to federal rules. It reflects flaws that must be addressed so that states and cities can set standards addressing local needs. Conflicts between federal and state programs must be quickly resolved.

4. Green Energy & Industries

> *Enormous New Industries Will Emerge*. The WWII effort lowered unemployment from 15% in 1940 to 1.9% within three years. Government had huge deficits that were paid off over time because wartime deficits were geared towards industrial growth. The economy flourished after the war. It could happen now if planned wisely, especially with enormous new solar panel and battery industries emerging similar to the quick emergence of TV's in the 1950s and smartphones after 2000. In the process, millions of new jobs could be created. The foundations of a new manufacturing and exporting economy would be laid. We would create new *American* manufacturers. With large federal deficits projected for years, new industries will provide much-needed tax relief.

> *Green Exports*. America can restore economic affluence by becoming a leader in green technologies and selling such products throughout the world. The future is bright if we invest at light speed in green technologies. The question is who will sell them 20 years from now? China or *us?*

> *Study the WWII Conversion Agencies*. Study WWII approaches as a model on how to quickly convert industries (the auto industry converted from cars to war vehicles, tanks and airplanes). The following industries and research projects will have to emerge.

- ✓ *renewable energy:* solar, batteries, wind, geothermal, tidal, etc.
- ✓ *electric cars*: retooling to manufacture 10 million green cars annually
- ✓ *mass transit:* subways, trams, green buses, "electric" pumps
- ✓ *Research & Development:* clean synthetic fuel, hydrogen fuel, nuclear *fusion* (not fission), efficient engines, powerful batteries, beaming electricity from space, tidal power, etc.
- ✓ *utility efficiency*: an estimated 70% of potential electric output is wasted. It must be addressed.

> *Carbon Absorption Technology:* In addition to national reforestation and efforts for worldwide cooperation, government must promote R&D for technologies that remove carbon emissions from the atmosphere. Sadly, new forests may not be enough to handle the problem.

> *No Ethanol:* Many synthetic fuels produce hydrocarbons and stress agriculture by raising food prices. We need ramped up R&D for truly clean fuels.

> *Global Warming:* America accounts for 25% of global warming though we are three percent of world population. Carbon emissions will be reduced if gas cars are replaced with green technologies. Industries producing high emissions must be regulated thoroughly. As world oil consumption is projected to increase 55%, America must be a role model.[165]

> *Outsourcing:* As new jobs are created, government must make sure multinationals do not outsource factories and jobs. Let the term "Built in America" mean quality and become a source of pride. U.S. tax code and trade policy must end corporate incentives to outsource or build factories abroad.

5. Conservation & Education

➤ *Utilities.* Shockingly, only 32% of electricity produced by utilities is distributed: 9% is lost traveling over transmission lines; one third of the energy in fossil fuel is converted into electricity at a typical power plant; only one third of electricity reaches its destination.[166-167] Government must work with utilities to change this. Imagine the efficiency savings and decreased carbon emissions.

➤ *Wide-Scale Conservation.* Electricity use accounts for 37 percent of U.S. carbon dioxide emissions.[168] Transportation (gas, diesel, jet fuel) accounts for vast oil consumption. Cutting transportation consumption could end oil imports. Conservation could wipe out oil consumption and carbon emissions, according to the government's Energy Information Agency. Energy-saving measures could lower household costs by $530 a year.[169] Americans notoriously waste energy.

➤ *Heating.* Many buildings and homes are poorly insulated. Government must offer tax incentives to abet progress. New buildings must meet high standards. Include efficient water faucets and showers (especially for water-plagued regions like California and the Southwest).

➤ *Hot Water.* When possible, all buildings should use solar energy to heat water.

➤ *Turning Off Unused Appliances & Lights.* Millions of people are sloppy about this. Education could change that. Further, only the most highly efficient appliances should be sold in the U.S.

➤ *Idle Appliances.* Studies show that on average about 50 devices/appliances in American homes use significant power even when "off" or in idle/standby/asleep mode.[170] It annually accounts for about 25 percent of residential energy use requiring 50 power plants. Government must work with industry to address this and provide truly efficient devices when on and "off."

➤ *Office Buildings & Roads.* Lighted roads, schools and offices can be more efficient in using light or heat. If anything, government structures must be a role model.

➤ *Vehicles.* Lower highway speed limits (estimated to reduce oil consumption by up to one percent).[171]

➤ *State Programs.* All states must study and embrace innovative and successful programs implemented by other states.

➤ *Education.* Changing habits means TV, radio, the Internet, newspapers, etc., offering ways to conserve energy. TV can lead the way through news and public service ads.

➤ *The Bully Pulpit.* The President (and all Governors) can prioritize conservation, solar panels and fuel-efficient cars in speeches.

➤ *DOE & FCC.* The Dept. of Energy must vigorously promote solar, wind, geothermal and other clean energy sources, and conservation programs through mailings, an "800" hotline, schools, TV, radio, and the Internet. DOE/FCC should focus on green energy conversion and conservation. The FCC can require TV, the Internet and cable networks to contribute to the effort through news programs and public service ads.

➤ *Government Bonds.* Selling "Energy War Bonds" sends a message to the nation: *this is serious.* War bonds were sold during WWII. Create patriotic support. Let people feel part of the effort.

> *Police Fines.* Empower police to ticket for wasteful practices like cars and trucks idling needlessly. It will send a powerful message.
> *Fine Businesses.* Closed stores aglow, empty skyscrapers lit up floor after floor even as they are empty all night. Fine them! The same is true for computers left on all night. Make a statement about energy waste.
> *Rewards.* Reward people for reporting street lights left on in daytime, closed stores with lights on all night, skyscrapers leaving lights on deep into the night, etc. Let people fear waste, but also reward good behavior: utility rebates for reduction in electricity use; rewards to bus and taxi companies for converting to green/hybrid vehicles; rewards to businesses improving conservation or converting from oil/coal to green technologies.

6. Clean Electric Energy

> *Electric Car Demand.* Electricity demand will soar as electric cars take over. Utility capacity must increase. It must come from clean and renewable sources as much as possible.
> *Utilities Inefficiency.* Utilities inefficiently transport electricity. Promote innovative means for reducing waste; promote efficient new technologies like superconductor materials.
> *Renewable Energy.* Only 6% of energy is created through renewable sources. We can do better by investing in wind, solar, ocean-tide energy, and solar panels on roofs everywhere.
> *Geothermal.* This intriguing clean and reliable idea uses heat from inner earth to drive turbines. A 2006 MIT report noted geothermal power could be an important energy source. The Bureau of Land Management opened up 190 million acres for geothermal exploration.[172]
> *Tidal energy.* Using the tides of the sea is intriguing. It would be clean and endless.
> *No Coal.* Coal power plants produce some 83% of electric sector carbon emissions.[173] End coal reliance and view "clean" coal with suspicion.
> *Jobs Creation.* People who lose work as coal and other industries shrink must be helped. Government must act to encourage emerging industries to build factories in areas hardest hit by the winds of change.
> *Space.* Sunlight in space is far more intense than on earth. It is worth researching ways to use it and transport that energy to earth.[174]
> *Nuclear.* Nuclear power though fission is potentially lethal. We need better solutions.
> *Fusion.* *This* is the game-changer if scientists figure it out. Fusing hydrogen into helium powers the sun. We use nuclear *fission* involving deadly radioactive materials. The historic breakthrough of mankind would be the unlocking of fusion. The complex process has confounded physicists for decades. We need a modern-day *Manhattan Project*. The only "pollution" is helium that harmlessly floats away. Fusion is a long-term solution. Godspeed to California's National Ignition Facility.
> *Experimentation.* During WWII, innovation was in the air. We need new industries. Trial and error is normal when exploring visionary plans, but it means occasional failure. Politicians must not be punished when things go

wrong. We must give them some room to maneuver and experiment.

A 21st CENTURY ECONOMIC MIRACLE

We can succeed just as the WWII generation did when the President, Congress and industry cooperated. Millions of Americans patriotically supported efforts; conservation and recycling became a way of life. There are lessons for us to learn from their focused cooperation and patriotism. As Nazi Germany invaded Poland in the bleak September of 1939, U.S. armed forces were feeble and weapons were dated. After Pearl Harbor, a flurry of change commenced. America was soon at the forefront of technology. War material was cranked out at unprecedented rates. GM and Ford ceased production of consumer cars and instead built tanks and war vehicles. Quickly retooled factories manufactured 324,750 aircraft.

With a bold, comprehensive plan we can make extraordinary achievements just as the WWII generation did. We should study their story. The economic boom was historic. In 1941, unemployment was a staggering 14.6%; it was 1.9% in 1945. After the war the economy converted to consumer industries. Government ran massive deficits to fund the war accounting in 1945 for 50% of the budget; debt was over 110% of GDP.[175-176] By 1948 the budget was balanced and within a few years public debt was under control.[177] The economy was robust and America ran trade surpluses until the 1970s. These were unusual times, but there is a message: well-planned investments encourage growth. Transform the economy from oil to green energy. *This is the historic challenge of our generation.*

Chapter 8

SOLAR AMERICA
Power Every Building By Sun in 10 Years

The idea of powering American homes, offices, malls, and factories by solar energy is hardly something that would bother most people. In fact, the process is already underway, but slowly. Converting to solar energy is expensive. A price around $15,000/house and up is common. Federal and state government programs encouraging conversion to solar power are spotty. That must change. It's time for a *Solar America.* At present, only a tiny amount of U.S. electricity is generated from the sun. Consider this 2015 quote from *Business Insider/Tech Insider.*[178]

> *"More power from the sun hits the Earth in a single hour than humanity uses in an entire year, yet solar only provided 0.0039% of the energy used in the US last year."*

It is time to change that. A President who has vision and thinks out of the box can convey these facts and rally the country to take action immediately by presenting a bold plan to place the country on the path to clean solar energy. Let's get it done in 10 years.

STRIDES IN COSTA RICA, DENMARK & GERMANY

It is already happening in Denmark and Germany. We are behind tiny Denmark in terms of innovation. If the words *America is the greatest country in the world* are true (a cliché our politicians often repeat), let's walk the walk. How can we allow little Denmark (but with a large heart) outpace us in technology and innovation? The Danish government is working towards the goal of 35% of energy from renewable sources by 2020 and 100% by 2050.[179] Costa Rica is already at 100% electrical energy independence. They make smart use of volcanoes throughout the country.

Tiny countries outpace us. They don't pollute as we do or pay huge amounts for imported oil. They put us to shame. Our leaders in Washington must take note of these small but innovative countries and how much they accomplish because their politicians try to innovate. Denmark also offers a powerful lesson to America in terms of wind power. Note the following 2015 report from *The Guardian.*[180]

> *"So much power was produced by Denmark's wind farms on Thursday that the country was able to meet its domestic electricity demand and export power to Norway, Germany and Sweden... Interconnectors allowed 80% of the power surplus to be shared equally between Germany and Norway, which can store it in hydropower systems for use later. Sweden took the remaining fifth of excess power. 'It shows that a world powered 100% by renewable energy is no fantasy,' said Oliver Joy, a spokesman for trade body the European Wind Energy Association."*

It's striking how far behind we are. Germany is also making strides towards the goal of energy from renewables. Note this excerpt from *MIT Technology Review*.[181]

"Now the [German] government is about to reboot its energy strategy, known as the Energiewende. It was launched in 2010 in hopes of dramatically increasing the share of the country's electricity that comes from renewable energy and slashing the country's overall carbon emissions to 40 percent below 1990 levels by 2020 ... renewable sources accounted for nearly one-third of the electricity consumed in Germany in 2015. The country is now the world's largest solar market. Germany's carbon emissions in 2014 were 27 percent lower than 1990 levels."

Skeptics must note the remarkable strides made by Denmark and Germany. The U.S. lags. Political fighting plagues us and thwarts innovation. It shuts down economic progress and innovation for no good reason. The dual goals of ending reliance upon foreign oil imports and dangerous nuclear energy (Google the Daiichi nuclear disaster in Japan) can be met through nationwide conversion to solar energy.

A NATIONAL PROGRAM FOR SOLAR
ENERGY & JOBS CREATION

Suggesting American homes be powered by the sun is not fantasy. This technology is available and in use. It would accomplish another important goal. It would create vast new industries potentially providing millions of new well paying jobs. What holds us back are cost and apathy. That could change with an enlightened President, a bold plan, and government cooperation with industry to encourage consumers to quickly convert.

In the spirit of *walking the walk*, government must promote solar energy through tax credits, tax incentives for merging industries, and perhaps a major program to actually subsidize homeowners installing solar panels. (More on this later.) *A Panel On Every Roof* should be the motto of our generation. Ten years should be our giant goal. It should be made a priority with wartime urgency.

The upside of making America solar-powered is enormous. The benefits include the creation of millions of jobs (alongside other clean energy industries), massive new industries that manufacture solar products and batteries, exports of those products throughout the world, the elimination of trade deficits, 100% energy independence, virtual zero carbon emissions in conjunction with converting the country to electric cars (as outlined next chapter), and an America no longer captive to foreign oil imports from countries using petro-dollars to fund criminals, terrorism and mischief.

If you want to talk about a gigantic industry in the waiting and an enormous jobs creation program, support the creation of a mega-industry that will provide solar panels and batteries (alongside millions of electric cars) for the estimated 131 million American homes and millions of commercial buildings. If America does not do it, other countries will. We will lose out on a historic opportunity to embrace emerging new industries and prevent economic foes like China from monopolizing this new market.

Anther important consideration is federal debt, at close to $20 trillion. As the post-WWII generation of politicians understood, wise investment in the economy can actually reduce federal debt as a problem. Note this: [182]

	Debt / U.S. GDP	as % of GDP
1945	$259 / $228 million	116%
1967	$340 / $867 million	339%

Debt was *higher* in 1967 yet lower as percent of GDP. Investment in solar energy, even if with borrowing, can *reduce* our debt problem. We can grow our way out of debt as did the WWII generation. A *Solar America* is a bold vision that will transform our future in every sense, from clean environment to a growing economy.

END PETRO DOLLARS FUNDING ENEMIES
Going 100% solar would likely reduce electricity demand so much that it would end the need for oil imports, averaging annually around $300 billion in recent years. That is $300 billion that would stay in America and not enrich countries that use that money for ugly purposes. Going solar would not end America's thirst for oil, but it would likely lower oil demand to the point that domestic production could satisfy needs. The 10-year goal is ending oil imports, which American oil companies may not object to since imported oil revenue mostly goes to countries like Venezuela and Saudi Arabia. Hardly friends.

Emerging solar industries could profitably supply Europe with this technology. Europe could wean itself off oil dependence from Russia. Imagine an enfeebled Russia once it cannot generate adequate oil revenue. Petro dollars fund Russian arms and aggression. Take away that money and obnoxious countries would lose petro dollars they use to fund terrorism or create mischief.

Going 100% solar is a win-win proposition. A 10-year conversion program could jump start the economy, create vast numbers of well paying jobs, end oil import deficits, and help us reach the goal of zero carbon emissions thereby providing a path for ending the nightmare of melting glaciers and a rising ocean. The sooner we convert the better.

There are powerful reasons why both Democrats and Republicans should support a sweeping and ambitious national program. As you read further, you will note the economic benefits. The idea may grow on you. This is a non-partisan plan whose time has come. It provides a compelling national goal that everyone could buy into, much like the World War II war effort and the way it united the country in purpose.

THE WORLD WAR II EFFORT IS A MODEL
Helping industries harmed by emerging new industries – industries that no doubt would lobby Washington to stop such a national program – is crucial to turning this plan into reality.

Instead of placing the utility and oil industries in a position of defending their turf, we must include them in the process and create a plan where they have more to gain by joining the effort than opposing. We must be pragmatic. Industrial conversion is a concept well known to those familiar with the changes quickly made during WWII as the country converted to a wartime economy. We have a model. The only excuse for not studying this successful model and taking action is apathy and those who fight progress.

Industries that have the most to lose from conversion should benefit from the emerging new solar industry.

Government should cooperate with vested interests that lose out from conversion by helping them lead the way. Work with utilities and oil companies to build the newly emerging solar and battery industries. In brief, the plan would encourage companies that would potentially lose out by conversion by granting non-interest loans for building infrastructure for the emerging new industries (factories, transportation networks, training, etc.) and agreements to offer zero-tax incentives for at least five years. It is a necessary step towards getting the task done. Politics means being realistic. During WWII, government focused on winning the war. If it meant enriching powerful companies, so be it. We had to win the war and did what was necessary.

Industries that initially lose out from conversion to solar (and electric cars) can be "gifted" the opportunity to benefit from conversion. Let's get those companies to back the plan because they stand to gain... and because they know that sooner or later their industries will fade. Anyone who studies business knows that products come and go. Kodak was once a giant and among the bluest of blue chip stocks. That company sure faded. Remember Polaroid? Computers and digital technology doomed those industries. IBM once sold *typewriters!* (And great ones.)

IBM, to its credit, transitioned to emerging industries. It no longer sells computers or typewriters yet continues to exist. AT&T in the 1970s was a landline telephone company (and monopoly). They transitioned very well to emerging telecommunication markets. ExxonMobil and others, if they do not convert to emerging energy markets, could become the next Kodak in 50 or 100 years once oil demand collapses. Let's simply speed up the clock and bring them aboard. Somehow, everyone has to talk and figure out a path that works for all.

The need to convert is something government must impress upon the oil industry. This will be a chance to convert to emerging industries with lucrative tax-free and interest-free incentives. The goal of 100% electrical energy from solar power (and wind and other renewables) is within reach if government, in conjunction with industries, works for that gigantic goal. Conversion of industries is not unprecedented. Study the World War II efforts led by government. A similar wartime-like plan is needed now. We should not wait until the ocean floods Florida, New York and South Carolina.

SOLAR CONVERSION IS REALISTIC

A question that comes to mind is the amount of land needed by utilities to produce sufficient electricity from the sun. Here are answers: 1) energy needed to power the entire world would require land the size of Spain and we can use uninhabited deserts;[183] and 2) a small portion of the enormous Sahara Desert roughly the size of the small state Connecticut could power all of Europe.

Better yet, we should use "land" right above our heads: the roof of the structure where you live, work or shop. We may not have to use up that much land for solar farms. We may be able to provide electricity needed by placing solar panels on every rooftop. Our country need not be covered by unsightly "solar farms" everywhere. Let panels on roofs be unsightly to birds.

A typical home uses about 48 kilowatts/day.[184] Using standard solar panel technology (readily available of about 20% efficiency) in a sunny state like Arizona, a house roof would require 409 sq. feet (20x20 feet). Quite doable. In less sunny regions like the northeast, 615 sq. feet of rooftop (25x25 feet) is needed using more efficient panels. Also doable. Further, when a home is not in use (and less electricity is used), batteries would store energy.

This could meet the energy needs of most every home. In cities, with more limited rooftop space, solar panels would offer a portion of electricity and needs would have to be met by utilities that could convert, over time, to wind, geothermal, offshore ocean turbines, or solar farms in deserts transferring power along the national grid to cloudy regions. With time and planning, the goal of a fossil-fuel-free electrical network is achievable and would pay for itself as oil imports (typically $200-300 billion annually) eventually disappear.

Reduction in utility bills, pollution and carbon emissions are among the huge benefits of going solar. Consider these facts:[185] [186]

1. A typical American home creates 2,700 pounds of pollution annually.
2. About 115 million homes in America (circa 2010) created nearly 310 billion pounds of pollution in the air.
3. Solar panels generating energy for about five hours a day would create one trillion kilowatt hours.
4. A typical home pays about $1,255 annually for electricity, or $144 billion nationwide. Savings through solar panels would pay for the cost of those panels in a matter of a few years. This, alongside generous government subsidies and/or tax credits, could provide enormous incentives to act quickly to install solar panels.
5. Entire electrical output for the U.S. in 2015 was four trillion kilowatt hours.
6. Conversion of all homes *alone* to solar power would eliminate 25% of electrical output by utilities and reduce the need for coal and oil.
7. Some 25% of electrical output is derived from burning filthy carbon emitting coal.

Do the math. The conversion of 130 million homes and millions more buildings could eliminate a large portion of earth-warming carbon emissions and eliminate all oil imports. The savings would be huge. This does not even consider the effect of solar panels on top of factories, stores, and office buildings, nor the potential for solar farms in deserts to service cities where buildings have insufficient roof space for panels.

END RELIANCE UPON RISKY NUCLEAR POWER

Nuclear power (and deadly radioactive poisons if there is an accident) accounts for about 20% of electricity in the U.S. Making use of solar power could allow the country to retire nuclear plants and end the nightmare of figuring out where to bury poisonous material left over. We could avoid the nightmare Japan endured following the meltdown of the Daiichi nuclear plant. Solar energy paves the way for eliminating risky nuclear power. Creating a solar America would be a historic step forward in terms of creating a safe environment without reliance upon risky nuclear fission, uranium and plutonium.

COST & A BOLD JFK-LIKE GOAL

Converting to solar power is not cheap, but the investment will pay for itself in several years. Your utility bill could vanish. If you pay $1,500/year (typical), conversion to solar panels would take 12 years to pay for itself as typical panels are about $17,000. With tax credits, the years needed to pay off the investment will decrease even more. Mass production and huge increases in demand for panels will further lower the cost.

Rapid conversion nationwide will require tax credits and incentives. This, alongside industry-wide lowering of prices once production efficiency improves, would enhance a successful 15-year goal for conversion. It needs a bold Kennedy-like challenge, as he eloquently stated in his 1961 speech asking Congress to fund the space program with the goal of landing a man on the moon and returning him safely to earth.

Quick conversion requires commitment not seen since WWII, when dormant and consumer factories were quickly converted to war production. It was done in the 1940s. It can happen again *with political commitment to this goal.*

There is an intriguing alternative to the slow process of convincing homeowners to convert. The federal government can subsidize the cost. Here are facts as to cost and economic arguments favoring this option. Overall cost boils down to this. a) There are about 131 million homes in the U.S.; b) average 2016 cost is $17,000/home[187]; c) if government paid the cost (through bond sales), it would cost $2.2 trillion; d) depreciated over 25 years $2.2 trillion is about 73 billion/year (minus recent low interest rates).

Let's put this $73 billion/year in perspective: *crude oil and refined petroleum import deficits totaled $2.87 trillion from 2002-12 (over a ten-year period).*[188] Were the U.S. to fully convert to solar energy, oil imports would likely vanish. This would mean, over the following ten years, the following:

1. $2.87 trillion (or a similar amount) would remain on American shores. That is $2.87 trillion American homeowners and businesses would *not* have to pay for oil imports from unsavory nations. That's a lot of money kept in America.
2. The economic benefit from eliminating that drain of money is intriguing. That is $2.87 trillion American homeowners and businesses could better use to buy American-made products or invest in business, much of which will be taxable revenue that will help pay off the accumulated federal debt incurred in monetizing the solar investment.

3. The cost of converting the country to solar panels, at $2.2 trillion, is nearly $700 billion *less* than we would otherwise pay to buy foreign oil.

Add to this an economic boom as new industries manufacturing solar equipment and batteries supply 131 million homes and millions more commercial buildings. Then add the huge number of jobs created to man factories and installation. Then add increased tax revenues for federal budgets from increased economic activity and millions of new well paying jobs. Then add foreign markets for American-made solar products. Europe is eager to end reliance on Russian oil. China, with its 1.36 billion population, is an enormous market.

When you consider these facts, it makes sense for government to subsidize solar energy nationwide. A *Solar America* initiative would be a giant step forward. It would be an economic engine unprecedented in modern times. It is an investment worth making.

Solar America is an idea whose time has come.

Chapter 9

FUSION ENERGY
The Holy Grail of Endless Clean Energy

Fusion energy. If physicists could figure it out, it would solve all of our energy, oil, pollution, carbon emissions, rising ocean, and planetary warming problems. If only...

Fusion involves creating energy the same way our sun does: by fusing hydrogen atoms into helium. It requires as fuel something as common as water (to get hydrogen) and produces as "pollution" harmless helium, which floats away into space like a child's balloon filled with helium. Fusing hydrogen into helium is what goes on inside our sun. We certainly feel the enormity of the sun's power as sunlight shines on our face – coming from 93 million miles away. Imagine if we had such fusion machines on earth!

Indeed, imagine...

If we had fusion power plants everywhere, instead of coal- and gas-fired utilities (or nuclear *fission* power plants that would wreak radioactive havoc with a meltdown), we could have endless power to light our cities, cleanly run billions of electric cars and trucks, power our homes, and allow mankind to move forward without an ounce of pollution and heat-causing carbon emissions. Pollution, global warming and rising oceans could end in a single stroke.

Indeed, imagine...

The energy earth gets from sunlight *in a single day* is more than enough to satisfy the entire world's energy needs for a year. If only we could harness the endless energy emanating each second from the sun. If only...

It requires creating temperatures in the millions. The sun creates such temperatures. How do we do it here on earth? Indeed, *how?* As Shakespeare so eloquently put it in *Hamlet*, "Therein lies the rub." Fusion has been the holy grail of physics for decades. Physicists and mathematicians worldwide are working on this astronomical riddle at this very moment. Inventing the atomic bomb in the 1940s was seemingly child's play compared to fusion.

Physicists have a quip: *we're always 40 years away.* Well, we have been *40 years away* for the past 50 years. So how do we change that? For starters, what has to change is a choice by society and, especially, our government: a decision to once and for all figure out this history-changing technology. We must not endlessly go on being *40 years away.*

The intricacies of scientific efforts worldwide, from number crunching supercomputers to accelerators, are complex to the point where most of us (including myself) would be a bit baffled. It involves heavy-duty physics and brilliant people with doctorates from the likes of MIT, Harvard, Cambridge, Caltech, and Oxford... and decades of experience. Wonderful thinkers. But this chapter will not go into details, for such information is easily found in a Google search. In fact, a search will provide plenty of information – thousands of pages of worth. But we seemingly forever remain *40 years away.*

This author, for one, has nothing but admiration for the incredible efforts of physicists, mathematicians and scientific minds now at work on this technological challenge of epic proportions. I relish news and TV programs updating their progress, but I rarely see it. It strikes me how little I see news on the topic of fusion on the major networks or in newspapers. It is not a topic we often see. I never hear politicians talk about it. *Aye, therein lies the rub.*

This chapter is brief to make a point. Let's not get caught up in the details of nuclear physics. The point is that half of the problem is science and the other half is *political* – political because our leaders are not doing enough to broadcast the potential of fusion or finance research projects. Were our leaders to support this effort with the same vigor of the 1940s atomic bomb program or the 1960s space program, perhaps *40 years away* would really mean 40 years. What if our leaders committed to fusion energy with such passion?

Imagine if this technology became real 40 years from now. Imagine clean, endless, safe energy that would flow once fusion power plants are built worldwide. Imagine how things would change if we no longer needed oil or coal. Imagine if our beloved planet were no longer heating up, glaciers no longer thawing, the Arctic icecap no longer melting, oceans no longer rising.

Indeed, imagine…

Would our economy change? Absolutely. Would economic conversion occur? Yes. Oil and coal industries would suffer, people would be out of work. Not quite. New technologies mean new industries, new opportunities and new types of work. Man transitioned from the horse and buggy era to cars, from radio to TV, from *nothing* to radio. Wonderful things come from new technologies: new industries, new jobs and new opportunities for fortunes to be made.

Standing still makes no sense. It's not what made America great and powerful. Moving tentatively on fusion energy is unwise. It keeps us on the same risky path: astronomical burning of oil and coal, carbon emissions, melting of glaciers, rising oceans, filthy air – pictures of Chinese people wearing masks because of overwhelming air pollution. This list of harms, of ominous planetary changes, goes on and on. All *that* needs to change.

This chapter ends with one simple message: government leaders must fund and support the fusion efforts of nuclear physicists with the same national urgency and vigor that government gave to the 1960s space program and the 1940s atomic bomb program. Anything short of that would be foolish.

Each morning you rise and look up, therein lies our answer. *It's in the sky.*

Chapter 10

ELECTRIC CARS
Take The Quantum Leap

If you want to get the best bang for the buck when deficit spending, consider this. It is estimated that a tax cut of $100 billion produces about $125 billion in benefit whereas $100 billion in infrastructure spending reaps nearly $350 billion.[189] The historic economic boom following World War II, when government invested in the economy, is an example. Public debt was over 110% of GDP at the end of World War II yet the result was three decades of economic prosperity.[190-191] If we invest money wisely in the economy, the economy will grow and tax revenue will increase. It makes objectives of both Liberals and fiscal Conservatives reachable.

Cars define our way of life. The thought that we should be reliant on foreign oil is anathema. Government should work with the American auto industry just as it did during WWII, only today we must build not tanks and airplanes (as they did) but electric cars. Think of the implications: the worldwide demand for fabulously fuel-efficient American cars; the massive exporting of electric cars; and the fast track to ending oil imports. *Take the quantum leap.*

Rebuild the auto industry so that it will be able to sell millions of electric and ultra fuel-efficient vehicles. In terms of redesigning cars, let's blow away anything ever done before. Ending our annual $500-700 trade deficits will justify this.

Naysayers will find reasons to kill the effort, like insisting that automakers cannot convert to such a radically different concept as electric cars. Or government should stay off our backs. Where has that approach taken us? In fact, the auto industry in 1942 ceased making consumer cars and converted within months to tanks and airplanes. There is precedent. What was done in 1942 can be done today. GM, Ford and Chrysler can convert, but markets must be created. Government can make it so through bold policy, tax credits and incentives. Here's the plan.

Goal #1: Unprecedented Fuel Efficiency Standards

GM, Chrysler and Ford must retool and focus on electric cars or ultra fuel-efficient hybrids that average at least 75 mpg. Tesla's Roadster is pure electric and has a range of over 245 miles. If auto executives say they cannot do it, let Tesla management take over. Auto makers must retool to manufacture electric and ultra fuel-efficient hybrid vehicles — ones that are *better* than foreign-made cars. The long-term solution is building electric cars with the same range as gas cars. Charging must be quick. Another idea is "volt stations" that can quickly *replace* your spent battery with a fully charged battery. Do this and gasoline becomes *obsolete.* The oil companies will not be happy about this, and government must work with them, too, to be on board with the plan. How about the oil companies building those batteries and ensuring this lucrative market for them? Innovative leaders must be nurtured.

Goal #2: Major Strides & Battery Technology

In close cooperation with the EPA, industry and academia, experts must conduct rapid and major research into creating ultra fuel-efficient technologies involving electric motors and batteries. Technologies must be converted into cost-effective products that can be sold at an affordable price. With government subsidizing and an industry-wide retooling of all factories geared towards producing millions of electric cars, the cost per unit will drop to the point of being affordable. An entry-level $15,000 electric or hybrid car must be the goal. This innovation will certainly create huge markets that justify the cost of innovation and retooling auto factories. It will allow for mass production that will dramatically lower the cost of such green vehicles.

Close government and auto industry cooperation is needed, not unlike the approach taken during WWII, which had a quick turnaround in terms of designing new war vehicles/airplanes and retooling factories. The intent is creating affordable electric cars with a range of over 200 miles on a single charge, but larger ranges should be our goal. Other companies (like Tesla) that now specialize in these technologies could be merged into GM and Ford, thereby merging innovation with those already experienced at manufacturing affordable cars. Hybrids with larger ranges will also be manufactured, but must reach far higher levels than now mandated. Let's find ways to get 75+ mpg. Don't let China sweep this industry away from us.

Goal #3: Manufacture 100 Million Electric Cars

As retooled factories mass produce these new electric or ultra fuel-efficient hybrid cars, government will subsidize the purchasing of these cars by the entire nation with interest-free loans with the goal of replacing gas-guzzling cars within 15 years. Let American-made electric and hybrid car purchases be tax deductible! All together it would end oil imports forever, and with stunning economic benefits once the car industry starts to sell these new cars throughout the world. Imports must meet the same stringent standards. Cars manufactured abroad will get no government support or tax deduction. The goal is to keep jobs here in America.

Goal #4: "Volt" Stations

We need to replace "gas" stations with "volt" stations. To make electric cars feasible, we must make sure everyone can recharge easily. Gas stations must retool so that they have electric charge stations. Technology must be developed so that cars recharge quickly – not the hours-long affair many know. A novel approach would be battery replacement. Instead of charging, "volt" stations will quickly install charged batteries then keep the old ones (and recharge them). With this, people could drive endlessly knowing they need only recharge overnight or locate a "volt" station to get a fully charged battery. The concept involves a national network of stations as common as gas stations. Gas stations can be encouraged to convert to lucrative battery and "volt" stations – emerging industries needed to power those millions of electric cars. It will take some convincing, but what choice is there besides teetering for decades as oil reserves dwindle... or oceans rise. It's time for courageous, bold changes and a plan for the long term.

LET'S BE BOLD - LET'S THINK OUT OF THE BOX

America did not become a prosperous nation by being tentative. We cannot give in to negativity and rigid ideology. Now is the time to do what we did in wartime: *damn the torpedoes, full speed ahead.* Now is the time to treat problems with the urgency of war and take bold steps – investing in technologies that have a fighting chance of transforming the future. If the bold steps outlined above become a reality within 15 years, the change of sea in our economy would be historic: no foreign oil dependence, a trade surplus, cleaner air, carbon emissions slashed, and a U.S. car industry selling millions of green cars each year domestically and internationally. Never forget what was accomplished during World War II. Never underestimate what bold vision and quality management can accomplish.

Let's be bold. Let's think out of the box. *Take the quantum leap.*

Chapter 11

TOXIC POLITICS
We Need A Political Geneva Conference

Uniting our nation to make giant strides means allowing the system our forefathers created to work: checks and balances, three branches of government, intentional gridlock so that leaders don't act brazenly. All are at the core of a democracy that was ever a messy business since early times, but toxic politics now creates extreme rancor in government, pushing gridlock into paralysis. The only exception seems to be times when one party controls all three branches. Even so, the minority party can shut things down due to the Senate filibuster, a rule that requires a supermajority of 60 Senators to allow legislation to go to the floor for a vote. Republicans used it effectively to slow or stop the Democratic agenda. When a Republican President is in power, it works the other way. The end result: nothing big ever gets done. It will remain like this until the two parties work together as they had in past times.

Years of mounting divisiveness climaxed in 2016. If there is any one warning, it is this: it is time for everyone, from politicians to the news media to the nation at large, to tone things down so that government can be effective, as it was during the Great Depression and post-WWII era. We need to restore to the vocabulary of government "bipartisan" and "cooperation" as followed by leaders from the WWII generation, who did not view these concepts as poison. Before we dream of making great strides forward, we need to restore healthy politics and use government intelligently rather than demonizing it. To cure the sick patient we call politics, we need a "Political Geneva Peace Conference."

*　　*　　*　　*　　*

POLITICIANS MUST TONE THINGS DOWN

There must be limits to what politicians say. Candidates and elected officials must rebuke dishonesty, end the predatory attacking of opponents, and spend more time studying complex issues. What used to be political disagreement has turned into feuds and hatred. It has all roiled millions of people into an unnecessary frenzy. Extremism, dishonest websites and news services fuel the flames. It has created dangerously divided political camps in hostile opposition.

Things have to tone down. Politicians seem to forget that dictatorships emerged from democracy. The time has come for politicians to come to an agreement to place limits on the toxicity and monitor themselves before things get worse – before the nation starts to talk of splitting apart. It already happened during the Civil War. It took four years of brutal war and 600,000 dead soldiers to put an end that that tragic episode of American history.

Sadly, the unthinkable has become thinkable. We can no longer hide from the fact that divisiveness of such intensity can lead to bad things. New nations formed in our lifetime. The Soviet Union collapsed into many independent countries to the shock of the western world. Scotland had a referendum for independence that came very close to passing. Czechoslovakia split into two countries. Yugoslavia split into many countries after years of regional war and the murder of thousands of innocent people creating a new term: ethnic cleansing. Spain now suffers from talk of dissolution.

The unthinkable is thinkable. The topic has not been discussed much in our country, but people think about it. Petitions for independence are heard about though it never goes far nor draws much attention... yet. People wonder if they belong to the same country. The divisions are strong. Texas and New York are like Venus and Mars. We too often talk in terms of *red* and *blue* states as if we are two different countries.

The politics of division mounts and must be put to an end by politicians themselves. The scary premise of regions seeking independence... well, we are not there yet, but you start wondering if we are headed there. Dissolution does not suggest violence or civil war. If it came, it would likely happen peacefully as in the Scotland or Brexit model: a referendum, a decision, a clean break. Done. The unthinkable nearly happened in Britain. If we allow extreme divisions to grow, we risk this type of thinking. We had better tone things down. Bad things can happen.

The point of this chapter is not to suggest that a separatist movement is about to begin, but then again perhaps we take too much for granted. The toxic politics has got to stop for many reasons: it's unhealthy, it leads to gridlock, it makes regions come to distrust or hate each other, it puts neighbors at odds, it makes politicians a negative role model for the young. The list of negatives resulting from toxicity is large. How long is the list of positives? This author can't think of any positives. Can you? Well, it generates jobs and revenue for TV networks that play to each political camp and fuel such bitterness. You call that positive?

Before things get worse (and they can)... before things drive people to talk of separate countries, let's all agree to tone things down. Let's demand that our politicians return to a more civil tone like the Reagan era. Back then there was conflict, but it was more level-headed and gentlemanly. Viciousness, dishonesty, brutal attacks – they were nowhere near what we now see. Change starts by people refusing to watch the extremist news "services" and refusing to vote for people who use such tactics.

Before we reach the point of the unthinkable, Democrat and Republican leaders need to create a "Political Geneva Conference" agreement. The concept of a Political Geneva Conference is an idea whose time has come – an agreement by all elected officials and candidates for office to place clear limits on what is said and threatened. The concept of the Geneva Conference is clear: even in times of war, all belligerents must abide by certain basic principles of human decency.

EXTREMISM & DANGEROUS WORDS REACH EPIC LEVELS

What we now see in America is disturbing. When a presidential candidate threatens to jail his opponent or suggest that gun owners take matters into their own hands, it starts to sound scarily similar to 1930s Germany. Killing and imprisoning political opponents are the hallmark of fascism. No one should ever utter such words, even in jest.

Even if politicians or "news" media saying such incendiary words are not trying to promote violence, nonetheless words are dangerous. Words can incite violent behavior. Words are the weapons of writers and politicians. Perhaps incendiary words were merely heat-of-the-moment comments during an intense campaign. We hope that's all it was. It's probable that such talk was meant to get votes and rouse voters, not incite violence. Still, words are powerful, especially when they come from politicians running for office where reporters and microphones and a large audience are in place.

It's time for all politicians to tone things down.

Our country is ripe for change. Millions of people are angry. They feel a better life they had in the past, better paying jobs, was stolen from them. They blame Wall Street, Liberals, free traders, Conservatives, anyone. Finding scapegoats has become common. The hate has become quite evident, but there is a right way to create change and a wrong way. Elections and civil debate are the right way. Extremist words are the wrong way. When prison or death is implied, that is dangerous extremism. Everyone must agree to place restraints on what is said. Major change came in far worse economic times like the Great Depression. Franklin Roosevelt steered the country through that disaster without bullying and threats.

Many politicians now push ethical standards too far in order to get their way or get elected. Standards have plummeted. From politician to citizen to news and Internet media, we all must work to tone things down. The so-named "Political Geneva Conference" agreement is not just between politicians. It is a concept everyone should abide by.

IN THE PRESS: INFLAMMATORY & DANGEROUS WORDS

Newspapers often reported on disturbing events in campaign rallies in 2016. A typical example was noted in a New York Times report. According to that report, a Donald Trump adviser, Al Baldasaro, told a radio host that Hillary Clinton "should be put in the firing line and shot for treason." According to the report, then-candidate Donald Trump praised Baldasaro despite the disturbing threat. It reflects the extremism that permeated the 2016 election.[192]

Reporters also reported on disturbing things commonly seen at a Trump campaign rally. People at one rally angrily and loudly yelled *"Kill her"*, *"F*ck those dirty beaners"*, *"Trump that bitch"*, and *"Build a wall — kill them all!"* People wore T-shirts with similarly disturbing threats. Reporters noted that such aggression and hatred was common at political rallies. Confrontations with reporters were also frequent, as were violent threats to reporters.[193]

Words inciting violence... words implying the murder of a political opponent... words urging mobs towards violence: this is more reminiscent of brown shirts and Nazi Germany, but this has now become a reality in America. Reports of bigotry and attacks spread.

Some say it was all in jest, not intended. Maybe so. But words are the foundation of politics. What people of stature say matters. There are some things that should never be said or implied in a civilized nation. Words can incite reckless actions by followers. The above incidents are scarily reminiscent of stories heard in the days of Nazi brown shirts as fascism overtook Germany. We witnessed extremism in America at rallies of a major party presidential candidate. These episodes (and there are many lately) show how extremism is getting out of control. This is why we need a "Political Geneva Conference."

SLANDEROUS NEWS MEDIA & WEBSITES FUEL EXTREMISM

There is growing recognition within political circles of the need to put a stop to extremism. It can start with an agreement by all politicians to shun those who resort to such tactics and refusal to support websites and news networks that promote extremism, violence, slander, lies, and unfounded accusations of criminal activity.

Our leaders have obligations to the republic and constitution prior to obligations to their political party or personal ambitions. All politicians must be guardians of the republic. They must protect something more important than political party loyalty: our democracy.

The basis of the Geneva Conference is that prisoners of war and civilians must be treated humanely. Even in times of war, all sides must abide by basic principles of decency. All sides follow these rules so that the enemy will follow the rules. The same concept must now apply to American politics. Republicans and Democrats, abiding by such an agreement, would follow it because they want to protect themselves from brutal attacks and dishonesty. What happened in the early days of Nazi Germany is something all politicians must be keenly aware of. Evil starts small and grows until it reaches a point where civilization collapses. We are inching towards it.

One of the problems we increasingly witness is the spread of disinformation and lies. The twisting of truth is almost at Orwellian proportions. With TV and the Internet, its reach has grown exponentially and affects how the country votes. It has become part of the problem and an abuse of First Amendment rights. Supreme Court Justice Oliver Wendell Holmes famously wrote in his 1919 opinion in *Schenck v. United States*, "The most stringent protection of free speech would not protect a man in falsely shouting fire in a theater and causing a panic."[194] Freedom of speech is not license for "news services" to spread lies and half-truths.

Key Republican and Democrat leaders can help in addressing this growing problem of disinformation. Included in the so-called *Political Geneva Conference* must be provisions requiring politicians and candidates for office to not support extremists and promoters of *fake news*. Incorrect facts, or twisting truths so much as to make the distinction between truth and fiction irrelevant, fuel extremism. Politicians must shun irresponsible TV and Internet media.

FAKE NEWS GAINING UNDESERVED RESPECTABILITY

Reporters have expressed apprehension about seedy news services or Internet websites that readily publish information or "news" from untrustworthy sources as if they were of high caliber and equal to established and respected news sources.

A 2016 New York Times article noted many disturbing things that have become rather typical of "news" services nowadays.[195] Internet sites like Facebook and Twitter commonly present unverified news stories, or reckless statements that are false, in such a respectable manner as to imply undeserved trustworthiness. One such story claimed that Hillary Clinton's chief campaign advisor, John Podesta, "practiced occult ritual involving various bodily fluids." Many thousands of people read this (and believed it). This "news story" never appeared in major TV networks or respected newspapers because it was ridiculous, but it nonetheless was seen in Internet websites as if it were real news based upon facts and professionally vetted news reporting. Sadly, such presentation of downright slanderous claims is becoming common on the Internet.

Another typical and disturbing example is an "alt right" figure who commented via Twitter that Donald Trump should disband the White House press corps. This comment appeared in Facebook and other Internet newsfeed alongside newsfeed from major newspapers like The New York Times, Boston Globe or Washington Post, giving the appearance of factual importance and equality to news reporting by highly respected and trusted newspapers.[196]

No doubt, people can find many more equally disturbing stories, but the point is clearly made: things have gotten out of control. Millions of people now read things on the Internet that, in past, never would have seen the light of day. It is one thing to say ridiculous, dishonest or slanderous things. It's a whole other matter when it appears alongside reports by the New York Times, NBC, FOX, CNN, or the Washington Post. It adds respectability to things that do not deserve attention. It is a dangerous trend that our national leaders, through the bully pulpit (and personal influence), must oppose and end.

THE PLAGUE OF EXTREMISM STARTED DECADES AGO

There was a time when leaders were admired and even set fashion. Theodore Roosevelt ("TR") had a mustache; a generation had mustaches. Woodrow Wilson shaved; the 1920s was a clean-shaven era. JFK took his hat off; fedora hat sales plummeted. It was fashion, but it reflected the mindset of a society that respected leaders. It has now gone full-tilt the other way. If politicians wear casual clothes, we think they're pretending to be one of us.

The changes started in the 1960s with Vietnam, protests, tie-dyed shirts, long hair, drugs, and distrust of the status quo. Given what happened in Vietnam, who could blame them for being angry? Lyndon Johnson was a target of scorn. Millions came to hate the President in a way never seen previously, only to be outdone in hatred for his successor, Richard Nixon, following the notorious Watergate scandal and his resignation.

LBJ entered office in November 1963 after the tragic JFK assassination. He won reelection in 1964 in a landslide after passage of the Civil Rights Act. His popularity soared (outside the South, anyway) after the Great Society and war on poverty. By 1968, he declined a run for reelection due to Vietnam. Things have not been the same ever since. LBJ's war disgraced the presidency. If *Vietnam* symbolized widespread loss of respect for government, *Watergate* symbolized widespread loss of trust.

THE ERA OF POLITICAL GAS WARFARE

The current state of politics is reminiscent of World War I in 1915. After stalemate overcame the trenches of France, desperation took over. German generals commenced gas warfare, launching chlorine or mustard gas into Allied trenches. Thousands died in minutes. Men went mad, gasping for air in agony. Soon, the Allies starting using poison gas. War escalated to new levels of evil, yet the front lines hardly budged. Political ads that slander good people, twist the meanings of 10-second sound bites, or destroy reputations – *this is political gas warfare*.

Like the trenches of France in 1915, it does not end stalemate. Character assassination, lies and slander serve no good purpose. It sends a terrible message. Ultimately, what ended the plague of gas warfare was the Geneva Conference, whereby all nations agreed to follow certain rules even in all-out war. Even Nazi Germany did not resort to gas warfare during World War II. Everyone followed certain rules, for it was in their interest. Democrats and Republicans need a political "Geneva Convention" in the name of a healthy new era of bipartisan leadership. The parties must sign a "treaty" as soon as possible. It should not be done quietly, by handshake, but on the record for the country to see.

Political gas warfare mounted during President Clinton's second term. The country heard lurid details about oral sex in the Oval Office and a stain on a woman's dress. Then came the brutal impeachment trial. A mother I knew summed up the era: "I'd like to thank the President for making me teach my 8 year-old what oral sex is."

During the Clinton era, the problems morphed into poisonous conflict between political parties. Division between Democrats and Republicans is at historic levels not seen since the years leading to the Civil War. That has scary implications.

In 2016 the problem reached new levels of toxicity that had political pundits and politicians in Washington shaking their heads. It emerged from years of mindless attacks by politicians who may not have recognized just where it would end up. Politicians created the problem and they will have to end it.

Following the Reagan years, we witnessed an era of stunningly toxic politics: slanderous 527 attack ads, politicians slandering each other, mocking of political philosophies, and humiliation of opponents. Poison gas warfare, in a sense. It's not as if past politicians were angels. Google Joe McCarthy, Huey Long, George Wallace, and Strom Thurmond. But those were also times of experimentation and bipartisan action. Modern political leaders can restore civility and honesty. The 2016 election pushed the lines way beyond what is acceptable. The nation is terribly divided. Lincoln warned, a house divided cannot stand. The Civil War began soon after. We all need to give more thought to the path we are following.

TOXIC POLITICS ONLY BRINGS STAGNATION

Lack of cooperation or negotiation is striking. Not a single House Republican voted for the 2009 stimulus package or the 2010 Affordable Care Act. The result, for years, was a unified Republican party that vowed to dismantle the whole thing. Look what happened once they became the majority. There is a lesson. Unless both parties agree on a direction, major initiatives may reverse every four to eight years when power shifts to the other party. That's no way to govern for the long term. Without bipartisan agreement, nothing lasts. Presidents cannot rule by executive order, for that can change as soon as we elect a new President. New executive orders quickly nullify the old. Only laws passed by Congress last. That requires bipartisan action.

How would our country have survived the Great Depression and World War II if *this* had been the attitude in Congress? Both parties are at fault. People don't like each other, cooperate or work together. Must politicians be Darth Vader? Destroy everything in their path? Politicians disagreed during the Depression and post-WWII era. There are theories why we face bitter conflict now. WWII bred a different attitude and patriotism. That generation understood that our real enemies were fascists, Hitler and communism. The current generation of politicians treats the other party with fear. Our enemies abroad benefit.

Gridlock and nastiness reflect a societal intolerance of new ideas. The parties become single-minded, shutting down dissent and innovation. Throughout the 1980s Republicans steadily vanquished its Progressive wing of the Teddy Roosevelt era. Democrats lost the south after the 1960s and became a Liberal Northeast and West coast party. Eight swing states seem to control the fate of the presidency. The political map, the "L" shape of staunch Republican states in the Midwest turning east in the South, looks strangely similar to the borders during the Civil War. *We should not underestimate the dangerous end result of continued political division.*

Divisiveness has a toll. Note this excerpt from a *McClatchyDC* report, "Congress Heads Home With Dubious Distinction: Far Fewer Laws Than Infamous Congress".

> *"The 113th Congress is heading home and into the history books with a record of legislative futility... this Congress will have passed slightly more than 57 bills into law... Critics say the current Congress makes the 80th Congress – dismissively dubbed by President Harry S Truman as the 'Do Nothing Congress' – look like workaholics. That Congress [in 1947] enacted 395 public bills into law by the end of its first session... By all objective measures, this is the worst Congress ever,' Tom Mann, a senior governance fellow at Washington's Brookings Institution, said of the 113th... 'They did a lot of stuff of no consequence... The 113th Congress didn't pass a single appropriations bill, a farm bill, immigration legislation, anything to change or improve healthcare or anything thing to curb the debt.'" [197]*

America has a long way to go if we are to return to the days of FDR, Truman, Eisenhower, and JFK, when Washington was seen as a place of action. Despite disagreement, politicians managed to pass important legislation. Compromise was not failure. It was how you ran government. It worked. We must restore their willingness to bang out agreements and work together. A new attitude among politicians is needed – not people always raising money for the next election and pressured to adhere to policies sponsors demand of them. Changing that would require blowing up the current system: a revolution like public funding of elections and getting money out of politics. That option is discussed in Chapter 11.

RECKLESS BASHING OF POLITICAL PHILOSOPHIES

The 2016 election brings things to a head: fake news and lies; websites twisting truths or creating false allegations of criminal acts. Every politician needs to tone things down before we reach a tipping point. It's one thing to disagree. It's a whole other thing to demonize others or lie. The bashing of Liberalism is one example where opponents need to tone it down.

Liberalism is an appropriate place to start for it is under withering attack. Government provides unemployment insurance, Social Security, Medicare,

Medicaid, and has many regulatory agencies that monitor Wall Street, banks, worker safety, air quality, water, and the food and medicines we use. Even Conservatives accept traditional Liberalism as part of government though they don't like to admit it.

Classical Liberalism was a doctrine evolving since the late 19th Century promoting social progress and economic regulation. It addressed the excesses of laissez-faire society like 16-hour workdays, sweatshops, disease-ridden tenements, poor sanitation encouraging disease, poisoned food, and cholera-ravaged water supplies. Liberalism promoted regulation so that people's wealth would not be wiped out by unscrupulous banking and stock market practices. It ended disastrous bank runs that wiped out people's life savings. It promoted justice for the working class so that people could live in dignity, have reasonable working hours, a safe workplace, and unemployment insurance or food stamps so that people never starve. Medicare, Medicaid, Social Security, Pell college grants, NEA support for the arts, FDIC, OSHA, FDA, SEC and EPA: these are the legacy of Liberalism. They help society function better, rich or poor.

There is no need to mock Liberalism. We all accept classical Liberalism – unless you want to return to Jim Crow segregation or 1920s laissez-faire economics, bank runs that wipe out your life savings, or children in sweatshops. Liberalism ended terrible injustices, starvation wages, 12-hour six-day workloads, child labor, rancid food, sanitation, and tainted water. The list of giant strides thanks to Liberalism is large, yet people bash it. Perhaps they should learn more about it instead of poisoning the well with ignorant accusations. Really, we don't want to live as people did before Liberalism emerged.

Conservatism should not be bashed either. Philosophies balance each other. In times of economic crisis we deficit-spend to stimulate an economy, and in good economic times government should pay off debt. Now, each extreme of the political spectrum bashes the other. Disagreement is a healthy part of democracy, but it becomes a problem when conflict leads to demonizing opposing points of view.

Trashing both Liberalism and Conservatism is throwing the baby out with the dirty bathwater. We are all Liberals and Conservatives to some extent, after all, if you buy a car or house with a loan, don't you pay it back? By analogy, economic stimulus by deficit spending eventually requires that debt be paid back. As in life, government balances conflicting goals. No one argues about ending Social Security or Medicare; they merely debate about funding them correctly. *Liberalism vs. Conservatism:* both part of intelligent fiscal policy. When we attack one, we attack ourselves. We need both. We all are both.

It is time politicians accept who their true enemies are. It is not the other party. It is totalitarianism, fascism and terrorism. It is governments intolerant of liberties and democracy. We need to tone things down and see to it that politicians of both parties grant dignity to each other. We are not all that different as we think. Agree to disagree, but resorting to slander, lies, fake news, and character assassination are unacceptable. In their desperation to get elected, politicians resort to poison gas warfare. Win at all costs. Things have to tone down.

TAXES & DEMONIZING COURAGEOUS THINKERS

If our nation is to restore its economic base, government must invest heavily in the future, but how do you do this when resorting to knee-jerk attacks on taxing? Sometimes we need to raise taxes. Economists often warn political leaders about it.

Remember George Bush (Sr.): "Read my lips: no new taxes."[198] He allowed a tax hike a couple of years later for the good of the country... *to lower government debt.* A conservative ideal! His own party – Conservatives! –brutally scorned him. He paid a big price for a reasonable decision. It was a shame that fellow Republicans disparaged him rather than see it as an example of common sense in recognizing that sometimes we must reverse course as conditions change. The disease of punishing politicians for doing what is necessary must end. *Compromise is not failure – it is the hallmark of competent leadership.*

We cannot always borrow. We cannot always keep low taxes. The obsession with cutting taxes is out of control with so-called Conservatives. Their brethren of the past were never so rigid. Republicans accepted tax hikes during WWII. Reagan agreed to tax hikes in the 1980s. They understood there were times when a greater goal overrode ideology. Sometimes taxes must rise to help government. Economists agree that deficit spending and/or raising taxes are essential tools when timed correctly. Franklin Roosevelt, a fiscal Conservative before becoming President, understood the need to be flexible and adjust to circumstances. The depression made flexibility necessary. Modern leaders must accept that no policy is perfect all the time. The disease of demonizing courageous decisions has gone too far. A portion from the Bible reminds all:

To everything there is a season,
a time for every purpose under the sun...
a time to lose and a time to seek;
a time to keep silent and a time to speak.
 – Ecclesiastes 3:1-8

SOLUTIONS: TERMS OF THE
POLITICAL GENEVA CONFERENCE

Party leaders must agree upon certain limits to political gas warfare: what they will and will not do. They need an actual document, signed, sealed and delivered to the public. There must be some agreement that everyone will abide by. The Senate and the House of Representatives are guided by parliamentary rules of civility. This must pass on to campaigns, the press and all interactions with the public. It would be a modern "Contract with America." As in war, everyone ends up having good reasons to abide by agreements: to prevent the enemy from breaking the agreement. Here is an outline for a political "treaty" to be agreed upon at this political Geneva Convention.

✓ Inflammatory Words. All politicians must agree to confront those who cross the line of decency. Words that incite violence, imprison opponents, charge treason, dangerous jokes, ethnic slurs, suggestions directly or by implication of totally false charges, and so on – all must immediately and severely be reprimanded by party leaders, especially within their own party. There are some things we must never tolerate. There must be an understanding that loyalties are first to country and second to political party.

✓   News Media, Fake News & the Internet. We witness an era where news networks and websites proclaim lies or twist facts. We witness a new term: *fake news.* The politicians themselves must attack these practices and refuse to have any interaction with such groups. Free speech is one thing, but freely proclaiming lies is not free speech. There have to be limits. The expression coined by Supreme Court Justice Oliver Wendell Holmes sums things up: *free speech does not mean falsely screaming fire in a crowded theater."*

✓   Gerrymandering. Politicians increasingly abuse the practice of creating voting districts that blatantly distort the vote. People have a right to elect the leaders they want. Abolishing this practice must be part of the "Geneva" agreement. It destroys the very premise of democracy. Case in point is a 2016 Wisconsin gerrymandering lawsuit noting that Republicans won 48.6% of the vote yet won 61% of the Assembly.[199] This is ruthless manipulation of districting – gerrymandering at its worst. It temporarily benefits one party but ultimately ruins democracy. Both parties need to ask this honest-to-heart question: do you value your political party more than our democratic republic? What marks us apart from countries like Russia that pretend to be a democracy but in reality create fake election results? Wisconsin gerrymandering raises questions about the health of our democracy and whether it is rigged. Simply put, 61% of votes should not elect 48.6% of representatives. This is deeply troubling, even to the political party that benefits... *temporarily.* The best solution is ending the cynical practice as a matter of law. In the meantime, let the matter of gerrymandering be addressed in the "Geneva" treaty.

✓   Common Cause & PIRG. Ethics in government, from campaign financing to honesty, must be addressed. Common Cause and PIRG (Public Interest Research Group) provide insightful concepts furthering the goals of better government and confronting corruption. Visit their websites and learn more.

✓   Sound Bites. Sound bites in ads must be truthful and factual. The practice of cutting up facts or quotes to distort an opponent's record must end. It's unethical. It's dishonest. Attack others for the position they hold, not the positions you create by cutting apart quotes and voting records into half-truths.

✓   Voting Records. Politicians must cease the use of voting records to distort a politician's beliefs. Legislation is filled with conflicting matters. A bill funding green energy could have a pork-barrel earmark for a museum in Iowa. A Senator may vote against that bill because earmarks are wasteful though he wanted clean energy. He might vote against the bill because of earmarks knowing that within days a revised bill will eliminate the earmark. The slander of advertising that the Senator voted against green energy would be a lie, but this is now common practice. Politicians know this and must stop the practice.

✓   Character Assassination. In the 2006 Tennessee Senate race, an African American candidate was hounded by sleazy 527 attack ads depicting a sexy white woman desiring a sexual encounter. It played on bigotry regarding interracial relationships. There was no excuse for such viciousness except that the candidate wanted to win (and did). Character assassination must be banned.

✓   Ban "527" tax loopholes. The 527s have sponsored slanderous TV ads about politicians, supposedly out of the control of politicians. Limiting the impact of 527s would allow candidates to focus on issues rather than pandering to special interest groups... and take full responsibility for all ads and statements. Not some. *All.* Third parties must not do their dirty campaigning.

✓   Public Financing. Our leaders should focus on governing, not fundraising. The cost of elections has skyrocketed and politicians waste huge amounts of time raising money. Eliminate this and you can eliminate corruption, undue corporate influence, and the influence of money. Politicians should agree to ease this burden so that they can focus on studying complex issues and running the country. This is truly the path to good government. There is an entire chapter on this plan. (Chapter 11: *Slay The Dragon.*)

✓   A Publicized Treaty & Follow-Up. There should be an actual document signed by party leaders so as to make a statement to the public and pressure politicians to follow agreements. Both parties must abide by "understandings" because it is in everyone's interest. A "convention of principles" should be held after each Congressional election (2 years) to resolve emerging problems and violations. Party leaders would meet to discuss violations of the political "Geneva Convention." It should create a healthy forum for eliminating new unethical problems that emerge.

✓   Vetting of Candidates. Party leaders and donors must agree to provide no support whatsoever to anyone expressing extremist and reckless tactics. Each party will act in advance to make sure demagogues expressing dangerous ideas won't get support from the parties. While Democrats and Republicans oppose each other, they also share the mutual desire to ensure that democracy and constitutional rights are safe. We don't want demagogues to emerge who use dangerous tactics of fascism. Some things must be off limits: attacks on racial groups, attacks on the press, targeting innocent people, lies, appealing to extremism, and outright hatred.

ESTABLISHING A DEMOCRACY TO ADMIRE

Abiding by this "treaty" would be a historic break from the past. It would lead to improved public policy, better government, ethical campaigns, and *civility*. We can end the era of divisive politics if our leaders make it so. The politics of 19th-century America still plagues our country. Our leaders need to professionalize their profession. What they have given us is not democracy of the 21st Century; it is a democracy of shame.

When politicians choose to act professionally, like most of us in the workplace, Washington will evolve into a better democracy. Before we attack others, let's clean up our own house – *disagreement, yes; gas warfare, no.* Rather than breeding a new generation of disrespect, lawmakers must set an example. The win-at-all-costs mentality must stop, and it stops when our leaders decide to stop it... and put pressure on each other to abide by understandings in the political "Geneva Conference."

Whether done in public, privately, or in old-fashioned "smoke-filled rooms," all that matters is that the political parties *do it.* America deserves it. Our children need positive role models. *Washington: end political gas warfare.*

Chapter 12

PUBLIC FUNDING OF ELECTIONS
Slay The Dragon

An idealistic new President enters the Oval Office with an ambitious agenda. He makes promises to millions of supporters. Now comes reality as the inertia of "business-as-usual" kicks in: 535 Senators and Congressman, each trying to raise money for the next campaign; the Byzantine agendas of many thousands of lobbyists; the conflicting goals of competing political factions. Legislation is proposed and now come the hordes of lobbyists from K Street. The banks want lax oversight. (The public wants accountability.) The oil companies want to drill in federal seas and parks. (The public wants the environment to be protected.) Multinationals want free trade pacts to allow access to yet more countries with cheap labor. (The public wants jobs and an end to outsourcing.) Welcome to Washington, Mr. (Ms.) President. (Are you sure you want this job?)

Money controls politics, as legislators need huge sums of money for their campaigns. They cannot get elected without donations from corporations and interest groups, whose hired lobbyists contact them to promote needs regarding legislation, taxes or regulations. Their influence is disproportionate. Legislators have to listen – they need money.

Legislators also spend a lot of time fundraising. They must not enjoy the constant phone calls to donors and tedious weekend trips to their district to fundraise. An average Congressional race cost $1.69 million in 2012. For a Senator, it was $10.48 million.[200] Congressmen must raise an average of $2,315 daily to fund campaigns. Senators average $14,351 per day.[201]

Lawmakers are part-time fundraisers. That's time raising money instead of focusing on legislating. What a drain of time. Such sapping of loyalty to voters. Instead of studying issues and learning, they endlessly raise money. They pay more attention to lobbyists working for cash-rich corporations than they do to the people who voted for them. The influence of campaign donors is far out of proportion. It's always been like this, only in the past money came from political machines (Prendergast, Daley, Tammany Hall) or tycoons (J.P. Morgan, Carnegie). Corruption is still common. Google Tom Delay, Jack Abramoff, Sheldon Silver and Joseph Skelos. As written thousands of years ago in the Bible, *nothing new under the sun* (Ecclesiastes, 1:4-11).

Corruption can be addressed by legislating ethics: limits on campaign contributions, preventing politicians from accepting campaign money for personal use, etc. Politicians enacting legislation on ethics… well, that's asking the drug addict to cure himself. Non-partisan organizations like *Common Cause* and *PIRG* (Public Interest Research Group) lobby leaders to enact laws requiring them to abide by high ethical standards, limit campaign donations, be held accountable, expose corruption, and eliminate politicians on the take for money. The efforts by *Common Cause* and *PIRG* are outstanding. Visit their websites.

But this chapter focuses on a specific goal. Rather than addressing problems piece-by-piece or asking politicians to self-police, simply *eliminate* the whole problem. Get rid of money in politics and change history. We enjoy 21st-century technology, yet government lives by 19th-century devices.

It's time to change the status quo. Take money out of politics by publically funding elections. A plan is presented at the end of the chapter. *Slay the dragon once and for all.*

LOBBYISTS & THE LURE OF MONEY

In the coming pages you will read disturbing facts − and a striking solution. Let's explore the extent of the poison brought on by corporate donations. We start with lobbyists. Lobbyists are hard-working and knowledgeable people providing useful services. If their client is the Sierra Club, they promote a clean environment. If it is a bank, they may promote deregulation. The issue is not lobbyists. It's their undue influence. It boils down to domination through campaign donations.

Many of the thousands of lobbyists in Washington are former Senators, Congressmen and Governors; former presidential advisors or cabinet members; or former Congressional staff (often paid better than when they worked for Congressmen). They are glad to speak with legislators (and former bosses). Corporate-hired lobbyists are paid well, averaging $300,000 per year and up to $2 million for former Governors or Senators with unique access to legislators. A former Assistant Dept. Secretary can earn up to $1 million. A former staff director for an important House or Senate committee can earn $500,000 to $800,000.[202]

Former Clinton Chief of Staff and Obama CIA chief Leon Panetta commented, "[T]he name of the game is money, and the fact is [legislators] still largely depend on lobbyists for the money to bulk up their campaigns."[203]

In their defense, lobbyists offer useful services. They are experts in their fields and offer insights about their respective industries. Their expertise may be of help in drafting legislation and addressing complex matters. Congressmen accept this help, but help comes at a price when it comes to upcoming legislation important to corporate-hired lobbyists. Aides are overwhelmed with work. Lobbyists lighten the workload: they will do research, provide detailed information, explain complicated matters, and even write legislation. But corporations are built for profit. They pay lobbyists well because they expect something important in return.

Corporations have a right to talk to legislators. The problem is they also control the purse. They have influence disproportionate to their numbers and because legislators need money to run campaigns, they are captive to corporations. That is the status quo. Many restrictions limit what lobbyists can offer to legislators. Direct transfers of money are forbidden. Lawmakers cannot accept gifts or meals beyond $50.[204] However, a firm can grant legislators access to corporate jets and pay for travel expenses. They can play golf and meet at resorts. Just what is discussed at the golf course?

527s & RESULTING CORRUPTION

While laws limit campaign donations, rules can be evaded. Terms like "hard" and "soft" money pervade Washington. Legislators face limits on how much money can be donated (hard money), but as for indirect donations (soft money), it's infinite. Corporations and special interest groups (like the NRA) are prime sponsors of soft money.

While campaign laws limit what corporations may contribute, rules are lax when it comes to fundraising *outside* rules. The "527s" (derived from U.S. tax code 26 U.S.C. §527 allowing political groups to form outside the scope of federal restrictions) advertise on behalf of politicians without money coming out of that politician's campaign fund. It is allowed because the Federal Elections Commission (FEC) determined that 527s are not covered. Campaign finance laws do not cover 527 groups unless they advocate the election or defeat of a candidate. A technicality created a monster. In 2008, 527s received $440 million.[205]

When 527s advertise, it is technically not under that candidate's control. If a TV ad is slanderous, the candidate can hide behind the excuse that it was not his/her campaign that produced the ad. That is why ads are followed by the words, *"I am *** and I approve of this message."* In a word, 527s are the attack dog doing the dirty work. Attack ads make it easy to spread dirt without candidates taking the hit.

There are many instances of scandal. One involves former Alaska Senator Ted Stevens, first elected in 1968. His long career ended in disgrace in 2008 when he was convicted on seven counts of failing to report gifts received from corporations and violations of the Ethics in Government Act. He lost a close election to Democrat Mark Begich. Nine former Stevens aides became lobbyists at firms known for ties to the Senator. The firms reported nearly $62 million in fees.[206]

The current system breeds stories like this.

Among notorious figures is Jack Abramoff, a former Republican lobbyist who was sentenced to over five years in prison in 2006, having been found guilty of fraud, tax evasion and conspiracy to bribe public officials. Among those disgraced (and now out of power) are former Republican majority leader Rep. Tom DeLay (R-Tex.) and Robert Ney (R-Ohio). Both pled guilty to charges related to the scandal. The influence of lobbyists can go right to the top.

If we changed the system, we might stop breeding stories like this.

CORRUPTION ALL THE WAY TO THE TOP

John Dean, in his New York Times bestseller "Broken Government," noted the following about past lobbyists:

• *The ousted Rep. House leader Tom DeLay wrote, "If you want to get government regulations off the backs of energy producers, for example, talk to the energy producers about how government gets in their way. Then get their government affairs people [lobbyists] to help you draft legislation. You'll certainly get better results than you would by talking to [EPA] and energy experts at Harvard."[207] ... DeLay boasted that he had lobbying firms writing the laws.[208]*

• *Former Rep. Duke Cunningham (R-Cal.) accepted $2.4 million in bribes, a record in the Guinness Book of World Records for the largest known bribe by a Congressman. He had agreed to help defense contractors who wanted to "buy" business.*

• *"The anything-goes atmosphere also led to the rise and fall of Jack Abramoff, whose multiple scandals, most playing off his access to Tom DeLay and other influential Republicans in Congress, along with players in the White House... threatened to mushroom into the biggest corruption scandal in Washington in 125 years."* [209]

Corporate lobbyists have enormous sway in Washington. Note, for example, lobbying efforts by the auto industry, which is typical among large industries. Auto lobbyists resisted, among other things, raising fuel economy standards. Some $95 million was spent on auto-industry lobbying over a ten-year period. The Washington Post reported that a group of 60 corporations, including Pfizer, Altria and Hewlett-Packard, paid lobbyists $1.6 million to meet with Congressmen about a low tax rate for money earned abroad, resulting in a 2004 law reducing tax rates by 5%. The bill affected some $300 billion in earnings and cost the IRS $100 billion. [210]

In 2009, bailed-out banks lobbied. Citigroup, which received $45 billion in bailout funds, spent $1.77 million on lobbying fees in the fourth fiscal quarter of 2008. In a sense, it was taxpayers' money. Other bailed out companies spending millions for lobbying included American Express, Capital One, Goldman Sachs, KeyCorp, Morgan Stanley, PNC, Bank of New York Mellon, GM, GMAC, Chrysler, and former AIG executives. [211]

THE PRESIDENT CAN INSPIRE CHANGE

Nearly half of all lawmakers returning to the private sector worked for lobbyists, according to Citizen's Congress Watch. [212] Among them are former Senators Tom Daschle and Bob Dole. Marc Racicot, the former Montana governor, earned over $1 million as president of the American Insurance Association. It raises troubling questions about politicians' motivations. The problem is that it's hard to find good people who have not worked for a lobbyist at some point. You can't blame them. They get paid well. But here's the rub: to whom is your loyalty? [213]

Public financing of elections is a solution. Today the White House can use its prestige to end our sad history of patronage. According to a 2006 national poll, 80% of Democrats and 65% of Republicans support public funding of elections. There is a groundswell of support. Liberate leaders from money and you will find a historic new atmosphere in Washington.

We depend on corporations for the products and services we need. They are not our enemy. We welcome useful exchange of ideas, but with a healthy balance. The only true long-term solution is to end our lawmakers' servitude to campaign donors. End the domination of money and pervasive conflicts of interest will evaporate. Once special interests and corporations get involved, the needs of the majority are lost. Who can protect the public? The White House. When Pfizer gave money, it expected attention when drug legislation came. When Ford contributed, it expected the Michigan delegation to stare down the next round of EPA standards. Their concerns were not necessarily what is best for the country.

Until this status quo changes, government will remain captive. Lobbyists thrive regardless of whether Republicans or Democrats are in power. To corporations, it is just a different list of names to endorse checks to. It could all change in a single stroke. Public financing of campaigns has revolutionary implications for our future. But would it be costly?

$4/PERSON: THE COST OF PUBLIC FUNDING OF ELECTIONS

Public funding of federal elections could be as low as $4/person per year. Congressional and Senatorial elections could be subsidized by voluntary contributions on our 1040 tax forms. If paid for by government, it amounts to $3.4 billion.[214] That's about 0.00085 of the federal budget. Yes, *0.00085*. What a bargain for a revolutionary change. Here are the numbers.

CONGRESS:

$3.4 million per race (for both candidates) x 435 seats = $1.48 billion
divided by 2 (as elections are every two years)
Total annual cost for each American: under $3 ($740 million/yr.)

SENATE:

$20.96 million per race (for both candidates) x 100 seats = $1.92 billion
divided by 6 (as terms are six years)
Total annual cost for each American: about $1 ($349 million/yr.)

TOTAL COST TO FUND ELECTIONS FOR 535 CONGRESSMEN & SENATORS: ABOUT $4/YEAR FOR EACH AMERICAN

Funding Congressman and Senator races comes to $4/person annually. The goal is a $4 contribution on each IRS 1040 for individuals (with option to opt out), $8 for small businesses and $50 to $100 for medium/large corporations. This will be enough to endow the campaigns fund. The individual contribution is tiny compared to the revolutionary change for the good. In the event of a shortfall, the deficit will be covered by the federal government. So to speak, it's the cost of doing business in a democracy.

It would bring unprecedented change. It will end the influence of money, clean up corruption, end fundraising pressures and the enormous time-drain, and allow lawmakers to focus on studying issues and running government rather than fundraising. Let's put it another way. No longer will a Congressman have to raise $2,315 *every day*. No longer will a Senator have to raise $14,351 *every day*. Think of the strain and daily pressure that would vanish!

Further, think of the fresh blood that would flow into Washington. Qualified people could run for office, not just the rich or gifted fundraisers. And without fundraising, politicians' schedules will clear up so that they can find plenty of time to read, study issues, talk to the public about needs, and not be forced to cater to wealthy sponsors day after day. Free them to do their jobs! It will create balance in power unknown in the past. Corporations and interest groups would remain, but more in an advisory role, for they will no longer fund campaigns. No longer will elected officials feel obligated or coerced to follow instructions.

The implications for wonderful change are historic. Had there been public funding in 1995, banks likely would have failed to get Congress to deregulate the banking system, which led to the subprime crisis and economic collapse in 2008. Congressmen and Senators would have likely studied the matter carefully, read more Congressional Research Service reports, and recognized the conflict of interest by banks pressing for deregulation harming the banking system. If Americans spent this $4/person to publicly fund elections back in 1995, we may have avoided the 2008 meltdown! This is just the tip of the iceberg in terms of change.

Another benefit would be the elimination of "underdog" politicians. There is a correlation: those who win elections typically raise more money. This advantage will be eliminated. Both candidates will have the same amount of money and will be granted equal TV and Internet time to explain their positions to the public. No longer would well-endowed candidates monopolize the airwaves. Candidates will be freed of it all and able to speak their minds and consciences because their campaign funds will be theirs as a matter of law.

We should also end the proliferation of 527 attack dogs and often-slanderous campaign ads. Instead, candidates would advertise issue positions directly and within their budget. Their values would better reflect what the public wants rather than what their contributors want. The President, by making campaign finance a key goal, could change history and be an agent of revolutionary change. This is a change of the status quo whose time has come.

12-STEP PLAN FOR PUBLIC FUNDING OF ELECTIONS

Just as Lyndon Johnson faced stubborn resistance from Southerners staunchly opposing civil rights legislation, the President will encounter opposition to public financing. The White House could rally public support for this revolutionary change. If the nation is behind the President, just as it was behind LBJ when he promoted civil rights, it will get done. Here is a list of reforms that will transform Washington.

1. *Public Funding of Federal Elections*. Finance all Congressional and Senatorial candidates nominated by the two major parties. Independents can be funded if they demonstrate significant support.

2. *Public Funding Cost Per American: $4*. It is a reasonable price for cleaning up Washington and shutting down corruption and money influence.

3. *Shut down All "527" Loopholes*. No campaign contributions shall be allowed by anyone: corporations, individuals, special interests, even charities. It will all be paid for by IRS form 1040 asking for a $4 campaign fund donation. There should be consideration of a tiny but permanent .01 percent "campaign tax" on huge S&P 500 companies.

4. *Hard & Soft Contributions*. Completely banned nationwide. This includes state officials.

5. *FEC Review*. A biannual bipartisan committee will meet to propose reforms to close fresh problems that circumvent the public funding system.

6. *Equitable Funding*. As campaigns in New York may be costlier than in Montana, the FEC will allocate money proportionate to demonstrated need.

Both candidates of each race will receive identical campaign funds. Level the playing fields.

7. *FCC Requirement of TV Ads*. All TV and radio stations will be required by the FCC to provide ample time for candidates to advertise their candidacy. This will remove the biggest expense to campaigns. This is the least we can ask of the TV networks for being part of a democracy and broadcasting over the airwaves that rightfully belong to the American people. The same shall apply to the Internet, Facebook, Twitter, et al.

8. *Primaries & Presidential Races*. Presidential candidates will be obligated to accept public financing so as to end the coming insanity of multi-billion dollar campaigns. There will be no option to "opt out." This also means shutting down fundraising on the Internet.

9. *Ban All Political Gifts*. Shut all loopholes allowing lobbyists and corporations to give gifts to politicians (corporate jets, golf, resorts, etc.). Criminalize gifts and impose tough ethical standards. Let lawmakers know no one is above the law or duty to act ethically.

10. *Ban Legislators From Lobbying for 10 Years*. A reform that will transform lobbying is banning former lawmakers from lobbying for 10 years after leaving office. This also applies to non-paying work and honorariums. Legislators must not be enriched for public service, for it attracts people to government for shady reasons. We cannot forever stop former legislators from lobbying, but we can impose a timeframe long enough to stop greed as a motivator. We should nevermore hear about a governor earning $1 million as a reward for public service.

11. *FEC*. The FEC was ineffective in controlling election violations and loopholes, according to The New York Times, and it was lax in policing unethical contributions and behavior. The *Times* called the FEC "dysfunctional" and said its six-member board has not served the public well.[215] The FEC should be depoliticized, or a brand new agency *with teeth* should monitor elections. It must be immune to corruption and corporate/lobbyist influence. It is time to professionalize the FEC (or its successor).

12. *527s*. Banning 527s would serve the country well though it is unclear how it would be resolved in the courts should legal action be taken. At minimum, limit 527s as a political force. Tax loopholes created them. Close the loopholes and as new loopholes emerge, shut them. Eliminating 527s could end slanderous and misleading ads, thereby uplifting politics. The precondition for accepting public funding must be the refusal of any help from 527s. Ads advocating a candidate must be paid for by the candidate's publicly funded campaign. If 527s survive, legislation should make 527s liable to lawsuit by anyone who is slandered or faces character assassination through fake news.

This would make 527s think twice about what they say. First Amendment rights must not protect slander and dishonesty.

CONCLUSION: SLAY THE DRAGON FOREVER

The implications of public funding would be historic. For perhaps the first time in American history, politics would be freed of the grip of the money. It is a path we should relish. The irony is that legislators must enact it just as an alcoholic must want to save himself.

Millions of people are outraged by Washington. Let them overwhelm lawmakers with letters, phone calls, petitions, emails, texts, and tweets rallying for passage of such historic legislation. Congressmen waste so much time raising money! Many might be relieved in shedding this burden, for too much time is devoted to matters that have nothing to do with legislating. It is time better used for studying complex issues they vote on.

Corporations and special interest groups will fight election reform, but once the fight is lost, they will move on. They should be heard from, but in a diminished role. They offer important contributions. Only disproportionate influence is at issue. We don't want them to dominate lawmakers. Just advise. Once made unable to contribute to campaigns, balance will be restored. Balance of power is important to a healthy democracy.

Our symbol of justice is the balanced scale. Multinationals will still have the right to promote their agenda, but, with lawmakers freed of donations, it would change relationships and restore balance. Also expect K Street lobbyist salaries to drop. Lower salaries will scare away sleazy elements.

If the President embraced reform, he/she would face resistance from wealthy corporations and the *two percent* who dominate politics. Well, what in the constitution ever stated they should have such outsized influence? Lyndon Johnson had to overcome opposition to civil rights legislation, but overcome he did as famously symbolized in his 1964 speech before Congress in quoting the mantra of the civil rights movement: *and we shall overcome.* It moved many and shamed holdouts from the South. He assembled a coalition of Liberals and Republicans (in itself a message) to get the legislation passed. It can work out the same now.

The President could transform Washington forever by choosing to use the bully pulpit to rally the nation to embrace public financing of elections. Public financing is essential if we are to truly change Washington and its disappointing status quo. *Slaying the Dragon* would rank among the greatest of achievements in a generational pursuit for a better democracy.

Let the Quixotic quest begin.

Chapter 13

GARBAGE
Boomerang!

Boom-er-ang (boo-mê-rang) *n.* 1. A curved wooden missile that can be thrown so that it returns to the thrower if it fails to hit anything, used by Australian aborigines. 2. Something that causes unexpected harm to its originator.[216]

No concept is so pervasive in our lives as *garbage.* No issue is so taken for granted. That's what garbage is by definition. You throw it out and it becomes someone else's problem. It becomes someone else's task to deal with it or make it disappear. The problem is it doesn't disappear. You bury the problem, but it has a way of coming back at you... *boomerang.*

It is among the most rancid of hidden diseases (literally!) that do not get talked about much. It is our ticking time bomb that mounts daily, invades the oceans and rots buried in our lands. It steadily takes up more and more land. While millions are numb to this reality, millions live with it. I remember it when I lived in Florida driving along I-95 by what my mom liked to call "Mount Trashmore." You could smell it miles away. You always knew which way the wind blew. Inside these huge "hills" were accumulated decades of human detritus. *Mount Trashmore* was apparently the tallest hill in the state (or at least Broward County). I remember closing my car windows though it helped little. I saw spouts sprinkled at the top of the hills spitting out flames like a vision from Dante's inferno.

People in New York's Staten Island knew about it if they lived near the notorious Fresh Kills, where New York buried its problems for decades until it ran out of room. Now it's exported to someone else's backyard. Now it's Pennsylvania's or Virginia's problem. They understand a real estate joke:

> *An agent says to a buyer looking at a house: there's good and bad news about the house. To the south there's a garbage dump, to the north oil tanks, and to the east a sewage plant. Buyer: so what's the good news? Agent: you'll know what direction the wind blows.*

THE PACIFIC GYRE
Things seem fine when the problem is in someone else's backyard. Truth is, it's now in everyone's backyard. I realized this when I saw a disturbing news report on the PBS News Hour. Have you ever heard of the Pacific Gyre? I didn't until that night back in November of 2008. It was a reminder of just why this garbage problem is our boomerang. Garbage and plastics flow into thousands of miles of the Pacific Ocean. Perhaps some of you saw a similar news report on CBS:[217]

> *"'Day after day after day, when I came on deck I saw objects floating by: toothbrushes, bottle caps and soap bottles,' says Captain Charles Moore. The trash he found floating, like a Japanese traffic cone, was from much of the world. Beneath the surface, a jellyfish was so entangled in a scrap of synthetic*

net that its tentacles had grown around the plastic strands. The trash was found in a patch of ocean called the North Pacific Gyre where the currents can trap floating debris for years. 'I have no doubt that some of these things that we're discovering out there have been there since the dawn of the plastic era in the 1950's,' says Moore. As plastic ages it crumbles, leaving so many tiny fragments that Moore found seawater in the Gyre contained more plastic than plankton, the tiny sea life that many ocean creatures feed on. To jellyfish, the plastic particles seem like food. 'It's like putting them on a plastic diet,' says Moore. 'It becomes part of their tissue.' ... After a heavy rain in Los Angeles, the plastic flows into the Pacific in torrents. Even with efforts to clean it up, some will escape, eventually reaching the synthetic sea of the North Pacific Gyre."

The Pacific Gyre: garbage that's now in everyone's tummy. Do you eat tuna fish or any seafood? Plankton consumes plastic particles. Plankton is the microscopic food that feeds the ocean's plants and fish. Perhaps those toxic plastics that we use − anything from supermarket bags to plastics you threw out (that could have been recycled) − make their way into the bodies of fish throughout the oceans. Are we now eating these microscopic toxic plastics?

WHERE HAVE ALL THE PLASTICS GONE?
Think of the billions of plastic items and bags that we throw out − items that could have been recycled. Living in New York, I see a lot of plastics in the garbage cans and on the streets − garbage apathetic people did not bother to put into recycle bins. These end up in dumps, sewers and, eventually, the ocean. It is well known that plastics are not biodegradable. Like that battery, they just *go on and on and on.* They do not break down for centuries and when they do, what do they become? According to the PBS report, plastics tend to simply get smashed down into smaller pieces. They end up in sewers, pumped into the waters, and smashed into tiny particles that fish and, eventually, *we* eat.

Simple calculations put things in perspective. Think about your shopping habits. You buy food at supermarkets, you carry them home in plastic bags. Do you recycle those bags? You know that answer. If each of us trashes just *four* plastic bags a week (multiplied by, say, 200 million people who shop), it means Americans are throwing out *over 40 billion* plastic bags every year. All could have been recycled. This does not even start to calculate the other plastics we throw out, like bottles, cleansers, deodorants, dry-cleaning and other wrappings, gifts, and countless food items with plastic covers or shrink-wrapping. How about the billions of shoes and sneakers we throw out? It's nauseating.

AND ALL THAT OTHER JUNK?
This just covers plastics. Then there are the newspapers, paper towels, used oils (car and cooking), chemicals, pesticides, clothes, furniture, metal cans, containers, and mountains of other products we use − all the things people do not recycle... but could. True, some is recycled; some is cleaned by sewage plants; and some decomposes over large tracts of time. Some. While places like New York

City are pretty good about recycling, not all parts of the country recycle well (if at all). Further, even in those places where waste is recycled, just how much do people actually recycle as opposed to being lazy or ignorant, throwing things out as normal garbage? When was the last time CNN, NBC or FOX mentioned how well the recycling industry is doing in fully reusing materials? Do we really know how much is recycled?

Actually, we do. An EPA report noted the following:[218]

- *"In 2006, U.S. residents, businesses, and institutions produced more than 251 million tons of municipal solid waste, which is approximately 4.6 pounds of waste per person per day. In addition, American industrial facilities generate and dispose of approximately 7.6 billion tons of industrial solid waste each year."*

- *From 1980 to 2005, MSW [Municipal Solid Waste] accumulation increased 60% for a total of 246 million tons of trash in 2005.*

- *Recycling and composting rates recovered 32.1% of MSW or 79 million tons, not including hazardous, industrial/construction waste.*

- *Only 50% of all paper products were recycled (about 42 million tons).*

We're not doing as well at recycling as we think.

FAST FOOD, FAST TRASH

What is striking about the EPA report is not just the huge amount of waste, but the strangely small amount that is recycled. After all these years of discussion and public awareness, perhaps half of paper products are recycled and worse yet, not even one third of waste is recycled! We have so far to go. The EPA notes that each of us produces about 4½ pounds of garbage each day. Most is not recycled.

How much do we waste? I defer to my own experiences – experiences that almost everyone sees day after day. I ate last December at Boston Market. Just one snack included a chicken pie that came with five napkins, a big plastic plate, a plastic fork and knife, and a tin container (I had no drink with paper cup, plastic lid and straw). It all got thrown out. I had no choice; there were no recycle bins. Am I to carry garbage home in my paper bag? (Oh yeah, I left that out.) I see overflowing garbage containers with hundreds of the same plastics. None will be recycled. In fact, in all of New York, rarely do I ever see a fast food restaurant (or any place) with garbage containers marked for recycling. It's the same with Chinese fast food chains, KFC, Burger King, and most any chain.

CORPORATIONS CAN RECYCLE TRASH, TOO

I remember recently visiting a McDonalds. One tiny snack (chicken fingers) required three plastic sauce containers, a bag, a bunch of napkins, a paper container, yet more wrapping, and a fork... oh yeah, the paper receipt. I threw them out and saw five huge, bulging containers filled with those same things. None would be recycled. Almost all could have been. This is typical of America. It happens millions of times each day.

We mindlessly throw out mountains of trash that could be recycled. It ends up in dumps, maybe the Pacific Gyre — unless you live along the Atlantic seaboard. When will we start hearing about the Atlantic Gyre? Or the Caribbean or Mediterranean Gyres? Are they far off... or already a reality?

Too often there are few options, for many businesses and fast food chains don't offer recycle bins. Government does not require it. Perhaps some think recycling infringes on liberties. Stop. Trash (and clean water) is everyone's concern. But becomes someone else's problem. It's dumped in someone else's backyard. It's government apathy — the hidden disease of ignoring problems. But it is *everyone's* problem. It ends up in the Pacific Gyre... the food chain... fish... you...

Boomerang!

THE WITCH'S TOXIC BREW

We are numb, just like that boiling frog. We throw out unimaginable amounts of things day after day after day and think little of it — perhaps not until the mountains of garbage reach our towns or the odors befoul our homes. Perhaps not until we start getting sick because the foods we ate, with microscopic plastic or other toxic carcinogens, start affecting us. Cancer has become commonplace. Is it related? Was your last fever or food virus the result of a rude sneeze or bacteria that ate microscopic plastics? Last time you used Rolaids or Tums... what really caused it? We are playing games with nature.

The plastics may already be in tuna fish we ate or the swordfish or salmon dinner — all of which ate the small fry that ate the plants that ate the plankton that ate the bacteria that ate the microscopic plastic particles floating somewhere out there in the Pacific Gyre... or the Atlantic Gyre... or the Caribbean Gyre. What about all those billions of tons of crushed, tiny plastic products sitting in thousands of landfills? Are they starting to get into our water supply? Are they starting to eat through the protective linings, sink deeper into the ground, or sink into the underground water supplies and rivers, and eventually get into the meats and fruits and vegetables we eat?

Boomerang!

These troubling questions do not even consider the toxic brews that we pump by the billions of gallons daily into our rivers, seas and oceans — the multitude of cleansers, soaps, shampoos, conditioners, chemicals (like turpentine or paint) that go into our sewer systems by the second. While water treatment plants reduce toxicity and poisons, are these plants removing *everything?* Perhaps some does not end up in those sewage treatment facilities. Do we know for sure what's happening to the ghoulish, decomposing substances in garbage dumps? Some may make its way into the rivers and seas. What happens when they enter the oceans and are absorbed by plankton, algae, plants, and fish? Do we know what is happening within the thousands of garbage dumps, how the materials decompose, where they go? Do they seep underground into water supplies?

Boomerang!

RECYCLE BAGS? GETOUTTAHERE!

Local communities can better address these issues by building more effective factories that recycle trash. Success will depend upon whether lawmakers cooperate and not fight progress. One such example occurred in New York City, where then-Mayor Bloomberg addressed the issue of plastic bags.[219] He faced huge battles and failed to convince state legislators to allow New York City to impose a mere 5 or 6 cent charge per bag to encourage people to use reusable bags. The resistance by politicians to reasonable efforts to control plastic bag pollution is stunning.

Reusable bags? How many politicians mention it? For sure, not enough. And no doubt corporate plastic and bag lobbyists would fight this idea. It touches on themes you read in previous chapters: lobbyists having disproportionate influence, politicians needing money from corporations for coming elections, the needs of the many outweighed by the two percent. Everything is interrelated.

The failed New York City plastic bags effort demonstrates how reasonable efforts fail. Many people complained that 6 cents per bag was too much money. Really! What would the WWII generation say? Government asked them to recycle anything from bubble gum wrappers to rags. Dear Lord, they recycled bubble gum wrappers! (Dropping the metallic lining was useful for airplanes trying to evade enemy radar detection). People just did it. They knew it was for the country's good. Civic duty, patriotism... perhaps things also floating somewhere in the Pacific Gyre.

This *bag* effort (still in its infancy nationwide) reflects initiatives that could make the nation's water cleaner and safer. But people just don't want to be bothered. Sooner or later, they'll have to be bothered. Remember the Pacific Gyre. When it comes to plastic bags, we are behind the Europeans. (What else is new?) As soon as Mayor Bloomberg proposed an initiative, he encountered resistance. The mayor, knowing New York State government for the paralyzed institution it is, tried to circumvent resistance by proposing a fee rather than a tax, therefore keeping Albany out of the picture. Sadly, it did not work. This is how politics works. In the mean time, yet more millions of plastic bags enter dumps and oceans each day as politicians avoid any duty to address it. Special Interest groups try to thwart progress. It's true everywhere.

I personally carry a bag when I shop. I rarely see others doing that. Whenever a supermarket cashier starts to put my items into a plastic bag, I quickly point to a bag I'm carrying and I start to put items in my bag. It seems perfectly decent and responsible, yet some cashiers look at me like I'm crazy. It's a sign of widespread apathy. It is a sign that supermarket executives give little thought to this matter.

However, there are positive signs of change. One such example of progress is San Francisco Pier 96 and its well-publicized facility recycling enormous amounts of waste. But elsewhere positive change often meets resistance. Too often, reasonable ideas are belittled by "government is the problem" politicians who reflexively want to deregulate and get government "off our backs." Our leaders too often protect harmful things. The industries that have something to lose by recycling – plastic bag manufacturers or fast food chains that dump millions of tons of paper and recyclable trash onto the streets for collection – prefer to thwart progress. Their hired lobbyists, no doubt, will reach out to politicians if serious legislation makes its way to a vote.

Problems are interrelated. If legislation addressing this came before Congress, you can just imagine what the hired mercenaries in Washington would lobby legislators *not to do*. In addressing issues like garbage, it may not change until the very nature of politics changes.

IT'S TIME TO TAKE *"TRASH"* ACTION

Too often, politicians avoid taking action until problems become a crisis. It does not have to be this way. The President can quickly transform the backwaters issue of garbage to the forefront of national debate. Problems are mounting and 1970s-era EPA and other regulations could benefit by a review of changed circumstances. The Pacific Gyre is one example of change for the worse.

Washington should let states and municipalities act on their own without federal interference, lawsuits or dated regulations. It is not too much to ask everyone to recycle more than currently done – and "everyone" includes the fast food chains that are irresponsible.

We can do better. It would not take much effort for the White House or Congress to give the issue a jumpstart. Plastic bags, for example, can be recycled. TV could help by jamming it into people's heads that they need to stop with the mindless habit of trashing recyclables. It's not too much to ask people to bring cloth bags to stores to avoid using plastic bags. The FCC can ask TV networks and the Internet sites to cooperate. Businesses that create unnecessary trash, like fast food chains, must be forced to act and be heavily fined when they violate laws (which currently may not exist).

The country needs to change its mindset. We need to think more about serving our community and cut out the "me generation" attitude. The WWII generation thought more about serving their country. We need to instill more of that in our value system nowadays. It starts by having more confidence in the good government offers. Washington can regulate trash more thoroughly. TV, the Internet and radio can help. Schools can encourage the younger generation to recycle more carefully. Local municipalities need to create deeper sanitation systems that recycle more than the standard paper, bottles and cans. But it will take money to build those recycling factories. If Washington helped, it can happen. Rigid ideologies and *government is the problem* attitudes prevent healthy progress. While we're at it, include energy and water conservation.

Many products that could be recycled are not – cups, plastic and paper plates, utensils, and plastic wrappings. This list is long. Local governments can enhance recycling efforts by providing fast food chains with special "green" bins for recycling. Municipalities will have to pick up the separated trash and build factories for recycling where they currently do not have such programs. And by the way, it also provides new job opportunities. Recycling factories can more thoroughly sort and remove recyclable trash. Government can require businesses to practice green-friendly policies. All fast food chains must have specially marked recycling bins for paper and plastics and signs asking customers to recycle plastic and paper products. They must be instructed to separate trash that irresponsible customers toss into the wrong trash bins. Chains can be fined when they violate recycling rules. Revenues from fines can be used to fund recycling and educational programs. A comprehensive program is needed.

During World War II, recycling and reuse of materials was a national obsession, a civic duty. We could learn more by studying our own history. Garbage is indeed one of the "hidden" diseases. Lawmakers and business leaders must not relegate this issue to the wilderness. We owe it to ourselves to bring sanitation disposal into the 21st Century, for if we do not, oceans may become one huge, poisonous "Gyre" – *our boomerang.*

Chapter 14

NUCLEAR TERRORISM
The Real Endgame

On a Friday afternoon in May at the port of New Orleans, alongside a shipment of fruits, a rail container is noted by customs officers as "assorted machinery goods, destination, Iowa." It is loaded onto a truck. There is no Infra-red machinery to check the containers. A week later, a container arrives in Baltimore labeled "scientific equipment." It is loaded onto a truck. In July, a private Pakistani jet airplane lands at New York's JFK airport. Men get off carrying briefcases. They flash diplomatic IDs and leave in rented cars. In early August, in northern Montana, men walk across the Canadian border to a town where a car awaits. They drive to a deserted barn outside a sleepy Iowa farming community. Four men here on expired student visas arrive. Boxes fill a shed. The leader, a man with jet-black hair, opens briefcases marked "diplomatic" and glances at documents. Others look on and soon open boxes containing delicate equipment. Nearby lies a box marked "toxic" in Arabic. Early on a brisk September 7th morning, they load a box into a rented U-Haul van. Four days later, two men driving that van pay the toll at the Lincoln Tunnel Manhattan-bound. Traffic is light. It is 10:58 a.m. Thirteen minutes later the van stops at a traffic light at 43rd Street and Broadway. The man in the passenger's seat moves to the back of the van and presses a button. A blinding flash is seen 20 miles away, then a towering mushroom cloud...

*   *   *   *   *

This frightening passage may be fiction of the likes of a Hollywood, but the premise of Armageddon-like proportions is feasible. Scary conclusions emerged in a report by the bipartisan Commission on the Prevention of Weapons of Mass Destruction Proliferation and Terrorism. Among those participating were former Senators Bob Graham (D-Fl.) and Jim Talent (R-Mo.).

The report by the nine-member bipartisan committee concluded that terrorists will most likely conduct an attack with biological, nuclear or other weapons in the near future. The committee, having reviewed classified government material and having interviewed over 250 experts, ominously noted that the United States is dangerously vulnerable. Among facts and conclusions noted: 1) terrorist havens in Afghanistan and Pakistan, which has large stockpiles of nuclear and biological materials; 2) a "nascent nuclear arms race in Asia"; and 3) nuclear weapons programs in Iran and North Korean. The committee also noted, scarily, that "Congressional oversight is dysfunctional."

NUCLEAR TERRORISM MUST BE HIGHEST PRIORITY
The article appeared on page 11, rather lost in the day's news. It is symbolic – a suggestion this matter is not getting the attention it warrants. It must be the focal political issue of our times and not be relegated to *page 11*. The International Atomic Energy Agency (IAEA) and experts on the Treaty on the Non-Proliferation

of Nuclear Weapons (NPT) have weighed in on the subject. Here is a perusal of the situation according to respected sources:

> *The Center for Arms Control and Non-Proliferation: "NPT has proven largely successful in stemming proliferation. But the nonproliferation regime faces new challenges: insufficient protections against the theft or sale of various nuclear materials in states of the former Soviet Union; nuclear black market activity such as the network operated by A.Q. Khan out of Pakistan; threats by North Korea to share nuclear technology with states or non-state actors hostile to the U.S.; and, most recently, violations of IAEA nuclear safeguard standards by Iran, a signatory of the NPT which is pursuing technology for producing nuclear materials as part of a possible quest for a nuclear bomb."[220]*

> *UN Secretary-General Kofi Annan during a 2006 address: "I fear, however, that the world is losing sight of this essential truth... One path can take us to a world, in which the proliferation of nuclear weapons is restricted and reversed, through trust, dialogue and negotiated agreement... The other path leads to a world, in which a rapidly growing number of States feel obliged to arm themselves with nuclear weapons, and in which non-State actors acquire the means to carry out nuclear terrorism. The international community seems almost to be sleepwalking down the latter path."[221]*

> *The Heritage Foundation: "Those who see the NPT as fatally flawed argue that the exercise of this right by a non-weapons state allows it to produce nuclear weapons with little or no chance that outside observers will be given timely warning that the state in question is actually pursuing a weapons capability.[222]*

The Congressional Research Service noted the following in a report to Congress:

- *"Several developments have led many to believe that the nuclear nonproliferation regime needs to be strengthened [regarding] the discovery of the [Pakistani] A.Q. Khan nuclear black market network [and] Iran's unreported nuclear activities, including secret uranium enrichment facilities."*

- *"The terrorist attacks of September 11, 2001 sharpened world focus on nuclear proliferation and the risk that terrorists might gain access to nuclear (and other weapons of mass destruction) technology. More states now are convinced that greater attention should be devoted to nuclear security."*

- *"The discovery of Pakistani scientist A. Q. Khan's sales of uranium enrichment technology, equipment, and a bomb design to Iran, North Korea, Libya, and possibly other states."[223]*

Nuclear terrorism must be the prime foreign policy issue of our time. All else pales compared to the possibility of an American Armageddon. Nothing else poses a threat like this – not even Iran, for should Iran obtain nuclear weapons, it falls under an expression used by military experts: *every missile has a return address*. But terrorists have no return address. Are the CIA, NSA and Pentagon so fixed on wars in the Middle East or crises in other parts of the world that they are not sufficiently vigilant on the real endgame of terrorism?

International terrorist networks want to obtain nuclear fuel and parts for a nuclear weapon. Is government so fixed on attacking Taliban forces in Afghanistan or sending drones into Pakistan that it has lost sight of terrorist groups trying to obtain uranium from weakly guarded Pakistani bases? Is it working with authorities to close security risks? Some seaports are still not using Infrared and X-ray machinery to check containers that enter the country. Our ports remain strangely vulnerable.

The detonation of a nuclear bomb in New York or Washington could shatter the foundations of the republic. Staying a step ahead of the enemy is crucial. The world is full of depraved, ignorant or financially desperate men. It is a constant threat. Will future Presidents be on top of this?

RUSSIA & PAKISTAN: WORRISOME TARGETS

Iran's nuclear ambitions are a hot issue, but it is Pakistan that we need to focus on. As of 2016, Pakistan had an estimated 140 nuclear weapons.[224] The country is filled with fanatics and terrorist groups at war with the government. In its northern regions, Taliban insurgency threatens stability, raising concerns about the security of Pakistani nuclear weapons. Could extremists infiltrate nuclear centers or steal parts and bomb-ready fuel? In a poor country, desperate or corrupt personnel could be ripe to bribery. Good relations with Pakistan are essential so that intelligence services are on top of the situation and America has input. It is not in our best interests to cause friction jeopardizing the important issue of keeping nuclear materials secure. Note this Congressional Research Service report:[225]

- *"The nations of greatest concern as potential sources of weapons or fissile materials are widely thought to be Russia and Pakistan. Russia has many tactical nuclear weapons, which tend to be lower in yield but more dispersed and apparently less secure than strategic weapons. It also has much highly enriched uranium (HEU) and weapons-grade plutonium, some said to have inadequate security. Many experts believe that technically sophisticated terrorists could, without state support, fabricate a nuclear bomb from HEU; opinion is divided."*

- *"The fear regarding Pakistan is that some members of the armed forces might covertly give a weapon to terrorists or that... an Islamic fundamentalist government or a state of chaos in Pakistan might enable terrorists to obtain a weapon. Terrorists might also obtain HEU from the more than 130 research reactors worldwide that use HEU as fuel."*

- *"It would be difficult for terrorists to mount a nuclear attack on a U.S. city, but such an attack is plausible and would have catastrophic consequences, in one scenario killing over a half-million people and causing damage of over $1 trillion."*

While CRS estimates 500,000 deaths, it does not consider the millions exposed to radiation or that the region would be uninhabitable. New York and Washington, D.C. would be in shambles. As CRS noted in the same report:

"This nation has many thousands of miles of land and sea borders, as well as several hundred ports of entry... Terrorists might smuggle a weapon across lightly-guarded stretches of borders, ship it in using a cargo container, place it in a hold of a crude oil tanker, or bring it in using a truck, a boat, or a small airplane."

It sounds eerily similar to the episode opening this chapter.

"I-START" ELIMINATING WEAPONS & A MODERNIZED "MAD" DOCTRINE

The Mutual Assured Destruction doctrine of deterrence ("MAD") was the foundation of U.S. foreign policy for decades. It was borne of the cold war between the U.S. and U.S.S.R. (Russia). Whatever friction America now has with Russia, Russia still cooperates regarding nuclear arms control and agreements and for good reason. Russia is just as imperiled by the threat of nuclear terrorism as we are. Perhaps more so. Russia has fierce enemies within. Google "Russian conflicts in Chechnya." Everyone's key threat is nuclear terrorism. Terrorists seeking nuclear weapons are the 21st Century threat. *Destroy the weapons and nuclear fuel.* It's the only certain way to keep it out of the hands of terrorist groups.

Only a small number of nuclear bombs are needed to keep MAD intact. Eliminate the weapons and fuel, and the threat of black markets, bribery and theft is shut down. To maintain MAD, Russia (7,000 nuclear warheads) and the U.S. (6,800), as well as Pakistan (140), France (300), U.K. (215), China (260), India (110), and North Korea (8) do not need so many weapons for self-defense or deterrence.[226] One hundred will suffice for purposes of deterrence. The weapons (especially in Pakistan) beg for theft. MAD is useless against terrorists. There is no deterrence to people hiding in caves, so to speak.

A modernized international strategic arms reduction treaty (call it I-START) is needed. All nuclear powers must eliminate vast stockpiles leaving only a minimum to satisfy deterrence needs. Russia, China and the U.S. can manage with 50; Britain and France with 10; Pakistan and India with five. North Korea must be bribed into giving up everything. India and Pakistan will more likely face nuclear attack by terrorists than from each other. The deadly 2008 Mumbai attack suggests that.

CYBER WARFARE & A CALL FOR ACTION

The ominous new threat of cyber warfare has emerged. It must be dealt with firmly. It is a threat of highest priority. When enemies attack or infiltrate computer

112

networks, terrible things are possible, from interfering with elections to shutting down utilities to crippling our banking system. What if they infiltrated our nuclear arsenal computer system? We face far bigger problems than hacked credit cards.

Most troubling is the possibility that enemies can play havoc with computer networks managing our nuclear arsenal. Could incorrect information be planted that lead to false indications of nuclear attack thereby causing Armageddon-like responses to false data? We hope our government and intelligence services are focused and vigilant. The point is that we may be more vulnerable to terrible things than we realize and had better be well prepared. Unplugging key computer networks from connection to the Internet may be the only sure way to protect ourselves. Is this possible.

What is also needed is a "Cyber MAD Doctrine." Mutually Assured Destruction can be applied to the Internet. Foes attacking computer networks must be attacked in return as a warning: stop or we will hit you equally hard. Proportionate response, as some call it. A warning. Can our government do it? Maybe we are not as prepared as we thought. Who knows? This is top-secret stuff. Let's hope our leaders know what they are doing and are giving cyber experts the resources necessary to engage the enemy: a new threat, a modern type of warfare.

A PLAN FOR ACTION

1. <u>Slash Nuclear Arsenals</u>. Modernize nuclear arms policy by minimizing nuclear fuel to prevent theft. Nuclear fuel is the hardest part to create. Severely cut weapons stockpiles via an *International Strategic Arms Treaty* ("I-START").

2. <u>Terrorist Funding</u>. We could never too thoroughly monitor international financial networks for suspicious money transfers.

3. <u>Intelligence.</u> The more America is perceived negatively, the more difficult it will be to spawn cooperation. Everyone must work together in terms of sharing information on terrorist networks. Muslim nations must continually provide crucial intelligence.

4. <u>Russia.</u> However offensive Russian actions are, we must maintain a good working relationship to control nuclear proliferation and, especially, Russian nuclear bases and fuel.

5. <u>Use of Military</u>. Waging war in the Middle East must be weighed against the harm of diverting resources away from the real objective: preventing terrorists from getting nuclear weapons.

6. <u>Ports & Border Security.</u> Borders and ports must be better secured. Imports must be inspected more carefully. Lax security along the Mexican and Canadian borders must be addressed.

7. <u>Rogue States</u>. Regarding Iran and North Korea, enemy or not, we are better off cultivating constructive relations. We are better off dealing with them to prevent them from supplying key nuclear components to terrorist groups.

8. <u>Cyber Warfare</u>. This emerging threat must be of highest priority. Necessary resources for keeping up with evolving Internet threats must be given to cyber experts. The 2016 hacking by Russia into the Republican and, especially, Democrat email servers (which raises the specter of Russian influence in a Presidential race) is an example of the grave threat we face. What if an enemy infiltrated our electrical grid or a nuclear power plant? What if they hacked computer networks handling nuclear-armed submarines, airplanes and silos? The implications are horrifying. Each generation of leaders in the White House must remain ever vigilant in granting resources needed to keep up with foreign cyber attacks – especially threats that could infiltrate our nuclear arsenal and monitoring systems. We don't want a war started because some rogue group (or nation!) planted false information in military computer systems. It's not just us. They could infiltrate *any* nuclear computer network worldwide.

AN OMINOUS "FOREIGN AFFAIRS" WARNING

An article in Foreign Affairs sums up the situation:

"Intense fears of nuclear terrorism have led to a search for a perfect defense: destroying all terrorist groups that threaten the United States, sealing U.S. borders against loose nukes, or locking up all existing nuclear weapons and materials. Yet none of these strategies is a silver bullet. It is fantasy to believe that terrorism can be eliminated or that thousands of miles of U.S. borders – not to mention the borders of U.S. allies – can be sealed. Initiatives to secure nuclear weapons and materials are vital, but they will always fall short, too... terrorists do not have superhuman powers; their plots are imperfect and contingent and can be derailed.[227]

"Can be derailed" means being a step ahead of the enemy. Millions of people in New York and Washington, D.C. (or Moscow or Paris) are depending on government to do its job competently... and so is the entire world. When it comes to foreign policy, nuclear terrorism is the real end game.

Chapter 15

GOVERNMENT DEBT
Coming Disaster? It Depends…

This book, so focused on long-term "hidden diseases" overlooked due to gridlock and kicking the can down the road, cannot avoid the 800 pound gorilla in the room: government debt, now approaching $20 trillion and projected to reach $30 trillion by 2026.[228] Debt is a topic that bores many people, but it is something that cannot be ignored for it is a monster problem steadily unfolding. Monsters do not necessarily appear as ugly beasts. Rather, they seem ordinary until they bite you. Such is debt. In some countries, debt led to economic collapse. That scenario could happen to us if we are irresponsible in managing the growing debt. On the other hand, debt could also end up as little more than normal course of business for government, which borrows just as we borrow money to finance a house, business or car. So which scenario will it be? Well… It depends. There is no clear answer.

Facts are presented in the form of opinions by respected sources. You will find disagreement about the path our country will take, for as you will see, the end game for government debt is unclear. Terra Incognita. To explain this complex problem, this chapter breaks down into eight parts: 1) basic principles to understanding debt, 2) the Weimar Germany disaster, 3) the cold facts & numbers, 4) ballooning interest payments & currency reserve, 5) the WWII generation's fiscal ethic as a model, 6) what experts say, 7) to whom do we owe money, 8) the effect of huge tax cuts, and 9) varying scenarios.

1. BASIC PRINCIPLES TO UNDERSTANDING DEBT
Two types of government debt are discussed here: overall debt and annual deficits. Public debt is what the federal government borrowed over the years. This is the $19 trillion figure noted earlier (as of 2016). Annual deficits – the government budget deficit each calendar year – add to the overall debt. Annual deficits ranged since 2008 from $400 billion to over one trillion. The focus here is on overall debt.

Is the staggering $19 trillion (and growing) debt a harbinger of disaster? Well, it depends… and *it depends* is the theme of this chapter. Disaster is something that is hard to predict because in this case it may unfold gradually – or not at all. It's kind of like water leaking into a ship. At some point the ship starts to sink.

The ship need not sink. Debt can bring disaster if managed poorly for years. Debt can also be normal and healthy. Borrowed money for a car, house, business, or college education are examples of healthy debt. Debt becomes unhealthy when you cannot pay back the loan… or borrow for the wrong reasons. If you need to borrow money to cover food and rent, well, that's not a good sign. Either way, the ability to pay down debt (or honor interest payments) is what determines whether it is normal or a path to disaster.

It is important to recognize that government debt is not always analogous to personal debt. We save for retirement then live off of those funds. One must view government borrowing differently for government does not age or retire.

Government will forever generate tax revenue, and more of it due to inflation. Government also has inflationary, banking and business principles on its side. It can sell treasury bills and print money. Analysis by Josh Zumbrun and Nick Timiraos in The Wall Street Journal sums things up well:[229]

> *(Zumbrun) "A lot of people want to make this analogy between individuals and the government. Economists think this is a really bad analogy. The U.S. government is 238 years old and isn't planning to retire one day. If you were going to live forever, and bring in revenue forever, and issue bonds in money that you print, then you'd have a much more similar situation. Governments aren't like people. They can fail, yes, but they don't need to pay off their mortgage to enjoy a comfortable retirement. The goal is for the government to be a going concern. So with that in mind, the only thing the government needs to do is hold its debt at a sustainable level. If your interest payments are stable at 3% or less of the economy, for example, there's no reason you couldn't carry this debt forever."*

Inflation is another crucial aspect of understanding debt. Government debt can be postponed and, in time, made irrelevant as inflation eats away at its real value. For example, if debt is $20 trillion, with decades of inflation that debt could easily be honored. Think of it this way. If you take out a mortgage for a house, you pay it off over 30 years. The monthly payments remain the same, but 30 years from now those payments in real terms are perhaps a third of what they were at the onset of the mortgage due to inflation. It works like this. If your salary was $50,000 annually at the onset of the mortgage, that same salary, in real terms, might be $150,000 30 years from now. A loaf of bread today is $1, but 30 years from now the loaf may be $3. In other words, your $50,000 salary today will buy the same amount that your $150,000 salary will buy in 30 years. Similarly, as your monthly payment stays the same, it will be one third the cost in real terms due to inflation. It is the same with Government. If government keeps debt at the same level, that debt could be cut in half in real terms 20 years later due to normal inflation. This has to do with the *rule of 72*.

In analyzing debt, it is important to understand the *rule of 72*: divide 72 by the interest rate and you learn many years it takes for your money to double. So if you invest $1,000 at 5% interest, money doubles in 14.4 years. Similarly, 5% annual inflation will cut the value of money in half over 14.4 years. Thus, each trillion dollars of debt is cut in half by inflation over time, depending on the inflation rate. If inflation jumps to 6%, the real value of money is cut in half in 12 years. If inflation is 36%, value is cut in half in a mere two years. Put another way, how do you cut $20 trillion debt in half? Wait 14.4 years with 5% inflation... or allow the economy to collapse and let huge inflation take charge. So as you see, debt can become a disaster if market forces cause high inflation. Inflation erodes the real value of debt (and your pocketbook). Note this chart:

year	Debt	GDP/as % of GDP
now	$20 trillion	$20 trillion/100%

| 14.4 years later | $20 trillion | $40 trillion/50% |

So as you can see, by merely keeping debt stable over time, government will cut that debt in half. Absorb *the rule of 72* and you understand the effects of inflation. You come to understand government debt as professionals and economists analyze it. That is why they see debt differently from personal debt. So the alarm over debt is uncalled for. Or is it? Debt becomes a big problem if it is not managed well. If the borrowing continues well out of proportion, the "favor" of time and inflation is lost. In other words, if debt doubles from $20 to $40 billion, the benefits of inflation will not help that much. The real question is this: does debt increase proportionately to GDP? Perhaps now you can see why the answer to the nagging question of whether debt is dangerous is... *it depends.*

2. THE WEIMAR GERMANY DISASTER

One frightening example of debt shattering an economy was the catastrophic hyperinflation in the early 1920s in Germany, the so-called "Weimar Republic." Government-created inflation so destabilized Germany that it set in motion all kinds of horrible things. Massive inflation wiped out the national wealth and the middle class. It paved the way for disaster. Economic collapse... political chaos... fascism... Hitler... World War II. This is the extreme of the spectrum of possibilities.

No one today believes such a calamity can happen again, but then again who would have predicted World War II or the Holocaust back in 1928? Hmm... maybe we should take debt more seriously. Here below is an explanation of how Germany moved from relative stability to the barbaric fascist country it became. The economic path of how the Weimar Republic managed debt shows us just what can happen when debt is managed miserably.

Germany, unable to honor staggering war reparations to the World War I victors (France and Britain), resorted to recklessly printing money. It caused unprecedented hyperinflation. Germany encountered massive inflation. The Mark, four to a dollar in 1914, plummeted to *4 trillion* to the dollar. A Mark was worth less than the paper it was printed on. An impoverished middle class resulted. Imagine today having $1 million and two years later that $1 million can only buy you a loaf of bread. Now you understand what happened to Germany in the early 1920s (as Hitler emerged as a political force). Debt handled like that can lead to a doomsday scenario. Let's not be naïve. The U.S. Federal Reserve can print money.

In truth, events plaguing Weimar Germany are far off from modern realities. Their doomsday scenario is unthinkable as long as debt is managed intelligently. We have learned from the past. Then again, how many of our politicians read history?

Will hyperinflation come? Probably not. The modern banking system is better run and government leaders see to it that banks and government debt are managed correctly. Then again, the near collapse of the banking system and economy back in 2008 raises troubling questions. We are not so immune to recklessness as we think. The Weimar scenario makes a point: there are consequences to handling debt poorly. There are more precedents of reckless government management of debt.

Google hyperinflation in Argentina.

Government funded by endless, excessive borrowing is like borrowing money to pay for food. Not smart. Same for printing money, perhaps worse. It creates the potential for soaring inflation. Printing money did not serve Weimar Germany well. Our situation is different, but the point here is staggering inflation is one way to deal with enormous debt. A bad way. Poor leaders could follow that bankrupt Weimar model and resort to printing money to honor debt. Now *that* would be a disaster.

Fiscal Conservatives believe debt must be paid off and not allowed to geometrically grow year after year. On the other hand, politicians want to fund programs to help the poor and middle class. Both objectives make sense. What is the right balance? In modern Washington, there seems to be no coherent plan for managing debt. The chart above shows how $20 trillion in debt is cut in half by 14.4 years of 5% inflation. However, what happens if the debt grows well beyond inflation or the ability of government to honor debt? The answer is not a happy one.

Tax revenue is an aspect to consider. It is normal to buy a house with a mortgage, but can you afford it? If you have a $500,000 mortgage but income drops to $30,000, you are in trouble. But if you earn $250,000, you are in fine shape. Similarly, $20 trillion in government debt may seem enormous, but with sufficient tax revenue debt can be managed.

The ability to honor debt depends on adequate tax revenue. If revenue is insufficient, the problem may eventually bring on disaster. The choices are stark: raise taxes, cut spending (and only about a third is within Congress's ability to cut; more on that later) or do nothing and resign ourselves to fate (an ugly choice). Part of the issue is whether government is willing to raise taxes. As you see, there are solutions to honoring debt, but those solutions – raising taxes – are politically unpopular. Better put, many Republicans refuse to consider that option. This makes things really difficult.

Republicans in the WWII and later eras were more flexible about raising taxes. They accepted the need to raise taxes in times of crisis. The question that all leaders must honestly address is this: is debt due to spending too much or the refusal to tax adequately? There are solutions, however politically unappetizing. There are times when unpleasant steps must be taken to save a house on fire.

3. THE COLD NUMBERS & FACTS

To get a feel for things, look at the charts below to get acquainted with debt past and present.[230] It can get a bit dense, but if you patiently examine each chart the debt situation becomes clearer. Think like an economist or accountant. Sift through the meaning of numbers. Let's start with the below chart showing debt as a percent of GDP.[231]

Year	Debt / GDP	As % of GDP
1941	$49 / $129 *million*	38%
1945	$259 / $228 million	116%
1967	$340 / $867 million	39%
1979	$829 / $2,670 million	31%

1999	$5.6 / $9.7 *billion*	58%
2009	$11.9 / $14.4 billion	83%
2015	$18.15 / $18.10	101%
2026 *(projected)*	$29 / ? billion	?

The "?" as to GDP in 2026 will eventually explain whether debt becomes a disaster, a drag on the economy, or merely normal business as usual. If debt as percentage of GDP and government spending is excessive, the possibility of dollar devaluation, high inflation, threat to the dollar as currency reserve, or severe fiscal government problems could potentially have a terrible impact on the economy. Will that happen? *Well, it depends...*

As noted above, government debt varied over time, rising, falling, and being paid off following years of heavy borrowing. While debt was a seemingly trivial $49 *million* in 1941, that amount was 38% of GDP! At the time, it was very significant. Reading numbers in real value is important. Putting things in perspective, you could buy a cup of coffee for a nickel in 1935 and people earned $30 a week, which was enough to get by. A nickel meant a lot back then. Be mindful of this when analyzing numbers. *Inflation changes values.*

The modest government debt of the 1920s reached 70 percent of GDP by 1933 (reflecting economic collapse), decreased to 45% by 1941 as the economy improved, then rose to almost 119% by 1946 due to war borrowing.[232] Over the following decades, debt decreased as a percentage of GDP as it was gradually paid down. Inflation (as discussed above) also eroded at the value of debt. To better understand this, note comparisons of the cost of living:[233][234][235]

	1946	*2006*
Avg. annual Income	$2,600	$37,900
Monthly Rent	$35	$950
House	$5,150	$266,000
New Car	$1,125	$28,800
First-Class Postage	3 cents	39 cents

If you had a $5,150 mortgage on a house in 1946 (a huge amount back then), that same mortgage today would be a joke. And who wouldn't want to buy a brand new car for $1,125? ($10 extra for A/C?) As you see, inflation can be a powerful tool in paying down debt! This is why government debt must be seen through the prism of *the rule of 72*. The message is this: keep debt stable and decades later the debt sum, even if the same, becomes far smaller relative to tax revenues that likely doubled. You can pay down debt by letting inflation and *time* erode its value. Bear this in mind when considering debt years from now.

Debt accounted for 32% of GDP in 1980.[236] It was about 101% by 2015 (and grows by millions each hour we breathe) yet politicians tend to be mum about dealing with it. These are not hopeful trends, but let's put things in perspective. Debt was similarly high back in 1946, accounting for 119% of GDP due to enormous war spending. It had been paid down by 1960, when it was at 53%. The percentage now approaches peak levels reached after World War II (101% vs. 119%). It's gotten seriously high again. So the question is how do we pay it down? Studying the WWII generation's approach will help.

Doom-and-gloom predictors say catastrophe looms. Perhaps some said that in 1946 as well. Others say no harm will come of large debt, reasoning (remember, *the rule of 72*) that time, reasonable inflation and economic growth will take care of things (as it did following the war, with the percentage dropping from 101% in 1946 to 58% in 1960). The denouement still unfolds; our fate is in our hands.

If modern leaders act responsibly as leaders did after WWII, the problem could be put under control. It will be far better if leaders address matters rather than leaving it to chance (taking no action on government expenses) or using horrible short-term solutions that lead to disaster in the long term (Weimar Germany).

The debt problem worsened since the Great Recession erupted in 2008. Funding wars in Iraq and Afghanistan contributed to debt. The choice by leaders to not raise taxes to fund those wars hurt the situation. There are similarities to the WWII era, when economic turmoil and war increased debt. But unlike today, Republicans and Democrats in that era understood the need raise taxes in order to fund wars or pay down debt in times of economic growth. The one-size-fits-all ideology of refusing to raise taxes under any circumstances did not yet exist.

Since 2008 debt as a percentage of GDP rose from 83% to 101% and now approaches the post-WWII peak at 119%. The danger posed by the *projected* debt increase to $29 trillion in 2026 depends on factors ranging from inflation to tax revenue to economic growth. That $29 trillion sounds scary, but if government tax revenue grows (or taxes are raised), these (alongside the effect of inflation) could make debt a smaller percentage of GDP than the $18 trillion is now. That would make the $29 trillion debt an improvement! Go figure.

Inflation and solid economic growth can eliminate debt as a problem. In other words, we can grow our way out of debt problems (through wise investment in the future) if the economic grows enough. You see that in these numbers: [237]

Year	Debt / GDP	As % of GDP
1945	$259 / $228 million	116%
1967	$340 / $867 million	39%

Debt was actually *higher* in 1967 than it was in 1945, yet lower (39% vs. 116%) as a percent of GDP. Experts rank the severity of debt based upon ratio to GDP. It is another way of saying this: the U.S. can grow its way out of debt problems. A growing economy makes past debt, even if higher, far less relevant.

It all shows how complex things can be and how meaningless numbers are unless seen in relation to inflation and the value of money. So could debt become a serious problem? *Well (here we go again), it depends...* it depends on actions leaders take (i.e. spending cuts and tax hikes) and how much the economy grows. Odd as it sounds, with inflation, intelligent government investment in the economy (as done by the post-WWII generation of politicians) and foresighted economic policies, government could actually *spend* its way out of debt. It may not make much sense at first, but that is the reality of economics. This is why one-size-fits-all ideologies are out of touch with economics and expert advice. Politicians who refuse to study the facts will not likely make smart decisions.

This is why our politicians need to read more and stop playing to the microphone. Simple-minded explanations don't account for the realities of a complicated world that cannot be analyzed by simplistic campaign rhetoric (smaller government, cut taxes) or cliché sound bites that get votes but do not pave the way for intelligent policies that get good results.

4. BALLOONING INTEREST PAYMENTS & CURRENCY RESERVE

Another troubling matter to be factored in is the cost of honoring debt. In a word, interest payments. According to the President's Office of Management and Budget (OMB), a government agency providing reliable numbers, interest payments alone are estimated in 2016 at $240 billion and are projected to rise to $574 by 2021.[238] That is money that cannot be used to fund government programs or pay down debt.

Without paying down debt, the country ends up trapped by interest payments that take up more and more of the government's limited resources. Striking the right balance is important, for interest payments will eventually swallow up our budgets and leave our leaders with few options. That's a scary future we may face. Examine these CBO net interest payment figures for debt:[239]

	2014	2024 (projected)
Interest	$231 billion	$799 billion
as % of GDP	1.24%	3%

The chart indicates interest payments will more than triple in coming years and double as percent of GDP... unless our leaders act sensibly and with political courage. In 2024, projections indicate some $800 billion will be needed just to cover interest payments! That's money unavailable to fund entitlements, grow the economy, improve infrastructure, support the military, or pay down debt.

Here is another fact to consider. About 65% of the federal budget is *non-discretionary*. In other words, it's mandatory (required by law). That arcane term has implications. It means most of the budget, by statute, is out of the control of Congress or the President (without changing entitlement laws, anyway). Government must honor statutory-required expenses like government and military staff salaries, veteran healthcare, pensions/healthcare, unemployment insurance, Social Security, Medicare, Medicaid, SNAP (food stamps), and so on. Social Security alone accounts for about 23% of the budget. Short of changing mandatory entitlements (which is complicated), only about a third of the budget can be addressed (or cut) by Congress.[240] It makes debt management harder.

Congress has a recent record of, so to speak, shooting itself in the foot: threats to shut down government or not raise borrowing limits are common. In 2011 government shutdown loomed due to Congressional bickering. The result was bad. There was serious threat of default or delay in honoring interest payments. Standard and Poor's downgraded government debt from AAA to AA+ causing stock markets to swoon and government interest rates to rise. It added to the cost of borrowing. It was avoidable. This is not a smart way to run government or manage debt.

Congress made things worse through inaction or refusal to cooperate. Self-imposed harm is the result when leaders bicker rather than dealing with economic realities. Being fact-driven is important. Congressmen have choices. Do you decide based upon fact or mere opinion? We are our own worst enemy. Spendthrifts need to show restraint. Fiscal Conservatives need to recognize that spending cuts can impede economic growth and, rather, wise investment in the economy (and GDP growth) can actually *raise* tax revenue, thereby decreasing the debt threat. Stubborn iconoclasts need to recognize that sometimes a tax rise is healthy, nay, essential. Spenders must recognize there are limits to resources. We cannot borrow endlessly to honor social programs and entitlements. Something must give. Ideologies must reconcile economic realities.

In brief, fiscal Conservatives want to cut government spending and taxes. Liberals want to increase social programs spending. Both think the other is completely wrong. Truth be told, both are *right* and need to listen to each other. It is a just matter of timing. Spending can grow an economy, but we cannot go on spending (and borrowing) forever. When the economy is stable or growing, there comes the time to pay down debt (and raise taxes). The post-WWII generation of politicians understood that. Our leaders now, ever in conflict, seem to miss this much-needed balancing of philosophies. One cannot live without the other, yet both are at war with each other nowadays. That will have to change, else we may face a tragic debt crisis.

The balancing of contrasting philosophies requires our leaders to listen more to experts, study facts, and stop fighting economic reality. There is a time to spend and time to pay down debt. Winning elections is not the same as governing. Post-WWII politicians, both Republican and Democrat, found ways to balance the need to encourage economic growth while managing debt responsibly.

If our leaders do not balance conflicting philosophies in the coming decades, economics and market forces will take over. That implies ominous possibilities: high inflation, reduced ability to fund essential needs (like military) or important entitlements (like Social Security and Medicare/Medicaid), economic contraction, and rising debt and interest payments. Even scarier is the potential for the end of the dollar as international currency reserve. The implications are disastrous to our economic future and status as a world power supporting democracy, human rights and keeping the peace worldwide.

The dollar, as international currency reserve, allows the Federal Reserve to help government control the economy, manage debt, print money, or lend money to banks to ease economic problems and recessions. The Fed often acts with money government technically does not have… in a word, its acts freely to address debt and economic downturns. Currency Reserve status allows that. We want to keep this prized ability.

The devaluation of the dollar (through poor government policies, inaction or currency trading markets) is also at play. The result would be big-time inflation, not Weimar-like, but bad enough to harm our economy. We saw the harsh effects of high inflation in the 1970s and 1980s. Were the dollar to shrink in value by 50% (or due to 10 years of 7% inflation) while income remains stagnant, prices would swoon yet debt would also be cut in half. That is one way to pay down debt, but at terrible cost to our economy and way of life. Think about the scary effect this would have on all of us, let alone our ability to remain an economic and military superpower.

There are better alternatives to inaction. With sensible debt management, limits to spending, appropriate taxation to raise sufficient revenues to fund programs and pay down debt (particularly when the economy is doing well), our country may do just fine. Extreme and irreconcilable positions – spending vs. never raise taxes – won't cut it. With present political attitudes (refusal to raise taxes especially), debt pay down is unlikely. Stubbornly promoting social programs or never raising taxes may win elections, but in the long run, it may lead us to debt disaster. Both political parties must be smarter by relying upon facts and economic realities. Balance conflicting economic agendas, the same as we learned in college Economics 101. There is a time to spend and a time to pay down debt.

5. WWII GENERATION'S FISCAL ETHIC AS A MODEL

The WWII experience (our recurring focus) offers a path to our getting our fiscal house in order. Debt in 1945 was over 100 percent of GDP. From 1946 to 1950 government actually ran *surpluses*. Tax revenue provided adequate funds to both run government and pay down debt. Government invested in the economy. Striking examples of such investment and social programs include the following:

- *the G.I. bill providing free or low-cost college education for millions of soldiers returning from war;*
- *the national highway system;*
- *state universities and public schools; and*
- *Infrastructure like bridges, parks and public works (utilities, dams, water, sewage treatment, rail, etc.) throughout the country.*

Thus, the balance of investment in the economy and fiscal management led to war debt evaporating as a serious problem within a few years. Debt was paid down by the 1960s. Government policy – Congress and the President in cooperation! – recognized the need to balance taxation, entitlements, Social Security, Medicare, the military, infrastructure, and low-cost college education. That's a pretty good role model for leaders nowadays. Alas, if only modern politicians studied their predecessors for guidance... and recalled what they learned in Economics 101 back in college.

Tried and proven fiscal policy is best respected and applied. Divisive politics will not provide for intelligent planning for future fiscal management. If sensible ideas come from the opposition, bash 'em. Don't listen. That's no way to run a country. Irrational divisiveness between political parties solves little. Did the WWII generation let political division get that out of control? No. Fight or not, at the end of the day they took care of business.

The result now, if politics does not change, may be recklessly leaving things to the winds of economic chance. If anything, our situation recalls American debt levels of 1945. Given that politicians in those days paid down debt to healthy levels some 15 years later, it makes sense that we study what they did as a sensible model for action. In fact, it was less paying down of debt and more economic growth (with resulting increased tax revenue) that put debt to the backburner as a problem. Republicans and Democrats should study the post-WWII model and put differences aside insofar as managing debt responsibly. *The alternative is worse.*

It is important to recognize that responsible fiscal management also requires intelligent investment in (for example) the economy, emerging technologies, infrastructure, and education. The post-WWII generation, both Republicans and Democrats, understood such investment.

In building a prosperous future, modern leaders must not leave things to chance... *for the winds of fate will intercede if we do not plan for the future.*

6. WHAT THE EXPERTS SAY

Too many politicians ignore studies by the respected Congressional Budget Office (CBO), an agency created *by Congress* to provide expert and trustworthy analysis. Ignoring carefully researched CBO reports is reckless. Note this ominous excerpt about debt from a report by the Liberal-leaning Brooking Institute:

> *"[B]y 2020 under CBO's alternative fiscal scenario, we will once again return to annual deficits above a trillion dollars... One wonders if members of Congress or the President read these CBO reports. What's the word for our fiscal situation? Stunning? Shocking? Desperate?...CBO's debt estimates do not take into account the full financial obligations the government is committed to honor, especially for future payments of Social Security, Medicare, and interest on the debt... We're headed toward a fiscal black hole."*[241]

The Brookings Institution and Princeton University Press noted the consequences of unchecked government debt: reduced "future national income and living standards"; reductions in government spending, higher marginal tax rates, higher inflation, larger future budget deficits, and decreases in purchasing power and income."[242][243] According to U.S. News & Reports:

> *"The nonpartisan Congressional Budget Office has looked at where we will be in 25 years and, though that may seem a long way ahead, it will come rushing at us as we fail to deal each year with excessive government spending. Millions of retiring baby boomers will bring along with them increased Social Security obligations as well as soaring Medicaid and Medicare costs ... by 2025, tax revenues will be sufficient to finance only interest on our national debt, leaving no room for anything else at all. Everything from national defense to homeland security to education and research will have to be paid for with borrowed money."*[244]

U.S. News & Reports reported this regarding baby boomers and Social Security:

> *"Barron's cited a CBO estimate that by 2038 there will be 79.1 million residents at least age 65, compared to 44.7 million now. Meanwhile, "the*

working-age population, 18 to 64, will grow at a much slower rate, to 214.7 million from 197.8 million" so that the "dependency ratio" of working people to retirees "will plummet to 2.7 working-age people to support each senior in 2038, from 4.4 today." [245]

A Wall Street Journal article, featuring analysis by Josh Zumbrun and Nick Timiraos, noted that debt is mostly a political problem and not a fundamentally economic problem.[246] Noted economist Paul Samuelson wrote in a Washington Post op ed that debt is far less serious than scaremongers suggest, noting that debt included "debt held by the public." Government itself, including treasury security and government trust funds (Social Security being among the largest) is one of the largest debt holders. (The chart below shows debt holders.) Samuelson notes that a large portion of debt is held by government. As Samuelson wrote: "It's comparable to lending yourself money. Congress could cancel these debts."[247]

The message we can take from these above conflicting opinions is further support for the moniker of this chapter: *well... it depends.*

7. TO WHOM DO WE OWE MONEY?

Who does government owe money to? China? Japan? Good guesses, both wrong. Remember that old expression, robbing Peter to pay Paul? Well, that's kind of where we are, for the largest single holder of government debt is... government! Government borrows heavily from the Social Security Trust Funds and the Federal Reserve. Here is a breakdown of debt owners as of 2015.[248]

Foreign/International	47%
Federal Reserve	19%
Mutual Funds	9%
Other Investors	7%
State & Local Govt.	5%
Private Pension Funds	4%
Banks & Savings Inst.	4%
Insurance Companies	2%
State/Local Pensions	2%
U.S. Savings Bonds	1%

The Federal Reserve, it turns out, is the largest single debt holder at 19% ($2.46 billion).[249] The Social Security Trust Funds and the Civil Service Retirement and Disability fund account for almost $3.6 billion of debt – in effect, government owing money to itself. It also suggests that the problem is more solvable than one might think. Simply put, government could wipe out a large chunk of debt by mere bookkeeping. Tax hikes and inflation would help to pay down the rest, but nowadays tax hikes are political quicksand. Politicians have needlessly boxed themselves into rigid positions with no "out" or good solution. It's time to "unbox."

Politicians could eliminate this arbitrary shutting down of an important tool by ending the one-size-fits-all jingoism that tax increases are never possible. Their

Republican ancestors sometimes granted tax increases – during WWII and Reagan's second term. Now, they merely back themselves into a corner by shutting down options. They ignore what we learned in college Economics 101. Politicians in the past were not so rigid and inflexible.

The likelihood is that progress will sporadically come at a time when the situation becomes so unbearable that even the most intransigent will have to cut a deal. Sooner or later that bitter pill of raising taxes will have to be swallowed, for the alternative is worse. Perhaps this is in part why optimists (as quoted above) are confident the issue of debt will not amount to much. It's part political, part bookkeeping, and part will to tax. We are not a poor nation. We cannot claim poverty with GDP of 18 *trillion* (and growing).

Truth be told (and this quiet truth is something many leaders prefer not to admit) is that we don't tax enough and use that money to pay down debt. Even in good economic times, we do not pay down debt. Politicians can electioneer as much as they want about taxes, but quietly they must accept economic truths. Congressmen should read their CBO and CRS reports. It's all there on their desks.

Congressmen and Senators would have plenty more time to read those important reports if they were not forced to raise campaign money all the time. *But that's a whole other issue.*

8. THE EFFECT OF HUGE TAXES CUTS

In 2017 the President and Republican Congress toyed with massive tax cuts including, among other things, reducing corporate taxes to 15%. Almost immediately government agencies and private think tanks reported that the legacy of such tax cuts could be anywhere from 4 to $7 *trillion* added to the national debt. That could move us from 19 trillion to nearly 30 trillion within a decade. Honestly, does it make sense?

Doing the math, it means annual deficits for 10 years would be $400-$700 billion higher. Debt would become astronomical. Interest payments could easily soar to half a trillion yearly. One must honestly ask: is this good fiscal policy?

It is dangerous conjecture at best as to whether enormous tax cuts will grow the economy enough to pay for such massive tax cuts and debt. It plays to the Laffer Curve, the 1980s-era theory that lower taxation leads to higher government revenue. The theory did not pan out and most economists agree. So our leaders now promote this largely discredited 40-year-old economic theory? It this smart policy?

In promoting such steep tax cuts without corresponding spending cuts (which, by the way, were not on the table), leaders are playing Russian r]Roulette with the economy. If the economy does not grow enough (5%, a nearly unprecedented amount) to support such tax cuts, we would be in horrible shape. It was all an example of a political obsession to cut taxes without prudent consideration of debt consequences in the long term.

Being concerned about the long-term is not a Democratic or Republican value. It is something that everyone must be concerned about. As ever, pandering to the public by offers to cut taxes gets votes, but pleasing the public is not the same thing as responsible leadership. Most people are ignorant of macroeconomics and the consequences of massive and complicated government fiscal policy.

We go to dentists to perform intricate work. You don't leave it to the patient fix his own teeth. It works the same with fiscal policy. The public has to have some trust in leaders, and leaders have to defer to experts, economists, and the Congressional Budget Office with its staff of experts who do nothing but study complex topics 24/7. Ignorance is bliss. Bliss can be dangerous.

 Good leadership means thinking things through carefully and not worrying whether good ideas come from Republicans or Democrats. Good ideas are like a ball. Kick it over and over, but at the end of the day it's still round. Huge debt is like the laws of physics. Reckless debt management will destroy an economy as surely as a brick will fall due to gravity. We cannot escape the laws of physics or the laws of economics.

Notes a proposal often hidden within the 2017 tax reform debate. It relates to a proposal to get rid of a rule that allows companies to write off interest paid on loans.[250] It is an idea that would largely affect real estate developers (who no doubt will vigorously lobby against). The rule change could raise *$1 trillion* in revenue yet probably would have a negligible effect on the economy. It is an example of sensible tax reform that responsibly addresses debt.

Whatever comes of tax reform or cuts will take years to assess. But this disturbing question lingers: are leaders giving careful thought to the consequences of tax policy 10 and 20 years down the road? The answer would probably worry us. Leaders have a duty to the public: to tell the truth and not pander with ill-conceived promises to cut taxes. Our leaders need to defer to experts and not endlessly pander. Fiscal health is more important than getting reelected.

9. VARYING SCENARIOS

As you read above, experts provide various scenarios ranging from disaster to pretty much *nothing will happen*. Balancing conflicting philosophies is important. Input from economists and healthy dialogue will help enormously. The hidden disease of debt presents no certainty. Where we head depends on whether leaders handle problems. Experts, as you noticed above, offer various perspectives. It's just another way of saying that our fate is still in our control, or… *well, it depends.*

You have probably seen someone with a sign saying something like "The world will end this Friday." Come the following Monday (with the world gladly still intact), you ask the fellow what went wrong (or right) and he answers, "Sorry; the end has been postponed to March 15th." It is likewise when it comes to debt. If you are waiting for the end of the world, don't hold your breath. The end result of debt is, well, you know… *it depends.*

Courageous and fact-driven leadership based upon expert guidance will help us avert disaster. As the Pogo cartoon famously noted: *"We have found the enemy and he is us."*

Chapter 16

THE SCOURGE OF DRUGS
The Ugliest of Hidden Diseases

Perhaps the most pervasive yet under-discussed issue in America is the extent of the use of marijuana, heroin, crack, meth, and other drugs. This chapter is short to make a point: facts speak for themselves. Read statistics and studies below from reputable sources. Bear in mind the singular question of whether drug use deserves greater attention by Congress and the President.

The National Institute of Health: [251]

"In 2013, an estimated 24.6 million Americans aged 12 or older − 9.4 per cent of the population − had used an illicit drug in the past month."

"Marijuana use has increased since 2007. In 2013, there were 19.8 million current users − about 7.5 percent of people aged 12 or older... Cocaine use ranges from 2.0 million to 2.4 million... Methamphetamine use: 595,000 current users, compared with 353,000 users in 2010.

"More than half of new illicit drug users begin with marijuana... In 2013, 22.6 percent of 18- to 20-year-olds reported using an illicit drug in the past month."

"Marijuana also affects [teenage] brain development... the drug may reduce thinking, memory, and learning functions... [smokers] lost an average of eight IQ points between ages 13 and 38... Long-term marijuana use has been linked to mental illness including hallucinations, paranoia, schizophrenia, depression, anxiety, and suicidal thoughts among teens." [252]

DrugWarFacts.org: [253] [254]

"1 in 10 individuals aged 12 or older in the United States used illicit drugs in the past month... In 2014, 27.0 million people aged 12 or older used an illicit drug in the past 30 days. (Source: Center for Behavioral Health Statistics and Quality. (2015)"

Drug Free World: [255]

"The United States government reported in 2008 that approximately 13 million people over the age of 12 have used methamphetamine − and 529,000 of those are regular users."

"[M]eth use can cause irreversible harm: increased heart rate and blood pressure; damaged blood vessels in the brain that can cause strokes or an irregular heartbeat that can, in turn, cause cardiovascular collapse or death; and liver, kidney and lung damage... Users may suffer brain damage, including memory loss and an increasing inability to grasp abstract thoughts. Those who recover are usually subject to memory gaps and extreme mood swings."

United Nations Office on Drugs and Crime (UNODC):[256]

"The amount of land used for cultivating opium poppies around the world is at an all-time high, says a UN report. Afghanistan is largely behind the increase, with its crop growing by 36 percent over a year, producing 80 percent of the world's opium... The UNODC classifies drug use around the world as stable, estimating that 5 percent of the world's population aged between 15 and 64 years used an illegal drug in 2012. It says that around 27 million people are considered *"problem drug users,"* about 6 percent of the world's population.

U.S. News & World Report: [257]

"The rate of heroin-related overdose deaths increased 286 percent between 2002 and 2013. In 2002... heroin seized at the border with Mexico quadrupled by 2013 from the 2000."

"During 2008-2011, there were about 1.1 million emergency department visits for drug poisoning each year... Abuse has increased most drastically in the Midwest."

Bureau of Justice Statistic (BJS)/ThinkProgress.org: [258 259 260]

"In 2004, 17% of state prisoners and 18% of federal inmates said they committed their current offense to obtain money for drugs [of the total 2,220,300 prisoners]... Almost half of federal inmates (46.4 percent) are in prison for drug crimes."

Columbia University Studies:[261]

"[C]hildren (12 to 17 years old) who use gateway drugs--tobacco, alcohol and marijuana--are up to 266 times--and adults who use such drugs are up to 323 times--more likely to use cocaine."

Consider the above facts (and there is plenty more online) then ask yourself these questions: should Congress and the President make drug use a high national priority, and are we too much in a rush to legalize marijuana? The public needs to better understand the extent of the drug problem. Politicians, using the bully pulpit, could do that. The seriousness of the problem is clearly noted in the above reports. *The scourge of drugs is indeed a much too hidden disease.*

Chapter 17
EDUCATION
From TV to Video Games to Texting

Improving education means dealing with "everything" at once, for seemingly unrelated matters are interrelated. There is no one solution. A theme throughout this chapter is that technology and modern society are pivotal reasons why schools get poor results. TV, the Internet, obsessive texting, video games, declining interest in the arts, drugs, gangs, poor mental health, poverty, broken homes, lax discipline – all are part of the problem. If you want change, consider the full texture of life.

This chapter features insights by teachers on ways to improve education and includes mental health services as a pillar of education. Having grown up on crime-ridden streets plagued by gangs, drugs and street killings, thousands of students from poor neighborhoods suffer from emotional problems. They endure broken homes, poor self-esteem and poverty. Such problems go unaddressed in schools. For many, mental health help can mean the difference between succeeding in life and ending up in prison.

This chapter also covers discipline and poor administrators. Interviewed teachers spoke of being handcuffed and unable to apply reasonable discipline or help students due to scarce options. What can a teacher do when a kid is constantly disruptive and the principal merely sends the troublemaker back to class? How can a teacher teach a child who has faced rape, street shootings, domestic violence, or gang warfare? Troubled kids need help. Are resources provided?

The framework of the chapter is (1) unaddressed problems, (2) rarely tried solutions, (3) innovative approaches and mental health programs, and (4) a comprehensive plan of action to revolutionize and improve schools. The author respects administrators and politicians working to improve education, but despite well-intentioned efforts, success eludes us. Too much goes unaddressed. This chapter tells it as it is, for harsh truths must be confronted. So to speak, we don't want to keep reading about America ranking 17th behind Bulgaria.

Our country has wonderful teachers. They are among the noblest people in society. During discussions with this author, teachers spoke about a societal culture that prevents them from doing their jobs (and explains why many teachers leave the profession). They feel ignored and commented about shabby treatment and intense disrespect by students and administrators. Teachers requested that their names be left out of the book. They feared retaliation from administrators. It reflects the oppressive environment they face.

If you want to understand problems, talk to teachers. Each school is different. This is a fault of "No Child Left Behind" (also known as NCLB and Nickelbee). As teachers said, what good does Nickelbee do if the culture (like the Internet, TV and video games) discourages education? Improving education will require a complete change in the way things are done, both in school and out. Future legislation, if comprehensive and innovative, could promote powerful change that will make schools much better. The goal of this chapter is to outline important matters that are part of the problem and, therefore, part of the solution.

THE CULTURE AT HOME IS PART OF THE PROBLEM

When it comes to schools, it gets personal. I spent much of my career in education. I've been in the trenches. I talked to students. I listened to teachers and their nightmarish experiences. Their disturbing stories appear in the coming pages. I wondered why they endure such insanity. I elected to teach at the college level, having heard how difficult it was to teach in public schools: disrespectful students, wildness, lax discipline, being unable to speak your mind, students not wanting to learn. Years later, having befriended schoolteachers, I learned this: everything I heard about schools was true. If anything, the situation had gotten worse.

Teachers are at war with a culture that breeds disrespect for education. You cannot have parents let kids spend the rest of their day after school texting, Tweeting, Facebook-ing, playing video games, or watching TV four hours/day (the national average for children) then expect kids to want to study and learn. You cannot have it both ways. Education must also be nurtured outside school.

In my discussions with teachers, the comments ended up at the same place: Nickelbee was well-intentioned and the results were "dumb" (their words). *We just had a lot of standardized tests to give.* Even so, teachers said administrators doctored test results and even instructed teachers to grade leniently or overlook errors. So much for mandatory tests. *So much for academic integrity.*

SOCIAL PROMOTION

Among problems teachers spoke of is what happens *after* kids go home. They do not study. Teachers cannot move ahead when kids don't study, don't show up, or run amok in classrooms and hallways. Teachers spoke of calls to parents. No response. They told me of parent-teacher nights where parents rarely come. As for the few who do come, the teacher explains the need for the parent to help the child. Nothing changes. By fourth grade, students could barely read and write. What happens? They are promoted to the next grade without meeting minimal requirements for that grade. Some teachers called this practice "social promotion."

Said one teacher, resist this practice, speak up, and you may end up in what he called the "rubber room" – a reference to being banished by administrators from teaching and forced to sit in a waiting room, sometimes for weeks at a time. The school system did not mind paying full-time salaries, perhaps $70,000 (plus healthcare and pension), for teachers who sat around all day reading newspapers and using laptops... all while crowded classrooms of 30-plus plague schools. Dare to offer suggestions for improvement and you face a reprimand. *Welcome to inner city schools.*

Students doing failing work still pass. Teachers are forced to do this or face repercussions. They commented about being demoralized and fearing arrogant principals threatening poor reviews if orders are not followed. Grades are inflated. Teachers fail students and grades are changed by administrators. Administrators mislead true academic performance. Teachers under pressure pass students who should have failed. *Social promotion.*

Widespread talk of progress and increasing graduation rates may be the result of watered-down grading and manipulation. The bottom line, teachers said, is that thousands of students graduate high school without basic reading, writing and math skills. A New York Times editorial commented about phony statistics, noting that "Vital statistics like graduation rates must rely on phony calculations cooked up by state governments that are determined to hide the truth for as long as possible... For too long the states have been allowed to talk a good game while piling up phony statistics and doing little to improve their schools."[262]

One gifted drama teacher lost her job; she said NCLB put so much pressure on administrators to raise test scores that they fired the fine arts faculty (a staff of one, by the way... a whole other problem). Instead, the school obsessed over test scores. Teachers were stressed. Grades were fudged to protect jobs and reputations. One wonders if test scores ever improved for real. Said another teacher, "administrators" changed grades or told teachers to grade liberally or, it was implied, face repercussions to job security. This is what happens in reality. Improvement in test scores may be a big lie.

Students do failing work yet get promoted to the next grade. Push the problem to the next level. Now the next teacher has to deal with it. I recall a joke from a teacher: "You know what Nickelbee stands for? No Child Left Back." How long can you postpone education until it blows up in our country's face? It already did. We rank low in many education categories worldwide.

We read about fading math and science skills, engineer shortages and universities on the lookout for foreign students. Perhaps it is the result of years of *promoting the problem to the next level.* I saw it at colleges where I taught. Students don't know basic history or geography. Whole classes could not place the Civil War within 50 years or had World War I in the wrong century. Who are Roosevelt and Winston Churchill? I have to do basic review before getting to the point of lectures – time teaching subjects that should have already been taught. I correct poor grammar and spelling. It is hard to talk about the Holocaust when they cannot locate Germany on a map. Science giants like Albert Einstein are unknown. At City University of New York, students had never even *heard* of Chopin or Shakespeare. What did they do in school for 12 years?

Social promotion.

COMPULSIVE TEXTING & LAX DISCIPLINE

In recent years, a new layer of problems has emerged. Students drifting in the hallways or seated in the classroom numbly staring at their cell phones. If I did not enforce the no-tolerance rule in class (cell phones must be off), they would continue to text. I have the support of the Dean, but many teachers do not have such support. In many schools, teachers just put up with it.

Many students roam the halls staring at the smartphone. Students are obsessed at every grade level. It is now commonplace to see 12-year-olds with smartphones. Some schools don't ban them and force teachers to deal with distracted students. In some schools, teachers cannot force kids to put away their cell phones because administrators do nothing about it. What could possibly be so urgent on that phone when you are 12 years old?

When it comes to texting, screaming, running amok in class, or taunting teachers, there is little discipline. Inner city teachers often commented that sending disruptive students to the principal has little effect; students return to class and resume the bad behavior. There is no belief that poor behavior will be punished.

Teachers spoke of an oppressive atmosphere. *The student is blameless, the teacher is scrutinized.* Some teachers commented how they just wanted to finish their careers and retire. One was in his thirties. Their desire to teach is dampened by apathetic administrators and students who resent learning.

One teacher was injured when an out-of-control student violently knocked over a desk. The teacher went to the emergency room and was out of school for two weeks due to a back injury. The student was not supposed to be in that classroom. The student showed no remorse. This typifies the attitude of many students and the lack of discipline, said the teacher. Students enter classrooms where they don't belong. Said the teacher:

> *"Students are not stopped from walking the halls. Teachers and administrators will tell kids to go back to class, but if kids ignore directions there is little that can be done to force them. No one can grab them and force them to go to class. Security doesn't do anything unless there's a fight. Security may yell at kids to go to class, but if students ignore directions there isn't anything they can do."*

Little is done to address this mocking of rules. It's like that in many schools. A teacher went to the emergency room, but as for the student the principal handed out a meager suspension of a few days. The student stayed home, probably enjoying himself eating and watching TV, the teacher said. "The student enjoyed the suspension." Teachers commented how kids are coddled and rarely punished for bad behavior. Said the teacher injured by the thrown desk:

> *"I would love to see teachers receive the same protections as police and bus drivers... If you assault a bus driver you serve jail time, but if you throw a desk at a teacher, you get a couple of days' suspension. To a student this is a short vacation."*

Kids are coddled (the teachers' words). Criticizing administrator decisions can get you in trouble, perhaps placed in the "rubber room" (as known in the New York school system). One teacher was placed in the "rubber room" for a full year because he was brutally attacked by a student (a strong, tough kid, he said). The teacher defended himself, pushing the out-of-control kid to the floor, nothing more. The teacher was suspended. And the student? Nothing happened though he brutally attacked a teacher for no reason except anger issues. This is what they meant by *coddling.*

It's not just the students who get away with things. In one school, the principal was seen smoking a cigarette in the bathroom. He was never disciplined. Sometimes students are destructive. A music teacher told me his school purchased new keyboards. Within weeks, students scratched a grand piano, destroyed two keyboards and pulled keys out of two keyboards. "To them, this was fun," he said. He contacted parents about the broken instruments. The parents were apathetic.

Where there is no fear of consequences for wrongful behavior, there is little meaningful learning.

What did Nickelbee do? Mandate standardized tests and cut the fine arts, one teacher said. What about discipline and options to permanently remove juveniles who traumatize students and teachers? When lawmakers drew up the No Child Left Behind legislation, did they bother to ask the teachers? Good generals don't just sit at desks. They talk to the soldiers.

DEAF GENERALS & THE TRENCHES

The gulf between teachers and Washington is reminiscent of the trenches of World War I. Millions of soldiers fought for king and country only to find that, once they entered the fetid 10-foot-deep trenches, their generals were never heard from. Those generals ordered the men to *go over the top* into mine-filled *no man's land* to face slaughter. This repeated folly killed millions of men without the front line moving more than a few miles. In the Somme offensive, some 50,000 soldiers died by noon. The generals never listened, never learned. In 1917, the French armies mutinied. Dozens of miles of trenches went undefended. They refused to fight. *Now, the generals listened.*

Government and administrators are often like this. Teachers are not unlike those overlooked soldiers. Politicians, principals and administrators don't listen and don't want to hear from teachers. It works both ways. Sometimes administrators do speak up, offering suggestions to improve education, and unions resist. Nobody listens and students suffer. Teachers want to teach, but they also want administrators to listen. Who knows better than the teachers who stand before the children day after day?

It's not just Washington that has to listen. It is principals, superintendents, school boards, and local politicians. Structural changes must be made. Troublesome juveniles need to be removed from classrooms so that the majority can learn. Teachers should have their say when a student crosses the line of acceptable behavior. A system of discipline must be in place, including the creation of "special-cases" schools where trained mental health experts will deal with troubled kids. Teachers note various problems that go unaddressed. Wasted money and "incentives" are other issues that were raised. Commented one teacher:

"There is a lot of money wasted in special 'deals.' At my old school, they are spending somewhere in the neighborhood of 2 million dollars to replace all of the windows (maybe more), but all the windows were installed within the past 5 years! Obviously, someone has friends in high places to grant needless building improvement contracts. Two million dollars is a lot of textbooks and pencils. I could put you in touch with veteran teachers who have seen more money squandering than I have... Principals and assistant principals receive bonus money when a certain percentage of students pass the regents exams. This is ironic, as the teachers who prepare the students do not receive any bonus. But this may also be seen as an incentive to principals to cut back on arts programs and pour the money into the academic subjects... they want their money!"

Administrators ought to address such problems. They turn a deaf ear to advice. It's not unlike those World War I soldiers – *deaf generals and the trenches.*

UTTER INCOMPETENCE MUST BE ENDED

The above episodes require more than reprimanding administrators (or ignoring things). It requires firing incompetent administrators. It requires granting teachers "whistleblower" ability to file complaints to boards empowered to take firm action. Teachers must speak up about bad things without fear of retaliation. Note this episode below by a New York City music teacher.

"They don't even give me heat. Very serious. The room hovers around 55 degrees. I've been complaining since October [it was then February]. They say there's a heating problem. So I asked for portable heaters and they have not provided me that either. I've spoken to the campus director already at least three times... I bought a thermometer specifically to measure the room temperature because this has been an ongoing problem. And I have probably sent 10 emails to administrators about the problem. So no instruments and no heat." [Author: it should also be noted, the teacher was given a budget to buy musical instruments. Administrators reneged. He taught music in a school that refused to buy a single instrument. The teacher was disgusted.]... "I'm not the only teacher without heat... most teachers just accept it and dress in layers. But that's no way to go to work each day. Some days I wear my hat and gloves in the classroom. Not to mention how it distracts students from learning."

Change is needed. Teachers need options for reporting unacceptable things.

WHISTLE-BLOWING & A TEACHER COMPLAINT BOARD

The above incidents demonstrate the extent of contempt by administrators in addressing obvious problems – like keeping a classroom heated or ordering teachers to fudge test scores. How could any administrator be so insensitive as to refuse to even buy a $10 heater for a cold classroom? Is this the type of person you want to run your child's school? Is this someone *you* want to work for? Perhaps you better understand how teachers feel.

It's time to repair a system nurturing incompetence. Local school boards must be empowered to act firmly and fire incompetents quickly. Unions must not protect incompetent administrators. All school districts must have an independent complaints board to receive complaints from teachers – anonymously if need be so that teachers won't fear being reprimanded or fired by vengeful administrators. Such boards must be empowered to take action quickly and without bureaucratic red tape. We must welcome whistleblowers. It's time for schools to fire bad people.

TRUANCY

Truancy is a pandemic problem. A PBS News Hour report about New Orleans noted the impact on those who attended class regularly.[263] Teachers said classes of 24 typically had only 17 students and sometimes as few as 10. Teachers noted drug use and problems in Mexico having a grave impact on schools, gangs and drug use.

In order for truants to catch up with class work, teachers repeat the same lecture. Those who are there regularly learn little new. Everyone falls behind. It gives insight as to why students move slowly. It also explains why social promotion is common. The responsible students suffer due to those who are routinely absent. The problem New Orleans faces is common to many cities. Teachers to whom I spoke in New York made similar comments regarding attendance. Their classes were half full on many days. It must be addressed nationwide.

NEGATIVE IMPACT OF TELEVISION

According to Nielson ratings, child TV viewership averages four hours per day. A Pew Research Center survey showed that 75% of adults want tighter government enforcement of broadcast content, especially when children are watching.[264] It is ignored despite widespread support. Note these surveys and statistics: [265-266-267]

60% of people want broadcast TV indecency standards extended to cable.
69% want fines for media companies.
68% believe the entertainment industry is out of touch with moral standards.
66% believe there is too much violence on TV.
58% say there is too much cursing.

3	minutes per week parents have "meaningful conversation" with kids
4	hours children watch TV daily
7	hours kids spend playing video game each week
9	years an average American spends watching TV by age 65
15	percent who use the V-Chip to limit TV for their kids
25	hours most children spend watching TV weekly
52	days the average person spends watching TV each year
54	percent of children who have TV sets in their bedroom
62	percent who say sex on TV and in movies influences kids to have sex
77	percent who say there is too much premarital sex on TV
99	percent of households that have a TV set
8,000	Simulated murders children see on TV by end of elementary school
16,000	Murders kids have seen on TV by the time they are 18 years old
30,000	TV ads an average child sees in a year
200,000	Violent acts kids have seen on TV by age 18

• *The American Psychiatric Association:* "For the last three decades, the one predominant finding in research on the mass media is that exposure to media portrayals of violence increases aggressive behavior in children."
• *The American Psychiatric Association:* "Children who watched violent shows were more likely to strike out at playmates, argue, disobey authority and were less willing to wait for things."
• 1 of every 7 TV shows has a portrayal of sexual intercourse.
• Children with exposure to sex on TV are nearly twice as likely to have sex.
• Nearly 70% of TV programs had racy or sexual content.[268]
• TV programs with sexual material had an average of 4.4 sexual scenes/hour.

• 46% of high school students have had sex. (Many may not even admit it.)
• 59% of Americans could name The Three Stooges, 17% could name three Supreme Court Justices. [269]

DEVICES TO SHUT DOWN TV & THE INTERNET

There are consequences to TV in a child's life. If there are messages that sum up these numbers, it is this: children fill their lives with empty TV, parents are fed up, government is not taking action, and TV executives don't care. If you want better schools, look at the above numbers and ask yourself what needs to be done, then contact your Congressman and Senator.

Parents must take action and not leave it to the schools. TV executives do not care (or at least that's the impression they give). Give parents options. Without action, kids will continue to watch TV four hours a day or excessively surf the net and play video games – time better used for studying. We (and Nickelbee) are in delusion if we think education will improve without addressing TV's impact. Schools, supported by wise government intervention, can take action by providing parents apps (free of charge) that can shut down access to TV, the Internet and video games during certain times of the day. It empowers parents to shield children from distractions. Working parents cannot control what their kids do after school. These apps could be made available. They should be easy to use and distributed by schools. Imagine the control parents could exert over children if they could do this.

BETTER TV & STRONGER FCC OVERSIGHT

TV and texting. Sugar highs and the Internet. Drugs and video games. It used to be just sex and hormones. Now a new generation grows up with far more distractions. What kids see on TV impacts values. Many TV executives appear to have abandoned any duty to society – especially children. It's all about money. TV programs often harm the cause of education. I cannot tell you how many times I have seen movies and TV programs that degrade, even humiliate, teachers and the fine arts. Hollywood scriptwriters seem to have a grudge against teachers and the arts. Why should *they* have such influence in the entertainment industry?

I personally feel the barrage of insults. Teachers and artists who do so much good for society are often depicted as weirdos, psychopaths and murderers. Google *Silence of the Lambs* and Lex Luther from *Superman*, atrocity-committing villains who adore Classical music. It sends a message. Teachers are also depicted as nerds always annoying cool teenagers. Yeah, teachers wake up in the morning thinking of ways to annoy students. Come on!

Teachers notice this grudge by TV and Hollywood. It's fashionable to make us look bad and make teenagers look smarter. It breeds student disrespect for teachers. It is an example of how Hollywood harms the cause of education... but could help instead. TV and Hollywood are protected by First Amendment rights. Still, the FCC can show some teeth. Free speech is a constitutional right, but even this has limits. One cannot scream "fire" in a crowded theater.

Our leaders can use the bully pulpit to address the entertainment industry (and pop music stars) regarding negative messages and urge the entertainment industry to accept some responsibility in terms of supporting education and the arts. The FCC was more forceful in past times in regulating TV content. Even the FCC fell prey to the "government is the problem" movement's obsession to deregulate.

Each time TV harms education and values, it empowers mediocrity. Entertainment executives can help. Transforming our culture into an education-valuing society does not require laws. It requires a grassroots understanding that change is necessary. It requires that Congressmen, Senators and the White House use the bully pulpit to encourage the cable and entertainment industries to be sensitive and supportive. Leaders can speak up. The FCC can to do more. Tools are available.

Teachers see the result of Hollywood's abandonment of duty to society. They see it when students are distracted, violent or pregnant, or have not studied. While parents are also at fault in allowing their children to watch so much TV, negative programs need not be so readily available. It reminds me of a comment a European made to me: "Your TV beeps when someone curses and blacks out a woman's breast, but you let your kids see torture and machine guns murdering dozens of people." Producers, scriptwriters and executives must patriotically act for the public good. They should love children more than they love money.

FEAR IN SCHOOLS

According to a *reason.org* study, these were the top-rated problems noted by schoolteachers in 1940: talking out of turn, chewing gum, making noise, running in the hall, cutting in line, dress code violations, littering. Nowadays, major issues include drug and alcohol abuse, pregnancy, suicide, rape, robbery, and assault.[270] Many inner city schools have metal detectors to prevent students from bringing in knives and guns. It's like airport security. Add to the list of modern problems obsession with cell phones, texting, sexting, Facebook slander, kik, surfing the net, and video games. Note these findings in a study by the *National Household Education Survey* regarding school violence:

• 29% of elementary school students and 34% of junior high students reported that they worried about becoming victimized at school.
• 20% of high schools reported they were worried about being victimized.
• 17% of middle school students reported being victimized.

The numbers get more troublesome: 1 in 7 students overall reported that he/she was a victim. Here are the percentages of students who reported "the occurrence of, witness of, worry about, or victimization through robbery, bullying or physical attack at school:"

Elementary School:	*60%*
Middle School:	*77%*
High School:	*71%*
All Combined:	*60%*

These statistics reflect a more violent society than in the past. Studies suggest TV is a cause. Children see 200,000 simulated murders by age 18. It must affect their personalities. Schools are not as safe or innocent as they once were. With cooperation, patriotism and civic duty, together we can all change this.

Education includes teaching proper behavior, ethics, and understanding the need to treat others with respect. When values are not taught, an important goal of education has been lost. Federal education programs could encourage the spread of these concepts in modern "Civics" classes. While we're at it, include better understanding of government, civic duty for the community and a more compassionate attitude towards others.

The desk-throwing incident (mentioned above), where a teacher ended up in the emergency room, is but one example. That "anger-crazed" act should have been addressed. Why was that student so angry, roaming the halls and out of control? The student should have been sent to a mental health expert to explore the cause of the violent outburst and find solutions. That type of program makes sense, but in most schools such a program does not exist. *It should.*

A student injured a teacher and little was done about it. It sends a pathetic message to other students: you can do sick things, perhaps battery or a misdemeanor, and get away with it. A system must be put in place that takes action. It's wrong to merely sweep it under the rug. Such rage in a student will not magically disappear. It manifests into something worse.

I heard teachers speak of students taunting and threatening to "have you fired." Students feel empowered and bully teachers! It's *One Flew Over the Cuckoo's Nest*: the insane running the asylum. A teacher meekly commented, "I cannot do anything about it; the principal does not care... the principal does not want incident reports because it makes the school look unsafe." So let's add "hiding problems" to the list. Administrators must be honest and take decisive action. It sends a message to students: there are consequences to bad behavior.

INVEST IN STUDENTS BEFORE THEY TURN TO CRIME

It costs about $31,000/person to incarcerate prison inmates (national average).[271] We could instead invest money in our children while they can still be reached – while at a young age when we can steer them towards a healthy future and out of the path of the criminal justice system and prison.

Prison gets even more expensive in several states. For example, the average cost per inmate in New York State is $60,000. In New York City, the cost skyrockets to $168,000/inmate.[272] Indeed, it behooves us to invest in students early in life, for the cost of handling matters once a person is in prison is quite high. Just how many among current prisoners nationwide may have avoided that terrible fate had there been intelligent intervention and mental health programs to help them while they were still in school?

It's time to find out. Commence nationwide mental health programs to help students before they embrace the dark path of drugs, gangs and crime. It makes more sense to invest in children than to let things go wrong. Bright young people would have a better path if government embraced such programs. It may not stop crime entirely, but it will likely prevent a large percentage of it over time.

An ounce of prevention is worth a pound of cure. Investing in our youth will likely steer many away from a dark life and prison. It's a generational challenge, costly at first, but likely to save far greater amounts of money a generation from now as we witness precipitous drops in crime and read articles about hundreds of prisons being shut down (at great savings to taxpayers) because those prisons are no longer needed!

It's worth the try. A new approach to education. A much-improved result. There are smarter and cost-effective solutions that leaders have yet to embrace.

SPECIAL-CASE SCHOOLS & THE "NORTHSIDE" MODEL

Society has created "special ed" programs to help learning disabled children. A new category must be created: *special-case schools.* Alternative approaches to helping children with problems already exist. One outstanding model is Northside Center.[273] Its mission statement sums up what it does.

"Northside Center provides children and families the support they need to overcome adversity and thrive. Our high quality outcome-driven behavioral, mental health and education services propel struggling children forward... away from the ill-effects of poverty and racism."

Various matters children and teenagers face account for violence and problems in schools. Mental health issues need to receive far higher priority nationwide. Experts in problems unique to children are better equipped to help troubled students. Public schools should be staffed with full-time mental health experts. In many school districts, entire schools should be devoted to these types of problems. They would be staffed by experts specifically trained to help students with emotional problems, violent tendencies, drug use issues, and association with gangs and crime – in sum, problems common to inner city life.

Northside Center has a track record of good results. It is an example of the nationwide system that should be made available to all schools so that they have an alternative for helping students who have problems. Troubled children too often head to crime, perhaps prison. There are far better ways to steer children to better lives. Northside provides a model. The federal government should provide financial support for a nationwide system of such institutions readily available to all school systems.

Troubled students, especially violent ones, must be removed from classrooms. Let trained personnel, as found at Northside Center, teach them. It will help students recover and improve. Doing so means more than removal from class. It means a separate facility. It will send a message to all teachers: the system will protect you and the integrity of the classroom. It sends a message to troubled students and their parents: we will provide solutions and staff to help.

Many students endure harsh environments. This can include broken homes, gang pressures, drugs, street shootings, and rape by parents or relatives. Parents may be indifferent to their children's education, unwilling to do obvious things like help with homework or ensure a child is fed. A parent might be a drug user or criminal or be in prison. Living with a grandparent is common. Imagine growing up with no mother or father? Teenagers desperately need healthy role models. What do they get instead?

Mental health issues and learning disabilities must be addressed in specialized schools. Perhaps the child has dyslexia and cannot read due to visual or perceptual problems. All children should receive tests regarding this condition. They need specialists to guide them. How many children with good potential end up troubled due to school systems ill-equipped to help their special needs?

Special-case schools must be staffed with trained mental health professionals. Too often, smart kids with fine potential suffer due to emotional problems that standard schools are not equipped to deal with. Children need help from professionals who understand their problems and know how to help children overcome those problems.

As for those students who are simply too violent and dangerous to handle, there must be staff equipped to deal with them as well. Simply keeping them in school and allowing them to disrupt classes, bully classmates and threaten teachers without consequences is not the answer. Without consequences for bad behavior, education cannot flourish. All students must understand that persistent troublemakers will be removed from school, but once they are removed, the system must try to help them in ways specifically designed to deal with their specific mental conditions and needs. Help them before it becomes a matter for police and the prison system.

THE "BOYS TOWN" MODEL

Another institution (made famous by a 1930s movie by the same name) is *Boys Town*, located in Nebraska. Troubled teenagers (often with criminal records) attend this live-in school that provides comprehensive help to get troubled teenagers on the right path. Does it always work? No, but it has a pretty good track record (and has received much publicity) for guiding troubled kids in the right direction.

This particular approach is quite expensive. The idea here is not that a live-in situation is the right solution, but that something along similar lines is the right path. Giving kids the professional attention they need can prevent many terrible things, but even if it is expensive to create schools modeled after Boys Town, it is a better investment than the cost of putting kids into prison later in life.

It leaves a gnawing question: just how many kids who end up in prison could have avoided that terrible fate had they received healthy attention early in life? It is worth recognizing that there are better ways. We need to think out of the box and try new solutions. Stop letting cost be the reason why we don't invest in our kids early in life... before they get in trouble. There is an old expression our leaders should absorb when it comes to investing in young people: *when you are stingy, you pay twice.*

THE FINLAND MODEL

The highly acclaimed and successful system of education in Finland provides yet another intriguing and innovative approach to education that should be carefully studied in America. Note the below excerpt from Smithsonian Magazine.

"Whatever it takes" is an attitude that drives not just Kirkkojarvi's 30 teachers, but most of Finland's 62,000 educators in 3,500 schools from Lapland to Turku – professionals selected from the top 10 percent of the nation's graduates to

earn a required master's degree in education. Many schools are small enough so that teachers know every student. If one method fails, teachers consult with colleagues to try something else. They seem to relish the challenges. Nearly 30 percent of Finland's children receive some kind of special help during their first nine years of school.[274]

The Finnish system is known to American teachers, many probably frustrated by the administrative resistance in America to innovating and trying new approaches like that of Finland. Said a teacher, *"The [Finland] education profession is very highly regarded and very competitive. It's on the level on being a doctor. Lots of rigorous training. More is expected from students, too. Finland is also a leader in music education."*

There is plenty of information online about Finland's approach. What is taking so long to innovate and try successful approaches that are well-documented?

THE "UKRAINIAN" MODEL

Schools in Ukraine also offer an approach that could revolutionize our education system. Students have teachers who remain involved for years at a time, monitoring progress and providing a mentor and compassionate advice – so to speak, a big brother or sister. We can try this approach. From grades 6-8 and 9-12, students will have one teacher who monitors their progress. In a word, they will always have a caring, knowledgeable friend who knows them for years – someone to go to for help and advice.

PARENTS OF TROUBLED STUDENTS

Interviewed teachers commented that parents are central to the problem. Parents refuse to help their own children learn and dump everything on teachers. Children go home to watch TV, text or play video games. Once parents abandon any duty to help their child, the situation is almost hopeless. Such students refuse to learn. They torment teachers and fellow students.

Teachers commented that they typically have several students like this – up to one third of the class. A teacher commented that parents typically do not show up on open school nights. So how can a teacher inform a parent of a child's problem? One answer would be the creation of a system where school personnel set up visits with parents at home to discuss the children.

Teachers have few options for removing such students and administrators offer few remedies besides "safe" classes or suspension, which are ineffective and brief. Students return to class and the problem resumes. A poisonous message is sent. It is at the root of struggling schools. Parents are part of the problem. Many do not create a home environment conducive to learning. It is a societal problem plaguing thousands of families. *Until administrators address this reality, we will not have good schools no matter how much money is pumped into system.*

Children spend their formative years obsessively texting, watching TV, playing video games, and witnessing neighborhoods with gangs, shootings, crime, and drug deals. *These* become role models. Many parents refuse to sit with young children and do obvious things like teach the alphabet, read stories or teach basic skills. By the time children of such families begin kindergarten, they already suffer from emotional problems and learning disabilities that teachers have difficulty addressing. It only gets worse as students get older.

Parents of such children often show little interest when teachers contact them. Teachers often noted how rarely parents attend parent-teacher conferences. When there is no interaction between parent and teacher, when parents are apathetic, how can teachers do their jobs? Society must not ignore conditions that plague millions of children and that have become pandemic and generational.

Solutions require a departure from current approaches – new programs that require parents of failing children (spotted as early as first grade) to attend mandatory counseling on how to promote a healthy learning environment at home. In the meantime, troubled children should be sent to special-case classes (or schools) specializing in troubled students so as to remove troubled students from classrooms that would otherwise be poisoned by their poor behavior and refusal to study at home. It should be done by court order if need be. This is a better option than spoiling the learning environment.

7 STEPS TO HELP TROUBLED STUDENTS

Give teachers the option of requesting removal of obsessively obnoxious and troubled students. Let this be the teacher's decision, for only that teacher knows what is best for the classroom. Administrators must then be given tools to address this. The process would be straightforward:

1. Teachers will remove students who are excessively disruptive. Administrators will place such troubled students in special-case classes and schools.

2. A staff of trained specialists will counsel and teach removed students. Other specialists, empowered with court orders, will go directly to parents at home or at work and try to find solutions that address the needs of the child. If a parent refuses to meet the specialists, he/she should be held in contempt of court.

3. Specialists will be trained to deal with problems unique to troubled children (poor nutrition, emotional problems, crime, broken families, gangs, drugs, etc.).

4. Parents will be counseled on ways to end disruptive behavior and help their child study and learn. Parents will also be given tools that shut down TV sets, smartphones and video games when children are at home.

5. Troubled children will receive tutors after school as well as sports and arts programs. Leaving kids on their own is a reason why problems arise.

6. If children improve and become capable of healthy learning and interaction, they will return to normal classes. If they act up again, they will be removed again.

7.   End "social promotion." Being left behind is a stigma, but being honest is the best option.   Don't move students to the next grade unless they satisfy requirements.   Administrators must not change grades!   Grant students tools needed to rebound and move deservedly to the next grade. *Help them earn it.*

The point here is to encourage lawmakers and administrators to commence and fund revolutionary new concepts that stand a fighting chance of addressing entrenched problems thousands of students face daily.

DECENTRALIZATION OF SCHOOL CONTROL

New York City runs an enormous school system with over 1.1 million students, 1,700 public schools and a budget of nearly $25 billion. It is a huge bureaucracy. Imagine trying to get things done.

Huge bureaucracies often are unresponsive and slow in addressing problems. Ask anyone dealing with Social Security and Medicaid.   Ask New York schoolteachers and they will tell you how hard it is to get things done. One teacher said he waited nearly six months just to get broken TV sets removed from his classroom. Administrators said "forms" had to be filled out and told him equipment can only be thrown out (recycled) once it reaches 50 in total. Huh? I had to toss an old TV and brought it to Staples. Staples accepts electronic items for recycling. It's easy, yet the New York school system creates obstacles for a simple matter.   It forced the teacher to keep broken equipment in his classroom for many months.

Teachers in that same school were also waiting months for the school to repair the boiler as they sat in 55 degree temperatures for months (along with students). I visited a classroom. I had to wear my winter coat! What insanity. Something is wrong with the system.   Would decentralization help?   Will much smaller headquarters be able to react faster? It is an idea worth investigating in major cities with large school systems.

Lethargy is an example of bureaucracy at its worst. Almost everything takes too long to get done. Even obvious matters become a time-consuming process. Teachers in New York routinely deal with it. How about Chicago, Miami and Cleveland? Perhaps they also endure bureaucracies that move at glacial speed.

Decentralization is a path large American cities should explore. If New York carved the Board of Education into 20 separate headquarters, each a fully empowered and vastly streamlined entity accounting *only to the Mayor*, perhaps things would get done faster. Administrators with far fewer layers of authority (and far less paperwork) might be able to act more quickly. Administrators must be able to quickly address teacher needs unburdened by paperwork and regulations that are out of touch with the modern world. Decentralization is a concept ripe for discussion. Will it work in every city? That is a question each State and city needs to consider. It's time to experiment and think out of the box.

IN THE PRESS . . .

Union Cooperation. Teacher unions sometimes stand in the way. Public interest is served when incompetent teachers are fired. Unions often protect poor teachers –

"dead wood" as they are often called. Unions must decide, is the priority protecting dead wood or helping students?

This touches on a system in New York known as "reserve" teachers, where competent teachers sit in rooms all day long awaiting notice if a teaching need arises. Many highly qualified teachers end up sitting around day after day. Schools can use paid staff more effectively and let more teachers teach.

American Schools in Decline. Note this editorial by The New York Times:

> *"Americans should be deeply alarmed by new data showing that the country is continuing to lose ground educationally to its competitors abroad. The U.S. once had the world's top high school graduation rate. It has now fallen to 13th place behind countries like South Korea, the Czech Republic and Slovenia. Worse still, a new study from the Education Trust, a nonpartisan foundation, finds that this is the only country in the industrial world where young people are less likely than their parents to graduate high school."* [275]

CHARTER SCHOOLS

Charter schools have been a source of controversy. Their success varies from school district to district. Is it a panacea for better education or a threat to public education insofar as siphoning off needed funds or allowing schemers to milk the system and make money? It depends on each state and city. New York, Florida, Chicago and New Orleans are different and should be analyzed case by case. The position the federal government should take is unclear for it is an evolving laboratory of education. It is an example where "one size fits all" does not work. The matter is better left to states to work out, but with firm federal guidelines and standards. The success of charter schools is real if schools provide superior education or put pressure on public schools to improve. If they fail to do so, they should be denied funding. As in the business world, competition of ideas and proven success are good for society. Charter schools offer potential for innovation where bureaucracy does not thwart experimentation – if efforts are sincere.

A COMPREHENSIVE PLAN

✓ TV & Video Games. Address excessive use of video games and TV by providing parents with apps that will shut down TV and video games.

✓ Smartphones. Smartphones must be banned during school hours. Upon entering school, students will place smartphones in lockers that are properly protected. When school ends they pick up phones. Teachers said students text and play with phones during class. This must stop. Administrators must cooperate. In schools that do not implement a ban, teachers must have the authority to order students to shut smartphones. Parents must cooperate and let schools take action. Smartphones defeat the goals of education.

✓ Tutors. Fund programs that let tutors help troubled students, go to children's homes, and meet parents at home or at work to figure out ways to improve progress; require students to stay after school if they are failing; keep libraries open late in inner cities and send tutors to libraries and community centers to help students; properly fund community centers and libraries.

✓ "Special-Case" Schools: Experts in Troubled-Student Issues. Fund special-case schools that hire specialists trained in problems afflicting students, including drugs, gangs, crime, domestic violence, and broken families. Move all troubled students to special-case classes/schools; hire mental health experts to work with troubled students and their parents; provide court orders forcing parents to meet with staff. School is for education, not babysitting.

✓ Class Size. Schools face overcrowding. States must fund schools to ensure adequate staff is in place. Schools can make better use of "reserve" teachers.

✓ Incompetence. Fire incompetent principals, administrators and teachers; unions must not protect "dead wood."

✓ Waste & Corruption. Monitor the mindless throwing out of furniture, books, and supplies; monitor waste by contractors; make custodial unions flexible about school repairs.

✓ The Fine Arts. Fund more music, theater and dance; buy instruments; fund programs that take students to professional symphony and jazz concerts, opera, and ballet; hire truly gifted artists to teach at schools.

✓ Food. Remove soda and candy vending machines to prevent sugar highs; spot cases of poor eating habits; stop serving junk food for lunch.

✓ Discipline. Deal firmly with juveniles who exact violence upon teachers and students or show disrespect; have a no-tolerance policy with deeply troubled students; move them to special-case classes.

✓ Drugs & Gangs. Counsel students on drug use; create mandatory programs to rehabilitate marijuana and drug users; remove drug peddlers from schools; have police patrol schools and nearby streets for drug sales; empower juvenile courts to prosecute juvenile drug peddlers as adults.

✓ Northside, Finland, Ukraine & Boys Town Models. These approaches would be a smart investment in our future that would lead to much-improved education and schools that put kids on a successful path early in life.

✓ Empower Teachers. Only teachers know students well enough to decide who should be removed from the classroom so that classes progress at a proper pace. Empower teachers to remove disruptive students from the classroom so that a healthy learning environment is in place. Schools shall be mandated to hire mental health specialists to remedy student needs.

✓ <u>End Social Promotion</u>. Administrators will be forbidden to change grades (punishable by law), water down standards or promote students to the next grade when students fail. Students who perform at sub-grade levels will have transcripts stating so. We must not let schools build upon lies. It is better to be honest and ensure that those who graduate *really* meet 12th grade standards.

✓ <u>Charter Schools</u>. Government can encourage charter schools, but lock out profiteers. Support innovation and experimentation. Where successful, let it be a model. Where unsuccessful or corrupt, defund and shut down immediately.

✓ <u>Mental Health & Learning Disabilities.</u> Children often suffer from mental health problems. Schools must help them. Dyslexia is also common. It impairs a child's ability to read and learn. A nationwide system of testing for dyslexia and other conditions at the elementary school level should be created. The sooner a child's condition is discovered, the sooner it can be addressed by trained professionals. Government must fund programs.

✓ <u>Prison</u>. How many people in prison could have been helped early in life? It is cheaper to treat problems early in life than to incarcerate later. Turn this into policy. Helping kids early on can prevent tragic problems later in life.

✓ <u>Whistle-Blowing & Teacher Complaint Centers</u>. Every school must provide a complaints board to receive complaints from teachers regarding incompetent administrators. Teachers should be allowed to do so anonymously if they fear job security due to vengeful administrators. Corrupt administrators must be fired; complaint boards must be empowered to investigate and act quickly. It's time to be firm with incompetent administrators.

Lawmakers can improve education with a comprehensive plan. Communicate with TV executives about values and encourage parents to shield children from bad influences. Administrators can better support teachers. Solutions require addressing *everything* – from TV to video games to texting.

Chapter 18

THE FINE ARTS
A Cabinet-Level Secretary of the Arts

An Elementary School: A class of some 35 nine-to-eleven year-old students rehearsed in a room filled with instruments and pictures of Beethoven and Mozart. They held violins, violas and cellos. One played a string bass taller than he was! They rehearsed a Beethoven minuet for the upcoming spring concert. The conductor sweetly cajoled them to play in tune. Nextdoor, 50 kids sang Broadway tunes. Among them was a nine-year-old pianist excited that in the spring concert he would perform as soloist a Bach minuet and 800 people would hear it. That afternoon students rehearsed a Sousa march. It was a band with clarinets, trumpets, saxophones, drums, trombones and flutes. They also were excited about performing in the spring concert. Everyone was. Music was part of their lives. It had always been that way... ever since kindergarten.

A Junior High School: A mile away some 35 students watched a conductor as they rehearsed a Mozart opera overture. Soon two young pianists entered and the orchestra rehearsed a two-piano concerto by the French composer Poulenc. Downstairs a chorus rehearsed Mendelssohn's oratorio "Elijah" and songs from "Cabaret." An hour later 25 students entered a classroom for a music appreciation class. They heard Mussorgsky's "Pictures at an Exhibition" and a Chopin nocturne. It was a typical day: science, English, history, math, gym, and music. It had always been that way... ever since kindergarten.

A Senior High School: Just up the hill, students, many of them siblings of the kids above, rehearsed Beethoven's 7th Symphony. During first period a band of 35 rehearsed a Holst march. At noon five students studied music theory, soon to compose a work the orchestra would play. After school, kids playing soccer overheard the jazz band in the distance rehearsing Duke Ellington. Young theater buffs rehearsed the musical "Gypsy". The 25-piece orchestra would soon join them. Nearby, Terpsichore rehearsed dance for an upcoming performance. All the students were well-rounded. In fact, 95 percent went to college and over 50 percent headed to top universities. Dozens were bound for Harvard, Yale, Brown, and Princeton. Many of them had performed as string, woodwind, brass, and percussion musicians in the spring concert. This was the life they knew. It had always been that way... ever since kindergarten.

These idyllic scenes are not fiction. They were what I experienced while attending public school in Great Neck, N.Y. The music mentioned is what we performed. I was that nine-year-old pianist. I respected students who danced and I saw their performances. Most of us did. Be it Broadway, jazz, orchestra, or dance, it was the life I knew... *ever since kindergarten.*

It is the life every child should know. I was a trumpeter in the high school band and orchestra when we performed Duke Ellington, Beethoven and *Gypsy*. I no longer play trumpet (and my neighbors are glad), but I relish the experiences. So did others who became successful doctors, bankers, lawyers and businessmen. The arts encourage good scholarship.

Mismanagement vanquished many school systems throughout the country. It is heartbreaking. We are becoming a cultural wasteland where tens of millions mock our greatest creators. I wish all students in grades K-12 could have that same warm experience I had. It's time to make it happen.

THE TIME HAS COME FOR A DEPT. OF THE FINE ARTS

At first one might think a cabinet-level fine arts program is odd, perhaps trivial. This type of thinking is dated and wrongheaded. As you'll see below, studies show that arts education *improves* academic results and decreases violent behavior. Such a change must be welcomed! It is time for our leaders to be fact-driven and think in new ways... *out of the box.*

Left unaddressed, opera, ballet, jazz, and symphony orchestras could be relegated to museums. We have a country with millions of students who know nothing about the arts or mock the fine and performing arts. Hollywood depicts people who like classical music as weird or psychopathic killers. (Google Hannibal in *Silence of the Lambs* and Lex Luther in *Superman* – both liked Mozart.) Kids never see a Broadway show, orchestra, ballet, or opera. They become adults with apathy for the arts, and their children become the same as adults. When school systems fire gifted music teachers, when "music departments" throw away instruments, when "No Child Left Behind" barely recognizes the arts exist, it reflects poorly on a civilized nation.

If children do not experience the arts in school, they will not support it later in life. This is not a legacy our lawmakers should be proud of. There were an estimated 98,817 public schools as of 2010 according to the National Center for Education Statistics.[276] The cost of funding all U.S. public schools with 197,634 fine arts teachers (two per school at $50,000 avg. salary) is less than the cost of *one aircraft carrier*: $9.88 billion. That's practically an accounting error in the $4 trillion federal budget. We must lobby for a Department of Fine Arts and take a giant stride towards making America a more cultured nation. It is the duty of civilization to respect its greatest artists.

A study by the Dept. of Education (DOE) noted that student achievement in the arts subjects is "mediocre." A *National Assessment of Education Progress in Arts* study concluded there are serious problems in arts education in public school systems throughout the country.[277] A cabinet-level department can repair the crisis in the arts. Congress must fund an agency that promotes fine arts education.

We must be more than a nation of money. We must be a nation of first-class education, and an important part of fine education means inclusion of the arts. This means hiring full-time fine arts teachers in every public school. The time has come for the mandate of overseeing the hiring of at least two fine arts teachers in every one of the 98,817 public schools in the U.S. This civilized nation needs to take a giant civilized artistic step forward.

THE FINE ARTS ARE IN TROUBLE

Support for the arts has collapsed. Arts education is good in rare cases. An article in the *San Francisco Chronicle* gives a sense of the situation in the nation's largest state:

"Of the state's 300,000 full-time public-school teachers, just 2 percent teach music or art. The scarcity of fine arts teachers is unlikely to change anytime soon because the state is short of teachers in general. Of the more than 30,000 new teachers hired this school year, only 635 teach art or music. Despite the grim numbers, experts say there are ways to bring art to more students. Solutions range from the philosophical to practical, from urging local boards of education to push an arts agenda to hiring artists to train regular classroom teachers."[278]

To end such stories, government must subsidize the hiring of performing arts teachers and the purchase of supplies, from sound systems to musical instruments to dance shoes. The Wallace Foundation noted this bleak assessment:

"Audiences for classical music, jazz, theater, visual arts and other art forms have all declined as a percentage of the population in recent years, and as this new RAND report argues, reversing that trend will require more than simply expanding the supply of art and people's access to it. It will also require cultivating more demand through arts education and other means.[279]

"[T]he arts are in serious decline due to ignorant or misinformed legislation. Take the No Child Left Behind Act (NCLB). Although it names the arts as part of the 'core curriculum,' the act falls short by not requiring schools to report time spent on art education; nor does it require students to meet any performance standards. Many blame the NCLB for causing budget cuts (35.6 million at the Federal level last year)."[280]

The Wallace article noted the decline of interest in the arts:

- Classical music sales have plummeted.
- One third of the nation's top 100 radio markets do not have a classical station.
- Many symphony orchestras are cutting back programs and suffering financial difficulties.[281]
- The New York City Opera is now defunct. (New York!)

An article in The New York Times portends a bleak future for the arts.[282] It noted that Chicago Symphony ticket and other sales fell by about a third since 1990, and that this typifies the problems faced by many professional orchestras, including the New York Philharmonic and the Philadelphia Orchestra.

ARTS EDUCATION IMPROVES OVERALL EDUCATION

As a college professor I personally see the results of gutted arts programs. In my classes, I ask students how many took music classes. Few raise their hands. This is coming from students from high-quality schools. What we consider "high-quality" is often not very high. That must change. Teaching the fine arts has been shown to improve overall academic performance. Students have higher test scores than those with little to no exposure. Note this *enewschannels.com* report:

> *"The arts are under attack in the nation's public schools and students are being denied the arts foundation they need to succeed in life, say the educators at Renaissance Publications, Inc... According to Stanford University and the Carnegie Foundation, students involved in the arts are four times more likely to be recognized for academic achievement, and four times more likely to participate in math or science fairs. They are three times more likely to win awards for school attendance, and they read for pleasure twice as much as their peers."[283]*

The *UCLA Imagination Project* concluded that the arts deter delinquent behavior and improve academic performance. According to *Americans for the Arts*, the arts develop many important skills: "Young people who participate in the arts for at least three hours on three days each week through at least one full year are

- 4 times more likely to be recognized for academic achievement;
- 3 times more likely to be elected to class office within their schools;
- 4 times more likely to participate in a math and science fair;
- 3 times more likely to win an award for school attendance;
- 4 times more likely to win an award for writing an essay or poem;
- participating in youth groups nearly four times as often;
- reading for pleasure nearly twice as often;
- performing community service more than four times as often."[284]

Americans for the Arts notes that in business circles, arts education offers benefits: [285] 1) a school climate of higher expectations, discipline, and academic rigor; 2) problem-solving and critical thinking skills, adding to overall academic achievement and school success; 3) alternatives to destructive behavior; 4) greater appreciation and understanding of the world around them.

RELATIVELY SMALL COST OF DEPT. OF FINE ARTS

The money needed to hire two fine arts teachers in every public school is tiny relative to what government spends. As of 2010 there were 98,817 public schools. Creating a lasting legacy for the arts means hiring two teachers per school. One teacher would focus on orchestra, jazz and band, and the second teacher would focus on chorus, theater and music appreciation. A part time dance teacher could collaborate with the choral teacher in teaching musical theater.

Each of the 98,817 public schools would be given a grant to hire two teachers (197,634 in total). At an average $50,000 salary/year, this comes to $9.88 billion. According the U.S. Government, $1.02 *trillion* was spent on education nationwide in fiscal year 2015.[286] The cost of hiring two fine arts teachers for each of the

98,817 public schools is barely a drop in the bucket of the $1.02 trillion spent on education: a puny 0.0097%. That's less than *a thousandth* of a percent! Is *that* too much to ask for such a noble purpose?

The Department of Fine Arts (DFA) would be part of the DOE. It would manage annual grants to hire fine arts teachers and a one-time $5 billion fund providing schools with a $50,000 grant towards the purchase of necessary equipment. A modest-sized staff would manage the program. It should be a model of efficiency. DFA will *not* hire teachers. It will merely enforce high standards and monitor schools to ensure money is used *only* for the purpose of the grant: hiring two fine arts teachers. Schools may add funds to their arts program to improve arts education and hire additional arts teachers. DFA would encourage this. The $100,000 DFA grant is in *addition* to whatever schools already spend. It is a minimum, not a limit.

Standards will be monitored to ensure that only top-quality teaching artists are hired. Top schools (Juilliard, Eastman, Curtis, Yale, Northwestern, etc.) graduate thousands of exceptional young artists who would love to teach unobstructed by bureaucracy and mediocrity. Once hired, let them do their job.

I have personally heard gut-wrenching stories about schools throwing out violins and cellos like they were garbage. Administrators who made such shameful decisions disgraced the education system. Discard mediocre administrators, not instruments. The DFA will help schools rebuild music programs gutted over the years. It means purchasing many items, including band and orchestra instruments, pianos, music stands, risers for choirs, and floor materials for dancers. Auditoriums that have been neglected would be upgraded. It is the price we pay for neglecting the arts for so long.

The program would require that all students attend performances of performing groups at biannual school assemblies. Students taking chorus may not be in the orchestra (and vice versa). Still, everyone will be exposed to the arts and will be required to attend performances. Everyone will benefit. Exposure is vital. Everyone will take music appreciation classes and be in a choir (particularly in elementary school). It should not be left to private sources, though help from foundations can add to the effort.

Union Public Schools, in Oklahoma, admirably demonstrates the movement towards innovation. They write on their 2017 website: [287]

> *"Union's Fine Arts Department proudly presents YouthArts!, an annual fine arts festival showcasing the creative works and talents of elementary and secondary students. YouthArts! is one of the longest running festivals of its type in the state of Oklahoma, celebrating its 38th anniversary in the spring of 2017... Under the direction of the district's 50-plus fine arts teachers, the multi-day event is scheduled in late April [2017] and includes a variety of performances and exhibitions all open to the public. Those include:*
>
> * *Combined Elementary Choir Concert*
> * *High School Repertory Theater Production*
> * *One Act Play Festival*

- *Visual Arts Exhibition*
- *Secondary Vocal Music Concerts*
- *Competitive Speech Exhibit*
- *High School Orchestra Concert*
- *Secondary Band Concerts*
- *High School Jazz Band Concert"*

YouthArts! is a model for schools that we, as a nation, wish to see at all schools nationwide. DFA can help make this happen! This is what happens when you have dedicated administrators and teachers. Imagine what we could see once DFA is created and gets to work! We would witness the blossoming of the fine arts if only we take action and create a properly-funded DFA.

DFA DIVISIONS & MANDATE: HIRE SUPERB ARTISTS

DFA will have four departments: 1) instrumental and jazz, 2) drama and musical theater, 3) dance, and 4) concert and museum fieldtrips. Its mandate will be monitoring proper use of grants and enforcing outstanding hiring standards for arts teachers. The DFA will not hire teachers, but will present guidelines for hiring. The DFA will override choices if competence is at question. The DFA will be on alert for cronyism, theft, embezzlement, mediocrity, and using funds for purposes other than the block grant for hiring two fine arts teachers. There must be no shenanigans like using funds to hire *non-arts* teachers.

Fine arts teachers would be required to provide video recordings to demonstrate accomplishment in their discipline. This applies to everyone from musicians to singers to actors. High levels of accomplishment will be required. Our children deserve this. Administrators would be prevented from watering down standards. The grant will come with the stipulation that schools will not hire mediocrities, cut or downsize arts programs, or use grants for non-arts programs. *Money granted for the arts must be used for the arts*.

Schools that obtain extra funding will never see their federal grants lowered. DFA will be staffed with people intimately familiar with the arts, raising money from Congress and networking. The Secretary of Fine Arts must be artistic yet politically savvy. He/she will have to constantly lobby Congress for more funding support to grow the department and arts.

A "NEW DEAL" FOR THE ARTS

We need a *New Deal* for the performing arts. During the FDR era, the *Works Progress Administration* (WPA) subsidized artists and programs throughout America. A modern, permanent WPA would be a revolution for the arts. Sadly, what FDR started disbanded a few years later. DFA will be the modern heir, a permanent agency properly funded. Its money would be distributed to needy artists, musicians, orchestras, and opera and ballet companies. Hiring thousands of musicians, dancers and artists would be the focus of the modern "WPA." Like the depression-era programs, artists must be helped. There are thousands of worthy musicians, artists and dancers who deserve opportunity and income.

The entire nation must come to believe in this reasonable goal and enjoy its fruits. Communities throughout the U.S. would see local talent perform in government-subsidized concerts and performances. We want to create a nation of working artists, not just hobbyists... and a more cultured nation that supports its local talent.

If we are to realize the dream of 98,817 schools with fine arts programs (and a modern WPA) there must be a sea of change. DFA can do just that! Let us all lobby the White House and Congress to create the DFA. Our country and education system will be energized by such a visionary concept. Education means more than English or math. It also means creativity. Our children deserve this. Once the fine arts are in place at every school, education will improve and a new generation will develop a healthy respect for the arts. We should welcome the dream.

"What marks man apart from beast? Certainly not strength, for lions shame man. Certainly not speed, for horses outpace plodding man. Certainly not grace, for the peacock outdoes man by far. What makes man different is art; music, dance, drama, the human voice, the creative mind able to soar the heavens without foot leaving soil. Deny the soul of art and what is left but emptiness? Deny the child the drama of Shakespeare, the towering emotion of Beethoven, or the majesty of da Vinci, and we deny the child a place near God. Man can dress or eat well, but without art, he is naked and famished. Only art can give the child knowledge of a higher world, and the will to strive for a mightier plateau amidst the universe of knowledge and wonder."

– Anonymous

Chapter 19

POPULATION GROWTH
The Elephant in the Room

Enormous population growth is a reality affecting our country and the world. Its discussion in political circles is taboo. The problem is real. Ignoring it, kicking the can down the road, is not in anyone's best interests. The issue is crucial yet a matter few politicians care to discuss. It would come off as an attack on precious values – family, intimacy and personal rights. It is uncomfortable to discuss it, but sadly we cannot hide from it. Each time you sit in heavy traffic, you feel its effect. It presents risks to our survival, the environment and our quality of life. Population growth is the *elephant in the room:* dangerous to discuss, too dangerous to ignore.

World population has surged since 1800. Look at this chart.[288] [289] [290]

1804	1 billion people
1927	2 billion
1960	3 billion
2016	7.4 billion

It took 123 years to move from one to two billion, 33 years to reach 3 billion, and a mere 52 years to grow from 3 billion to 7 billion (in 2012). If the current 1.07% growth rate (as of 2016) continues, world population will double to 15 billion by 2083. What will come of life as we know it? Population growth in the U.S. has also been strikingly geometric.[291]

1850	23 million people
1900	76 million
1930	123 million
1960	180 million
1980	227 million
2016[292]	324 million
2051[293]	400 million *(projected)*

EXPONENTIAL GROWTH IN CARS

Population growth also impacts development and the environment. As population grows, so too does demand for cars, fuel, electricity, land, water, food, minerals, metals, housing, parking lots, roads, malls, sprawling suburbs, exurbs... you name it. Demand grows for everything. Most notable is *land.* More is needed to build housing, malls, parking lots, airports, roads... almost anything you can think of.

Population growth means development. Forests and farms shrink year after year. It means millions and millions more cars pumping enormous amounts of pollution and carbon emissions into the atmosphere. This generation has witnessed geometric increases of cars in China. Just look at these statistics:

Year	# of Cars in China[294]
1980	1.7 million
2009	64 million
2015	140 million

Similar growth in car ownership was seen worldwide from Vietnam to Mexico, but growth applies not just to cars. It applies to *everything.* Demand for electricity (and utilities burning gas and coal), oil, coal, paper, metals, wood, housing, food, *land…* the list is endless. Cars are just the tip of the iceberg.

The elephant in the room.

The footprint of growth in developing countries dramatically affects the environment, atmosphere, earth temperatures (heating up, of course), pollution, sewage, garbage disposal, employment growth, and quality of life. There are countless implications to population growth.

STRESSES ON THE ENVIRONMENT

People create air pollution, garbage, carbon dioxide, and sewage. It requires ever-growing demand for landfills to dump that garbage and stresses oceans absorbing sewage or harmful fluids seeping into waterways. It is impossible to separate population growth from development and growing consumer demand for anything from gasoline to land for housing. All are linked. When air pollution and coal soot are pumped into the air in China, wind spreads it everywhere. Countries cannot hide from its effects. Air and sea know no borders.

China had 1.7 million cars in 1980. That shot up to 140 million cars in a mere 35 years and is projected to reach 200 million by 2020. Those millions of cars require roads that take up land… land that had been farms and forest. Those millions of cars belch pollution into the atmosphere… heat causing carbon dioxide. How many thousands of acres of farmland and forest were destroyed to build roads? The ominous implications are clear. Growth stresses the earth's ability to stay in balance.

Population growth, pollution, consumer demand, and development: you cannot discuss one without the other. People in developing nations desire the quality of life we enjoy in the U.S. It seems fair, but there are environmental consequences. We are feeling it. Global warming is a harbinger of things to come. Land and resources of planet earth are finite. The geometric increase of demand for *everything*, from China to India to Arizona, cannot go on endlessly without consequences. We need to respect nature's ability to absorb the legacy of human growth.

Forests throughout the world are under attack. The vast Brazilian and South American Amazon rainforests, accounting for nearly half of remaining rain forests, have shrunk due to development and consumer demand for food and products. Prior to 1970 the Amazon forests amounted to 4.1 million sq. kilometers. About 18% of Amazon forests, the size of California has been cut down.[295] Those forests absorbed carbon emissions. It is a disastrous combination.

We are playing with nature, and nature always has the last say. Thousands of animal species went extinct in the course of earth history. Many animals go extinct or near extinct now thanks to human activities. We should not be so arrogant as to think we are immune to the forces of nature. When we fight nature, we lose. Astronomically increasing cars. Shrinking forests and rural lands. *The elephant in the room.*

EXPERTS TALK OF ENVIRONMENTAL RUIN

The below excerpts from a 2016 report by *Negative Population Growth* (NPG at www.negativepopulationgrowth.com) summarizes problems mankind will face in the near future as the population reaches 8 billion... 10 billion... 12 billion... 15 billion...[296]

"Following a [2016] September 16th report in the journal Science outlining the world's 'sixth extinction' event – a serious ecological threat which scientists are increasingly convinced is imminent ... the paper begins with a warning: "One species, Homo sapiens, [is] expanding at the expense of most other creatures – and bankrupting biodiversity in the process."

"... NPG special advisor Leon Kolankiewicz draws on three decades of professional experience as an all-around ecologist ... [his] Forum paper highlight[s] our world's frightening reality – of all the species on the planet, fewer and fewer are able to withstand the pressure of human population growth. Kolankiewicz explains: "... never had there existed an organism this powerful and lethal in the 3.5-billion-year history of life on Earth."

"[H]is analysis considers multiple factors, which are worsening global biodiversity loss – such as intense farming and logging operations, and the unwillingness of most national governments to implement (or strictly enforce) policies to protect habitat areas... And our nation's population is growing every day – presently by an average of one person every 11 seconds ... increasing human population density accounted for 90% or more of increasing numbers of threatened species."

NPG President Donald Mann made these observations about political leaders:

"[T]he United States is already unsustainably overpopulated – and yet the Census Bureau projects that we will continue to grow, reaching 400 million by mid-century ... NPG hopes that the alarming reality – artfully relayed within Kolankiewicz's perceptive work – will reach more of our nation's citizens and elected officials. Only then can we foster broad public support for national policies which work to slow, halt, and eventually reverse U.S. population growth – until we reach a much smaller, truly sustainable level."

STRESS ON JOBS GROWTH

Population growth also places stress on the economy. According to a *Wall Street Journal* report, the economy has to create 145,000 jobs each month just to keep up with population growth.[297] It means that over 1.5 million new jobs are needed every year just to *keep the unemployment rate stable*. Those 1.5 million new jobs will not even *lower* the unemployment rate. It is a stunning statistic, a statement as to the gravity of population growth and its stress on the economy.

Other studies suggest the jobs growth number is lower. One states it is closer to 90,000 new jobs/month.[298] Whatever the actual number is (and it will vary depending on population growth and immigration), the effect of population growth is clear. Growth places pressure on jobs creation *just to stand still*.

Adding to the problem, growth continues in competition with industries becoming increasingly mechanized, efficient, and able to handle workload using computers, robots and machines. It creates a combustible brew of problems if worldwide economies cannot keep up with the growing population. Sadly, this seems highly likely. It implies higher unemployment, greater reliance upon government programs, increased poverty, frustration, and the possibility many will resort to crime or drugs as a way of dealing with poverty. All kinds of ugliness brews when people are out of work or struggling to make ends meet.

LAND USE, WATER & POLLUTION

The growing population diminishes resources and requires millions of acres of land for infrastructure and housing. Forests, farms and natural lands steadily recede. That is the legacy of development serving the needs of a growing population. New housing, communities, malls, parking lots, utilities, factories, and roads are needed. It places demands on water supplies in dry regions like California and the Middle East.

Many countries are not building sewage plants that properly clean waste or chemicals. The same can be said of air pollution. While the world endures mounting warming problems, China has built many coal-fired electric plants and now plans to build another 210 coal-fired power plants.[299] It's the wrong direction at the wrong time.

China's over 1.3 billion population desires a comfortable life, and electricity demand therefore grows. Here is yet another consequence of population growth and development. For China, coal is the answer. Filthy coal. It's the wrong solution for an environment increasingly under threat. We may not share land, but we share oceans and air where all that pollution ends up. We all eat fish that breathes in what we put into the ocean. We all breathe the same air. We all witness mounting evidence that the world is getting warmer, yet China continues to plan to burn coal. More than ever.

Mounting sewage, coal-fired utilities and garbage disposal test the world's ability to find landfills, improve air quality and clean the oceans. Will the sewage and pollutants in water endanger our oceans or harm fish and marine life that we rely upon for food? Will life become unbearable with overwhelming traffic as suburbs and exurbs expand and people buy more pollution-causing cars? And all the while, more farms, forests and countryside vanish. In the U.S., what happens when the population reaches 400, 500 and 600 million? What happens when the world population reaches 9 billion, 11 billion, 13 billion? Draw your own conclusions.

Elephant in the room.

OIL, RISING OCEANS & MELTING GLACIERS

Scary questions mount. Will gas-guzzling autos further clog cities and fill the atmosphere with more destructive gases that warm the earth and threaten Antarctic glaciers? According to studies, water stored in Antarctica, if it melts, would raise ocean levels over 200 feet. Cities and countries will vanish. It may not happen by 2100, but mankind is taking shocking risks by thinking this will all pass. What will happen 200 years from now? If those who believe this is nonsense are wrong, it will be too late to avert disaster. The melting of glaciers has already started. The ocean level is eight inches higher since 1900.

There are too many unknowns. When it comes to environment, population growth and development are part of the problem... and part of the solution. When the ocean floods the states of Florida, North and South Carolina, it will be too late to act. It's already starting. Ask anyone who lives on the shores of Florida and North Carolina. The flooding is getting worse. If only those who say it is a hoax would read the facts (let alone the entire chapter here about warming oceans). If only they would be open-minded and fact-driven.

IMMIGRATION

Population growth, leading to increased poverty, puts pressure on the poor to emigrate and cross borders. We see it almost daily on TV: people from Africa arriving in Europe in rickety boats. Some of those boats sink. We read about people from Mexico or Central America entering America illegally trying to escape drug gangs and poverty. Part of it is due to war and poverty, but these are also legacies of population growth. Nations that were poor decades ago are still poor, and their populations have grown. Pressure to leave mounts.

Emigration, jobs creation, economic growth. Everything is affected by population growth. The dry Middle East needs water. Israel, Syria, Turkey, Iraq and Jordan wrangle over water rights from rivers that are increasingly unable to meet the needs of cities in need of water – cities with growing populations that need more and more water each passing year. Poverty creates economic and job stress. It increases anger and political instability. By that measure, the horrible war in Syria (or Yemen or Libya) could in part be due to the stresses brought on by a growing population where jobs and opportunity are inadequate. Directly and indirectly, population growth affects many things from political chaos to unemployment to war.

GOVERNMENT CHAOS & VIOLENCE

To some extent, the violence and wars in the Middle East are a legacy of an extraordinary growth in population since World War II. Larger population creates enormous stress on jobs creation. Economies struggle to keep up with the growing population. Egypt, for example had a population of 23 million in 1955. In 2016 the population reached 94 million. That's a 300% percent increase in 60 years. It's hardly a coincidence that Egypt's politics are unstable. It is typical of many countries. It is hardly a coincidence that Egypt had a tumultuous outbreak of violence with President Mubarak ending up ousted from power. Motivations and reasons varied, but when people are poor, chaos follows. Poverty will do that. Poverty is the legacy of insufficient job growth in the wake of enormous population growth. Note this excerpt from an article in *The Population Institute*:[300]

> *"But the Population Institute's President Lawrence Smith says brisk population growth can quickly lead to overpopulation and instability in poor countries with stressed resources. 'Rapid population increases have an impact on virtually every environmental, health, education, economic and gender equity concern in the world. But when you look at global security, which is only one of them and is one that is important in our minds, you can see some of the changes that are taking place and how countries that are referred to as 'fragile states' are characterized,' says Smith. Population threats [in] Angola and Sudan, for example, are cited by the World Bank as extreme examples of 'low-income countries under stress.' The list also includes Haiti, the Central African Republic, Somalia, the Solomon Islands and Myanmar... Seventeen of the countries, for example, in the severe level [category] are going to more than double their populations by the middle of this century," says Smith... So, these things are run-away situations."*

CONCLUSIONS: UNHAPPY TRUTHS MUST BE SPOKEN

The adage *the road to hell is paved with good intentions* rings true. So does the term *tough love*. Tough love means saying what is for our good, however unpleasant it is to hear.

Question after question was raised throughout this chapter presenting troubling issues with obvious yet complicated solutions. We should try to control growth. How? Draw you own conclusions. But politicians reading this book need to recognize the need to speak more about this topic and to support, and not bash, NGOs and groups that work toward responsible parenting and family planning.

Preventing birth control may appear to be the Christian thing to do (and this author is highly respectful in that way), but there is nothing Christian about watching countries become so overpopulated that people increasingly suffer from the mere accumulation of growth, polluted air and water, and mounting demand for food, water and income. On this matter, good intentions could lead to horrible suffering. *The road to hell is paved with good intentions.*

Issues of family and children are painful. The notion that government should control our personal lives is troublesome and goes against everything we stand for in America. The goal of controlling population growth must come from people themselves. People must voluntary want to take action through responsible family choices. Through education and more publicity, the issue will become better known and understood. Politicians can jump start the process by ending the taboo of avoidance. Birth control and worldwide education on family planning are part of the solution. Plan for the future. Don't trash those who promote solutions even if they occasionally stumble or err.

It is a tough subject, but it needs to be addressed. Good leadership requires courage... the courage to stress upon people that sooner or later population growth may tear apart society. The sooner politicians recognize the need to act instead of beating up on groups that address population growth, the sooner we will be on the path to harmony with nature. Without intelligent planning and action, catastrophic shortages, suffering, and steadily diminishing quality of life will ensue. Scary things loom if we all choose to take no responsibility for our actions and act.

Elephant in the room.

Chapter 20
THE BULLY PULPIT
Inspiring With Bold Goals

BULLY PULPIT: an opportunity to present views and be widely heard by the public; a privilege enjoyed by a leader or politician.

What does it take to convince people to feel hope and work for giant goals? For starters, it requires a President with bold vision and a generational challenge. That is where Presidents like Theodore Roosevelt (TR), Lincoln, Franklin Roosevelt (FDR), Lyndon Johnson (LBJ), and Kennedy (JFK) succeeded where lesser men fell short. Progress involves more than ending gridlock. It means motivating a nation to act. This is what is explored in this chapter.

A LOST ERA OF IDEALISM & CIVIC DUTY
Americans no longer display civic duty or idealism as they once did. There was a time when people fought abusive industries and created unions to protect the working class. They fought unethical employers who abused workers. They fought a mean-spirited laissez-faire system. They fought to make sure the poor were fed, the unemployed received help in times of need, and the elderly were cared for. They fought for civil rights as shameful segregation spread its poisonous tentacles throughout the country. They marched in Montgomery and in the South. One in particular sat in the front seat of a bus to make a statement, then made history. Nowadays we see one of our most quiet hidden diseases: *apathy and loss of hope and dreams.*

As people fought for their rights, our better Presidents acted and steadily moved the country forward. A nation followed their leadership. The better Presidents asked people to take action, and people did. Over the past decades, "government is the problem" thinking convinced millions to fear government. We saw the results in the Great Recession. That is why it is time to revisit the lost era of idealism and civic duty. More than civic duty has diminished. Idealism has faded. Terms like the New Deal, New Frontier and Great Society were a statement that government and people can work together to improve society. Collective duty and sacrifice. Presidents can be summed up into two camps: the highly Conservative Calvin Coolidge ("The business of America is business") and the innovative FDR (the New Deal). We are better off being innovative.

The greatness of legendary Presidents who mastered the bully pulpit was not just towering ideas; it was *how* those ideas were expressed. To appreciate the wonder of FDR is to see his words in their original form, for only then can one begin to understand just why he was able to inspire his country and why he country responded to him.

Much of FDR's legend was in his eloquence. That is preserved on old recordings of his speeches and inspiring fireside chats. As we read his words in the coming pages, wisdom unfolds. He was a master orator because he was a man of vision and compassion for the common man, of professorial erudition and humility.

This always came across. He may not have always made the right decision, but he tried to do the right thing. It inspired people. FDR was a man of ideals and conviction. Great leaders are like this. Were FDR President today, he would have effectively used government to cure our ills and he would have convinced Congress to support him. People comment that we need a modern-day FDR, someone who can wisely use the power of the bully pulpit and offer a nation *vision* and *a plan*.

PATRIOTISM & SACRIFICE

Great leaders, from Lincoln to Martin Luther King, inspired people with a bold vision. They inspired people to act and sacrifice. Civic duty does not die. It simply goes dormant in the presence of lesser men. It needs a giant goal and a spark. The President has the potential to do so if he chooses. It could be oil independence, or public funding of elections, or building 100 million "green" cars. How about all three? Our greatest leaders gave the country a bold challenge. We need that today. We have gone too long without it. Great Presidents embraced problems and asked sacrifice of the country. They spoke the truth. Harry Truman did so when he desegregated the military despite fierce opposition from southern Dixiecrats and racists.

We need this again.

TR used the bully pulpit to advocate the regulation of ruthless business tycoons and protect national parklands and wildlife. JFK inspired civic duty in creating the Peace Corps while urging people to improve the world, and, unlike prior Presidents, he courageously supported the civil rights movement. He launched the moon program. And Lyndon Johnson chose, despite violent opposition, to push the nation to enact the 1964 Civil Rights Act and 1965 Voting Rights Act that ridded the country of injustices shamefully eroding the rights of millions.

We need this again.

The presidency is the greatest bully pulpit in the world. Used by visionary leaders, greatness comes. In the hands of lesser men, it is wasted opportunity. TR embraced the concept in his striking monologues. FDR turned it into an art form in his fireside chats. JFK brought it to the modern television age with his inspiring goals, but since then so much wasted potential, so little idealism.

We need idealism again.

There were moments in history when a President changed history. It does not come often, but when it does, people remember it. JFK did it in 1961 during a speech before Congress:

"We go into space because whatever mankind must undertake, free men must fully share. I therefore ask the Congress... to provide the funds which are needed to meet the following national goals: First, I believe that this nation should commit itself to achieving the goal, before this decade is out, of landing a man on the Moon and returning him safely to the Earth. No single space project in this period will be more impressive to mankind, or more important for the long-range exploration of space; and none will be so difficult or expensive to accomplish."[301]

Eight years later, sadly without JFK, Neil Armstrong walked on the moon. In his Gettysburg Address, Lincoln inspired many amidst divisive civil war:

> *"It is rather for us to be here dedicated to the great task remaining before us – that from these honored dead we take increased devotion to that cause for which they gave the last full measure of devotion – that we here highly resolve that these dead shall not have died in vain – that this nation, under God, shall have a new birth of freedom – and that government of the people, by the people, for the people, shall not perish from the earth."*

Three years later, sadly without Lincoln, slavery was abolished with passage of the 13th Amendment.

The great Presidents knew how to courageously lead the nation. Two paid the ultimate price. Now as much as ever, America needs a President to do what Lincoln, JFK and FDR did in their time: talk honestly to the nation and inspire giant goals.

We need this again.

FDR: OUR GREATEST MODERN ROLE MODEL

Great leaders did not resort to empty clichés and ten-second sound bites. There was substance beyond words, a vision and a sensible plan. Solving problems may take inspirational words, but those words will have to be backed by a plan. Franklin Delano Roosevelt was a great leader because he had vision, a plan, and the ability to rouse a great nation to action.

FDR was at his best during his radio *Fireside Chats* (in an era before television), speaking about three times a year on pressing issues during his four terms from 1933 to 1945. He did it sparingly. He understood that a President loses influence if he says too much or broadcasts speeches too often. Modern Presidents tend to lose grasp of this, especially in an era of 24-7 news, Facebook and Twitter. FDR spoke 33 times to the nation in his fireside chats over a period of 13 years. Among them:[302]

Fireside Chat 1:	On the Banking Crisis (March 12, 1933)
Fireside Chat 4:	On Economic Progress (October 22, 1933)
Fireside Chat 6:	On Government and Capitalism (September 30, 1934)
Fireside Chat 7:	On the Social Security Act (April 28, 1935)
Fireside Chat 8:	On Farmers and Laborers (September 6, 1936)
Fireside Chat 12:	On the Recession (April 14, 1938)
Fireside Chat 14:	On the European War (September 3, 1939)
Fireside Chat 15:	On National Defense (May 26, 1940)
Fireside Chat 16:	On the "Arsenal of Democracy" (December 29, 1940)
Fireside Chat 17:	On an Unlimited National Emergency (May 27, 1941)
Fireside Chat 19:	On the War with Japan (December 9, 1941)
Fireside Chat 20:	On the Progress of the War (February 23, 1942)
Fireside Chat 21:	On Sacrifice (April 28, 1942)

Notice the diversity of topics and how they were educational. FDR discussed his reasons for *Lend Lease* and tried to turn around public opinion about opposing the Nazis. He explained the banking problem in professorial terms that calmed a jittery nation. He spoke about inflation and food prices. He reminisced about his sad visit with impoverished farmers. He asked people to take action, and they usually did.

He often succeeded. When he did, great things happened. When he failed, he was not ridiculed or humiliated as often happens today. People in those days understood the concept of trial and error. If something did not work, you tried another way. People (and politicians) were more patient and forgiving of error. They were forgiving of a President who could not even walk unassisted due to polio. It is hard to imagine our nation and press nowadays displaying such grace, compassion and acceptance.

When speaking, FDR did not overdo it. His chats were broadcast about three times a year, so they remained fresh and influential.

Here is an excerpt from FDR's March 12, 1933 Fireside Chat on the banking crises. Notice his erudite and professorial tone and how eerily his words recall the 2008 banking meltdown:[303]

"I want to talk for a few minutes with the people of the United States about banking – with the comparatively few who understand the mechanics of banking but more particularly with the overwhelming majority who use banks for the making of deposits and the drawing of checks. I want to tell you what has been done in the last few days, why it was done, and what the next steps are going to be."

Like a professor, a friendly neighbor, FDR explains the banking system in straightforward terms.

"Let me state the simple fact that when you deposit money in a bank, the bank does not put the money into a safe deposit vault. It invests your money in many different forms of credit-bonds, commercial paper, mortgages and many other kinds of loans. In other words, the bank puts your money to work to keep the wheels of industry and of agriculture turning around. A comparatively small part of the money you put into the bank is kept in currency – an amount which in normal times is wholly sufficient to cover the cash needs of the average citizen."

FDR explains the crisis. (And how many truly understand the 2008 banking crisis today?)

"What then happened during the last few days of February and the first few days of March? Because of undermined confidence on the part of the public, there was a general rush by a large portion of our population to turn bank deposits into currency or gold, a rush so great that the soundest banks could not get enough currency to meet the demand. The reason for this was that on the spur of the moment it was, of course, impossible to sell perfectly sound assets of a bank and convert them into cash except at panic prices far below their real value. By the afternoon of March 3 scarcely a bank in the country was open to do business."

FDR then outlines steps taken to ease the crisis, offering a clear plan:

"It was then that I issued the proclamation providing for the nation-wide bank holiday, and this was the first step in the government's reconstruction of our financial and economic fabric. The second step was the legislation promptly and patriotically passed by the Congress confirming my proclamation and broadening my powers so that it became possible in view of the requirement of time to extend the holiday and lift the ban of that holiday gradually. This law also gave authority to develop a program of rehabilitation of our banking facilities. I want to tell our citizens in every part of the Nation that the national Congress − Republicans and Democrats alike − showed by this action a devotion to public welfare and a realization of the emergency and the necessity for speed that it is difficult to match in our history."

Notice how Congress (both Republican and Democrat) cooperated with the President! Different times indeed. Finally, FDR offers the permanent solution implemented to solve the crisis:

"The third stage has been the series of regulations permitting the banks to continue their functions to take care of the distribution of food and household necessities and the payment of payrolls."

FDR offered clear explanations, a plan, a solution. *And Congress cooperated.* It was the same with the farming crisis. Here are excerpts from his Sept. 6, 1936 Fireside Chat, "On Farmers and Laborers." He visited troubled regions, spoke to people, and was moved by what he saw. He clearly interacted with the people he visited:

"I have been on a journey of husbandry. I went primarily to see at first-hand conditions in the drought states; to see how effectively Federal and local authorities are taking care of pressing problems of relief and also how they are to work together to defend the people of this country against the effects of future droughts. I saw drought devastation in nine states. I talked with families who had lost their wheat crop, lost their corn crop, lost their livestock, lost the water in their well, lost their garden and come through to the end of the summer without one dollar of cash resources, facing a winter without feed or food."

Later, FDR eloquently offers encouragement to the discouraged:

"No cracked earth, no blistering sun, no burning wind, no grasshoppers, are a permanent match for the indomitable American farmers and stockmen and their wives and children who have carried on through desperate days, and inspire us with their self-reliance, their tenacity and their courage."

Soon, FDR summarizes the steps being taken by government to help those in need.

His words indicate an understanding of the problems farmers faced:

"We have the option, in the case of families who need actual subsistence, of putting them on the dole or putting them to work. They do not want to go on the dole and they are one thousand percent right. We agree, therefore, that we must put them to work for a decent wage, and when we reach that decision we kill two birds with one stone, because these families will earn enough by working, not only to subsist themselves, but to buy food for their stock, and seed for next year's planting. Into this scheme of things there fit of course the government lending agencies which next year, as in the past, will help with production loans."

Later, FDR defends government deficit spending and the attacks by fiscal Conservatives:

"Spending like this is not waste. It would spell future waste if we did not spend for such things now. These emergency work projects provide money to buy food and clothing for the winter; they keep the livestock on the farm; they provide seed for a new crop, and, best of all, they will conserve soil and water in the future in those areas most frequently hit by drought."

FDR then gives an unusually honest critique of the job government has done:

"In 1934 none of us had preparation; we worked without blueprints and made the mistakes of inexperience. Hindsight shows us this. But as time has gone on we have been making fewer and fewer mistakes."

How refreshing! He then makes a plea for people to help each other and show respect:

"The employer-employee relationship should be one between free men and equals. We refuse to regard those who work with hand or brain as different from or inferior to those who live from their property. We insist that labor is entitled to as much respect as property. But our workers with hand and brain deserve more than respect for their labor."

Finally, FDR attacks mean-spirited practices of businessmen who abuse workers and do not pay them enough. Unlike Washington of recent times, FDR agitates for the working class and it is sincere, not just clichés. He is pro-labor:

"There are those who fail to read both the signs of the times and American history. They would try to refuse the worker any effective power to bargain collectively, to earn a decent livelihood and to acquire security. It is those short-sighted ones, not labor, who threaten this country with that class dissension which in other countries has led to dictatorship and the establishment of fear and hatred as the dominant emotions in human life. There is no cleavage between white-collar workers and manual workers, between artists and artisans,

musicians and mechanics, lawyers and accountants and architects and miners."

Roosevelt is a philosopher!   He is direct, unafraid to lash out against corporations or the elite. He supports the rights of the working class. His decency as a leader is as good a role model as one could ask for. We were spared platitudes and rosy expectations. Would a man of such conviction, if President today, stand by and let corporations ship jobs and factories abroad?

FDR was captive to no one. He is not like our modern leaders. He was unafraid, spoke with substance, not merely reciting tired clichés and sound bites. Today's leaders could learn so much from him. He was not one to cater to lobbyists, special interests, or the pretentious, modern political world captive to television, image and sound bites. He was a victim of polio who could not walk without iron braces. He was crippled in the prime of his life. Imagine modern-day politicians or the press allowing a handicapped man to rise in our political culture. But it mattered not to the press or the nation in those days. He was a good President, clearly competent and on top of things, and that was all that mattered. His forceful idealism did his walking for him. How much decency and idealism we have lost from the past.

What is also fascinating is that FDR wrote his own speeches. He did not rely heavily upon speechwriters as Presidents do today. There is a message there. We need a giant intellect if we want a great leader. We need a man of substance, not someone created for TV and the modern era of image-making.

FDR was genuine, flawed, yet a giant. He endured the life of a cripple, being mostly confined to a wheelchair due to polio. But this merely made him greater. His personal suffering seemed to help him connect to the common man. It made him better able to sympathize with those who suffered during the terrible days of the Great Depression. He was also brilliantly sly, a clever leader who knew how to navigate dirty politics and get things done.   A great President needs both compassion and cleverness. A great President need not be a choirboy. He needs to be *effective.*

His modus operandi would work in our times. He was brilliant yet compassionate. He knew how to handle the slickest and most devious politicians, yet he (and his remarkable wife, Eleanor) understood the need to stand up to the rich and focus on helping the poor and disenfranchised. He felt compassion for them and knew how to make their lives better. He was not captive to money. He was captive to conscience, justice and painstakingly thoughtful innovation.

Let us hope a modern FDR someday emerges. He would transform the country in wonderful ways just as FDR did during the Great Depression. He would rouse the nation and lead us to glorious victory just as FDR did during World War II. Let us hope such a great leader comes again.   More importantly, let us seek and welcome that modern-day giant and intellect when he arrives.

FDR IS A ROLE MODEL FOR US NOW

Were our modern lawmakers to approach matters like oil, global warming, outsourcing, or trade deficits like FDR, we would probably be well on our way to recovery. If the President now chose to convert the country to electric cars or end the plague of outsourcing, think how much might change. If he could inspire us to greater goals and propel a nation to patiently address its grave problems, we might resolve so many frustrating problems within a decade.

Just as FDR spoke so eloquently on 33 diverse matters of crisis, so too could our modern President. But it is about more than talking – it is about providing solutions that are practical and doable. There is more a President can do than thought possible. We need not look any further than FDR.

The words spoken by FDR show what is missing in our times. It is no joy to read of the suffering he spoke about, but it is satisfying to read words of depth and erudition. With FDR, we do not see clichés, pandering, or dissection of words to fit the nightly round of 10-second sound bites. Instead, we read words of honesty. We see eloquence with links to a distant past, prose that of a philosopher, Cicero or a poet; sentences of classical beauty speaking not down to people, but with prescience so as to uplift discouraged souls. Honesty about government's failings shames the modern world of finger-pointing. No, his world respected intellect, much unlike present leaders where politicians are often cheerleaders pretending to be of the common folk, pandering to be someone they are not.

With FDR, there are no pretentious speeches, only thoughtful, intelligent analysis. No crowd-rousing words demanding roars; only reasoned explanations. No long-winded clichés saying little but with flair; just clarity as to what government was doing and how it would do better the next time. TV image-conscious lawmakers of the present have lost sight of what great leadership is: trial and error. They won't give a President some space to experiment. If one thing goes wrong, they never let up on the hounding.

However, FDR had that working space during the Depression era. A modern President needs some time and space: to honestly assess problems, experiment, confide to a nation the tough job ahead, ask people (and Congress) to accept the need for sacrifice and patience while government agencies address stubborn problems. If it does not work, we'll try another way. That's how things were done in the 1930s. It helped; it often worked. Sadly, modern politicians will not let the President say, "I made a mistake and I'll do better next time" without humiliating him and getting "debate" points. They are impatient – quick to viciously find fault. It need not be this way. Let failure be a lesson, a path to finding a solution. Don't always beat up on leaders because something tried did not work out. Experimentation is important. *And patience.*

We are now a nation of avoidance and pretensions because we allow our leaders to be this way. Would FDR have accepted outsourcing or oil dependence? No, he would have called a spade a spade, explained the problem, and given Congress a plan. If that failed, he would try something else. He certainly would not have allowed disgrace to drag on for decades. He would have had a new plan of action ready within months and a down-to-earth way of explaining his plan. And, of course, he would have gotten Congress and the nation aboard.

FDR ON PATRIOTISM & SACRIFICE

During a 1942 Fireside Chat, war raging throughout Europe, Asia, Africa, and the Pacific, FDR spoke to the nation in fearful times about the need for patience, sacrifice and patriotism. His words resonate today:

> *"We have had no illusions about the fact that this [war effort] would be a tough job – and a long one. But there is one front and one battle where everyone in the United States – every man, woman, and child – is in action, and will be privileged to remain in action throughout this war. That front is right here at home, in our daily lives, in our daily tasks... This will require, of course, the abandonment not only of luxuries but of many other creature comforts. Every loyal American is aware of his individual responsibility. Whenever I hear anyone saying 'The American people are complacent – they need to be aroused,' I feel like asking him to come to Washington to read the mail that floods into the White House and into all departments of this Government. The one question that recurs through all these thousands of letters and messages is "What more can I do to help my country in winning this war?"*[304]

If we are now going to win our battles for our country's future, our President will have to convince Americans to ask themselves, "What more can I do to help my country?" He must ask the nation to embrace urgency to act, sacrifice, and place country over selfish needs. FDR did that though the dire situation made it easier to reach the soul of a nation. The modern President must convince the country that it faces grave threats though not as clear and imminent as in FDR's time. We can benefit from the wisdom of an era long left in the past. FDR's words were blunt. His words were neither apologetic nor flowery – just to the point.

We need that today.

Most Americans would make such sacrifices given a bold vision. The President must do that now if he is to one day join an elite group of Presidents. Past Presidents had potential, but fell short. Success begs a visionary plan. Potential is a terrible thing to waste, as many lesser men have learned. Potential is omnipresent, but success must be crafted.

IMPORTANT LESSONS FOR US NOW

FDR's greatness was in being honest yet optimistic in presenting solutions alongside experimentation with government programs when efforts failed. His greatness was in his saying we could work harder to become *better*. We have forgotten where we came from. Our leaders are bright people, but they would benefit by studying history. We have better role models than polarized division. Lead, but do it honestly. Trust people to make sacrifices when given conviction and vision. They will not let you down when offered a sensible plan.

The greatness of America was not in being great, but in recognizing faults and addressing them. Lincoln did not start out in 1861 planning to abolish slavery, but events took over and he grew. We were a segregated society when JFK and LBJ took office in 1961, but they took us, as Martin Luther King said, *to the Promised Land...* and Congress worked with them. Inspired leaders used the bully pulpit. They made us better by reminding us that we had a long way to go and they showed a path. Let our modern-day leaders lead not by clichés about American being great, but by giving us a plan to *just plain get better.*

Chapter 21
LOTTERIES & TAXES
State-Sponsored Greed

A rose by any other name is still a rose – and so is a spade. Today, government is in the business of greed as both vender and sponsor. What else could you call lotteries or promoting casinos as a source of tax revenue? Lotteries now run daily nationally. According to *The Atlantic* in its article *Lotteries: America's $70 Billion Shame*, "People spent more money playing the lottery last year than on books, video games, and tickets for movies and sporting events combined."[305]

Lotteries and gambling are now pervasive. Not long ago gambling was something you only saw in Nevada. It spread to Atlantic City. Now it is everywhere. The Indian reservations are notorious for gambling. Huh? Indian reservations? Louisiana, a state with a history of being tough on gambling, joins the list. States promote lotteries and gambling as a source of revenue, but at a price: addiction and obsession by many millions of people. *Call a spade a spade.*

Lotteries and online gambling are forms of greed created by *our own government.* It's a cynical way for government to raise tax revenue. It makes government a quasi sponsor of greed. Lawmakers should reverse the trend by taking government out of the gambling business. Stopping does not mean letting private enterprise take over. It means ending it.

People now buy lottery tickets nationwide at tens of thousands of candy shops, delis and newspaper stands. It's everywhere. I see it advertised on shopping carts at my local supermarket. It is all over TV: the latest lotto numbers announced nearly every night, as if this were important news or newsworthy. This culture of greed – get rich quick schemes – spreads like wildfire. It's not healthy. It's not the right message for children. It is the poor, who can least afford to lose precious money on lotto tickets (or in casinos), who get sucked into it. It is an omnipresent obsession, an unhealthy one – a get-rich scheme where almost everyone loses. The poor should not be sucked into this. It is a cynical back-door way to tax the poor.

CASINOS AT YOUR LOCAL DELI

When approaching a cliff, if you cannot move backward, at least don't move forward. That's how government should handle lotteries and gambling. The number of casinos has grown dramatically. There are now 47 states with 1,511 legal gambling facilities.[306] Put a moratorium on expansion. We let the genie out of the bottle. It is online. New options like fantasy football grow. Will it next be fantasy baseball or hockey, all available on your smartphone? We cannot put the genie back, but at least stop the growth. Government can encourage ethics.

We cannot legislate morality, but we certainly can refrain from promoting greed and addiction for both gambling and lotteries. Let's draw the line. There will be no more casinos and hotels, be it in American territory or "Indian Reservations." Next, tax gambling dearly! If raising revenue is the point, then take the money from the addicts. If they wish to blow their money, let society benefit by using that money for good purposes like better schools (which was the original intent of lotteries). Casinos should not be entitled to windfall profits by drawing in sadly addicted people. Perhaps government cannot stop it, but at least don't make things worse than they are.

LAWMAKERS MUST STAND FOR INTEGRITY

End lotteries and casino expansion. Taking on such a policy would require courageous decisions by lawmakers. It would require that they be brutally honest and tell the public the truth, as FDR would. If you want good schools, social services, a strong military, a balanced government budget, or enough police to keep your streets safe, you will need to pay sufficient taxes. *We will not do it by promoting gambling resorts and lottery tickets.*

We are a nation of gamblers. Whether you gamble at a casino, buy lottery tickets, or bet on horses and sports events, you are a gambler. Gambling is defined in the Oxford Dictionary as "playing games of chance for money." Our government has become a bookie – a "person" whose business is taking bets. If "bookie" does not define what government does in selling lottery tickets, what does define what government is sponsoring nationwide?

Government must pull out of the bookie business and stop using dubious methods to raise revenue. Oh, and "privatizing" is no solution. Some $56.4 billion was spent on lottery tickets in 2007, coming to $282 for everyone among the 200 million taxpayers. Tax them $282 – it is a more ethical way to raise revenue than lotteries. Were state lawmakers to end lotteries and explain to people why, they would likely earn an outpouring of respect for having the courage to do the right thing – and angering the addicted so needing of help. Well, help them! Don't take their money then leave them out in the cold. Do the right thing. Run government ethically.

Government should not be in the lottery/gambling business. Those who would complain about ending lotteries remind me of a joke from *Saturday Night Live* after the Berlin Wall fell: the Berlin handball league protested. Government should not promote gambling resorts or sell lottery tickets. Government should not promote obsession and addiction. Be it in a decade or a generation, government must get out of the gambling business.

A nation is great because its foundation is based upon honesty and ethics. *It is time to see ourselves for what we have become.*

Chapter 22
A PARABLE ABOUT IRAQ
Lessons from a War

The war in Iraq. So much can be said. What went wrong? What lessons were learned? The answer (for this author) is not to try to answer. Instead, I wrote this parable with messages within. Literature addresses burning issues quite effectively.

A mighty land was attacked by an evil witch.
That land was led by a stubborn knight.
He was a dragon-slaying fella with a clear agenda:
He'd kill that witch once in sight.
His advisors said things not too smart
Based on facts from kingdom spies.
And the knight told his people all he heard
And it turned out not so wise.

The witch was never found though they looked far and wide
Putting the knight between "a-roq" and a hard place.
It turned out facts spies said were wrong
And the knight had to save face.
He said the witch hid in the land of Raq
And he'd smoke the witch out of his cave.
And this pretty much sums up all the knight said
In every speech he gave.

And the fellow bellowed,
"Peasants thou heed my words:
We all live in dangerous times."
And the kingdom listened closely for it truly feared
The dark witch's ghastly crimes.
Now those ghastly crimes were truly nasty.
On this everyone agreed.
The knight bellowed the king of Raq was also a threat
And in bed with the witch, indeed.

He said spies had learned the king of Raq
Posed a clear and imminent threat.
Raq had jousts of mass destruction,
Though no jousts had been found as yet.
The knight rounded up horses and cavalry
To smite the evil king of Raq,
Then asked saber-rattling neighbors in a foreign land,
"Would you lend a helping hand?"

Other kings also thought Raq had gone sour,
But what spies said was simply not true.
The French king then asked, "If jousts are not found,
Just what then will you do?"
So the knight shot back with a mighty roar,
"You're either with us or you're not."
But friendly kings whined, "We don't like this war,"
Which placeth a twist in the plot.

A young prince, Sir Roos, said Raq posed no threat,
Saying "People, there's no reason to fret."
But the stubborn knight replied, "We must stay the course.
Success is a sure bet."
So the war began and the knight beamed, "All's well."
'board his ship he roared, "Mission Accomplished."
Raq fell, but darn, no jousts of destruction were found.
The knight now rued things he had wished.

Throughout the kingdom vassals complained,
"Were jousts found anywhere?"
And the only effect this had on the knight
Was to send more brave knights there.
Brave knights looked wide and far for jousts,
But caught no more than a cold.
Many vassals asked, "What are we fighting for?
What's accomplished by this war?"

The young prince, Sir Roos, told angry crowds,
"There's nothing to fear but fear."
The stubborn knight fetched his horse and fled.
Many a folk did taunt and jeer.
And the wise prince said to the sullen crowds,
"Both friends and foes must talk,
For witches only rush away when they hear the hawk."

"For the hawk yells, 'Hurry, there's a dragon to slay'
When it turns out there was none.
And it's wrong if the hawk must get his way
By justice left undone."
And that's the story of the witch and the prince
With lessons there for everyone.
We can ill-afford wisdom ignored.
The pen is mightier than the sword.

EPILOGUE
An Innovative Era Looms

Sooner or later Conservative and, so to speak, Tea Party activists (or whatever new groups emerge) will have come to accept the emerging trends of global warming and automation, both with scary implications in the coming years as rising oceans swallow our lands, widespread unemployment mounts, and a choking middle class slips into poverty. If none of these occur over the next two decades, all the better, but chances are that they are going to come and the evidence will be come so strong that even the more stubborn holdouts will shift positions.

Shifting positions is the nature of politics. Isolationalists clinged to neutrality as late as Dec. 6, 1941. Opposition to American involvement in the raging wars in Europe and the Pacific was strong. Two days later, Congress voted 388-1 and the Senate voted 88-0 to declare war. Things can change things that fast. Similarly enormous change in our country's economic path, though over a period of several years, following the 1929 stock market crash the deepening economic collapse. By 1933, the country was ready for change and it overwhelmingly elected FDR and an overwhelming Democratic Congress to implement quick, massive change.

Things work that way. Sooner or later, events will trigger such a massive generational change for our times. The question is will such change come steadily with healthy acceptance of facts, or will such change be forced upon us in a convulsive serious of horrible economic collapses. That, too, is a choice our generation must make. If we do not accept the inevitable, change will forced upon us. The 2008 economic collapse was a warning: do we act wisely and prevent disaster or do we wait for disaster giving us no choice but change? Hopefully, we will choose the former. That chapter of our history steadily unfolds.

Change is inevitable and it will happen with insightful planning in a positive manner once Democrats and Progressives cease their bellicose and combative approach to conservatives and become fact driven, respectful and less combative. But one way or another change will come. It has to for the only likely alternative will be the collapse of American democracy.

Epic generational change happened in the past. It happened with the America Revolution and the Civil War. It happened, more relevantly to our current circumstances, in the 1930s as the Great Depression and economic collapse forced the transition from laissez-faire to an economic paradigm embracing government regulation of and invention with the economy. A new era of progressive change will come eventually – maybe not in a year or two, but *in time*.

Convulsive societal events will unfold. *Watch.* The chapter on automation, pointing out the inevitable consequences of automation, indicates we are creeping towards that point of a new economic paradigm – *a modern New Deal*. Sooner or later economic conservatives will shift just as past economic conservatives shifted (uncomfortably and reluctantly) during the 1930s. The question is whether it will come in a steady, healthy manner or whether disastrous economic disruption will be needed to create for a common sense, cooperative path towards an economic paradigm and government policies *designed* for the 21st Century of computer technology, automation and rising oceans.

Sooner or later we need to act. It *could* happen as a healthy evolution if political parties learn to respect each other and accept (happily or not) cooperation as a tool for government. It *could* happen if politicians reject bitter and vicious conflict. The choice will come one way or the other, be it through cooperation or being forced upon us through economic collapse or, worse yet, worldwide war.

America can boldly act or America can sleepwalk. Thus said, this book ends where it began: a parable about a stumbling, fading giant. The first chapter, *A Sleeping Giant,* and the WWII generation sent a message: things can quickly change for the better with comprehensive planning and a bold vision. A new era of progressive policies is inevitable. The clock ticks.

Parables are powerful. They offer guidance with subtlety. The metaphor of the sleeping giant has implications. He sleeps and stumbles, but is full of potential. But as he sleeps, some around him, depending on him, yearn for this giant to awaken. Others – petty, mean, eager to disrupt – take advantage of his slumber. The giant is alive, but how long must he lie dormant before he wakes up to find problems too difficult, his enemies too powerful?

If our country, sleeping as it did as Hitler laid siege to all of Europe except brave England, had slept longer – had Pearl Harbor not stirred the nation to war – would Hitler have won? Would Nazis have invented a nuclear bomb before us, used it to level New York and Washington, and place humanity in an ice-age of human depravity at the hands of ruthless, psychopathic killers? In those days, those who created that sleeping giant were "isolationists." We now face similarly fearful threats from terrorism and extremism in the Middle East (and spreading).

Prior to WWII, isolationists said war was terrible. Avoid fires raging in Europe. In a way they were right, but you have to be right at the *right* time. A similar message lies for us today with terrorism. Be right, but be wise enough to know when it is the wrong time to be passive, for there is danger to being a sleeping giant. The longer it takes to awaken, the harder it becomes to make the world right.

Mediocre leaders will lead us to a bleak future if citizens do not force leaders to improve. Spain and Portugal, centuries ago, were world powers. That changed. Corrupt leadership dooms mighty empires. We are not immune to these forces. If our leaders do not address problems, we could be the next Spain or Portugal. If Washington and leaders throughout the 50 states do not change the status quo, our country may drift toward irrelevancy and that is a scary thought for us and allies depending on us to protect democracy and the free world. Indeed, they (and our enemies) closely eye the sleeping giant.

Our country is a beacon of hope and decency to a world traumatized by tyranny and terrorism. It is a world in need of a righteous giant, but lasting power is derived from economic might. Such might defeated Nazi Germany and stared down cold war Soviet Union. Behind that power was a vibrant economy. We must never lose grasp of this.

Theodore Roosevelt famously commented, "Speak softly but carry a big stick." The "stick" derives from military might, but true power derives from a thriving economy... just not at the expense of social justice and planet earth. If our economic might declines, America will lose influence. Polarized politics is a risk foolishly taken by mediocre leaders.

We need steady, quality leadership, as we had in the days of FDR, so that America can effectively confront threats. Our country must remain able to project power and that means keeping our economy and schools healthy… key themes of this book. We defeated fascism not with words, but with tanks, airplanes, ships, and endless supplies. We rebuilt a shattered Europe after WWII with endless supplies. *The Marshall Plan.* A thriving American economy fueled both. A government of action and innovation was key.

Power relies upon innovation and a well-run government. Shutting down or bashing government is the road to disaster. It is oppression that we should fear, not innovative government. Anything less and we will become a feeble sleeping giant. This book presents a blueprint to keep us vibrant, but it requires that our leaders get their priorities straight. Future generations deserve this. Strive for greatness, but start by just getting *better.*

Citizens must put immense pressure on leaders to change the status quo and reinvent the culture of Washington. Thinking out of the box. Public financing of elections. Ending the corrosive effect of money in politics. And we need to restore political civility, a political "Geneva Peace Conference." *Division* should never again describe America.

We need a plan for the future – the future of 10, 30 and 50 years down the road. Once leaders improve, everything is possible. It is time that we as a nation return to progressive government that takes action, passes important legislation, experiments, innovates, supports prudent fiscal management, and tries to move America forward… and make us better…

   … and awaken a sleeping giant.

Acknowledgments

I appreciate the many suggestions from family and friends in helping me edit the book and remaining journalistic, objective and nonpartisan. I especially thank my loyal friend Michele, whose many hours of proofreading and whose vigilant eye for anything from commas to hyphens, were very helpful. She kept me grounded indeed on use of dangling modifiers – and an occasional laugh. In terms of researching topics covered in the book, the most striking acknowledgement is modern society itself. In a word, the Internet.

I see firsthand how remarkable the Internet has become in pursuit of a free society open to information, ideas and facts. Oceans of it! The enormity of information available online is a modern miracle. The openness of ideas and a government freely providing information to the public is underestimated.

I was struck during one discussion with my "aged" uncle (as he calls himself) when he said with sadness, upon my commenting how much I research online, that libraries have become obsolete. Well, I replied, libraries aren't obsolete. They've simply been made available to us at home at the touch of your finger on a smartphone, iPad or tablet.

For sure, the stunning amount of information online has reduced the dominance of libraries. I cannot say I miss those long days back at Northwestern University camping out in the library and thumbing through card catalogues. Now, I can do a thousandfold more in my living room. Now *that* is change for the good.

My extensive use of the Internet (and the miracle of Google searches) helped me recognize the modern miracle of the age of online information. Our generation has quietly witnessed the advent of a new media with stunning access to information that would be the envy of the past generations of writers and journalists. Every time you think about bad influences on the Internet or wasted potential, remember this: the Internet, in the hands of those who use it intelligently, is also the equivalent of having millions of books and periodicals in the palm of your hand anywhere in the world from home to a forest. It's one of the most unappreciated miracles of our times.

The Internet revolutionized access to information much as Gutenberg changed the world for the good when he invented the modern printing press around 1440. The information we can get on the Internet is a bottomless treasure chest for writers, reporters and students... if used intelligently. This gives me hope for the future. If the news media and free press are called the fourth estate, providing a check on government and power, I would agree that the Internet (used wisely) should be called *the fifth estate.*

- James Behr

About the Author. James Behr is an Adjunct Professor at Manhattan College and an attorney and journalist. Behr was awarded his Juris Doctor from City University of New York Law School and is a member of the New York Bar. He was awarded his B.A. in Political Science from Northwestern University as well as M.M. and B.A. degrees from The Juilliard School. Behr resides in Manhattan.

END NOTES

Chapter 1: The Sleeping Giant
1 http://www.amny.com/transit/jfk-airport-twa-flight-center-hotel-to-bring-swinging-jet-age-back-to-nyc-1.12762785

Chapter 2: Governing Creatively
2 New York Times, op ed, Dec. 24, 2008, "Time to Reboot America," Thomas Friedman, A25
3 http://earthquakes.ok.gov/
4 http://www.nytimes.com/interactive/2015/02/23/us/oklahoma-quakes.html?_r=0
5 www.chrisp.com.html
6 U.S. Primary Energy Consumption by Source and Sector, 2007," Energy Information Administration, http://www.eia.doe.gov/emeu/aer/pecss_diagram.html
7 Apteras, http://gas2.org/2008/03/12/apteras-26000-electric-car-and-300-mpg-hybrid-coming-soon/
8 http://www.chinahighlights.com/travelguide/transportation/the-fastest-train.htm
9 Teen Drug Abuse, http://www.teendrugabuse.us/teen_drug_use.html
10 MSNBC & Maplight, http://www.msnbc.com/hardball/how-much-does-it-cost-win-seat-congre and http://maplight.org/content/73190
11 CBS Sixty Minutes, http://www.cbsnews.com/news/preview-dialing-for-dollars/

Chapter 3: Taking on Free Trade & Outsourcing
12 http://www.cnbc.com/2016/07/21/adjusted-for-inflation-the-federal-minimum-wage-is-worth-less-than-50-years-ago.html
13 http://www.thesimpledollar.com/a-dose-of-financial-reality/
14 http://www.thesimpledollar.com/a-dose-of-financial-reality/
15 http://inequality.org/minimum-wage/
16 http://www.huffingtonpost.com/2013/02/13/minimum-wage-productivity_n_2680639.html?ncid=engmodushpmg00000006
17 China Labor Watch, http://www.chinalaborwatch.org/en/web/article.php?article_id=50304
18 Economic Policy Institute, http://www.epi.org/content.cfm/briefingpapers_bp147
19 Sources: Department of Energy and Maryland Energy Administration and Apollo PAC, Institute for the Analysis of Global Security)
20 Economic Policy Institute, http://www.epi.org/content.cfm/bp188
21 Associate Press, "Factory Jobs: 3 Million Lost Since 2000, Apr 20, 2008 By Martin Crutsinger, AP Economics Writer http://www.breitbart.com/article.php?id=D8OKGR480&show_article=
22 China Labor Watch, http://www.chinalaborwatch.org/en/web/article.php?article_id=50304
23 Sweatshops in Mexico, http://www.newint.org/easier-english/Garment/sweatmexico.html
24 Business Week, "A World of Sweatshops," http://www.businessweek.com/2000/00_45/b3706008.htm
25 Sweatshops in Mexico, http://www.newint.org/easier-english/Garment/sweatmexico.html
26 http://www.ibj.com/articles/57293-carrier-plant-closing-shows-vagaries-of-modern-manufacturing
27 The World Almanac, 2008, pg. 96
28 Source: Franklin D. Roosevelt, Inaugural Address, March 4, 1933, as published in Samuel Rosenman, ed., The Public Papers of Franklin D. Roosevelt, Volume Two: The Year of Crisis, 1933 (New York: Random House, 1938), 11–16. AMERICA%20On%20The%20BRINK%2012-16a/XX%20RESEARCH%20FILE/FDR%20Inaugural%20Address.html
29 The Telegraph, UK, http://www.telegraph.co.uk/news/worldnews/1567849/'Gap-sweatshop-children'-saved-in-India-raid.html
30 The Telegraph, UK, http://www.telegraph.co.uk/news/worldnews/1567849/'Gap-sweatshop-children'-saved-in-India-raid.html
31 http://www.statista.com/statistics/220041/total-value-of-us-trade-balance-since-2000/
32 http://cnsnews.com/news/article/terence-p-jeffrey/365694500000-merchandise-trade-deficit-china-hit-record-2015
33 http://www.investopedia.com/terms/c/corporateinversion.asp
34 Educating for Justice, http://www.educatingforjustice.org/stopnikesweatshops.htm
35 Educating for Justice, http://www.educatingforjustice.org/stopnikesweatshops.htm

36 http://www.maryferrell.org/wiki/index.php/Kennedy_Presidency
37 Kennedy press conference,
   http://www.jfklibrary.org/Historical+Resources/Archives/Reference+Desk/Press+Conferences/003
   POF05Pressconference30_04111962.htm
38 Source: Franklin D. Roosevelt, Inaugural Address, March 4, 1933, as published in Samuel Rosenman,
   ed., The Public Papers of Franklin D. Roosevelt, Volume Two: The Year of Crisis, 1933 (New
   York: Random House, 1938), 11–16. AMERICA%20On%20The%20BRINK%2012-
   16a/XX%20RESEARCH%20FILE/FDR%20Inaugural%20Address.html
39 http://thehill.com/opinion/op-ed/264136-reform-tax-code-keep-companies-in-us
40 https://www.recode.net/platform/amp/2017/3/25/15051308/us-uk-germany-japan-robot-job-
automation
41 http://www.economist.com/news/special-report/21700758-will-smarter-machines-cause-mass-
unemployment-automation-and-anxiety
42 https://mobile.nytimes.com/2017/05/31/business/economy/volatile-income-economy-jobs.html
43 http://whatis.techtarget.com/definition/gig-economy
44 https://futurism.com/is-universal-basic-income-a-good-idea-stick-around-because-were-about-to-find-
out/

Chapter 4: Deregulation & The Broken Banks
45 Oxford American Dictionary, Heald Colleges Edition.
46 New York Times, Dec. 18, 2008, "Wall Street Profits Were a Mirage, But Huge Bonuses Were Real,"
   by Louise Story
47 Oxford American Dictionary, Heald Colleges Edition.
48 http://inequality.org/99to1/facts-figures/
49 https://www.washingtonpost.com/news/wonk/wp/2015/05/21/the-top-10-of-americans-own-76-of-the-
   stuff-and-its-dragging-our-economy-down/?utm_term=.2d21f5375683
50 Interview with Paul Samuelson on The News Hour, PBS, Dec. 26, 2008.
51 http://blogs.wsj.com/economics/2012/10/01/total-global-losses-from-financial-crisis-15-trillion/
52 Foreign Affairs, Jan./Feb., "The Great Crash, 2009: A Geopolitical Setback for the West," by Roger
   Altman, pgs. 5-7
53 http://seekingalpha.com/article/97843-the-evolution-and-extinction-of-lehman-brothers
54 http://www.atimes.com/atimes/Global_Economy/JC12Dj02.html
55 http://www.nytimes.com/roomfordebate/2016/04/14/has-dodd-frank-eliminated-the-dangers-in-the-
   banking-system?nytmobile=0?referer=https://www.google.com/
56 Fireside Chat on banking, March 12, 1933 http://www.mhric.org/fdr/chat1.html
57 [For an informative analysis on this, see The America Prospect Jan./Feb. 2009, "A Global New
   Deal"] "A Global New Deal, by Harold Meyerson, pg. 10, Jan./Feb. 2008, The American Prospect,
   www.Prospect.org
58 http://www.google.com/search?client=safari&rls=en&q=runables+liability&ie=UTF-8&oe=UTF-8
59 New York Times, Dec. 25, 2008, "Federal Cases of Stock Fraud Drop sharply," Eric Lichtblau, A1
60 New York Times, Jan. 6, 2009, op ed, "Where Is Our Ferdinand Pecora?" Ron Chernow
61 New York Times, Dec. 25, 2008, "Couple Who Created Innovative Mortgage Fall Under Scrutiny"
   A1-24
62 New York Times, Jan. 15, 2008, A1, "Swindlers Find Growing Market In Foreclosures, John Leland

Chapter 5: Rising Oceans & Temperature
63 http://ngm.nationalgeographic.com/2013/09/rising-seas/if-ice-melted-map
64 http://usatoday30.usatoday.com/weather/resources/coldscience/aiceshet.htm
65 https://thinkprogress.org/were-aiming-at-200-feet-or-more-of-sea-level-rise-here-s-what-that-looks-
   like-5500c703671b
66 http://www.dailymail.co.uk/news/article-2945078/U-S-maps-major-cities-look-like-submerged-
   hundreds-feet-water.html
67 http://www.waterencyclopedia.com/Ge-Hy/Glaciers-Ice-Sheets-and-Climate-Change.html
68 http://usatoday30.usatoday.com/weather/resources/coldscience/aiceshet.htm
69 http://oceanservice.noaa.gov/facts/sealevel.html
70 http://www.climatecentral.org/news/antarctic-riddle-south-pole-melt-17938

71 http://environment.nationalgeographic.com/environment/global-warming/big-thaw/
72 https://www.epa.gov/climate-indicators/climate-change-indicators-glaciers
73 http://www.livescience.com/39147-arctic-sea-ice-melting.html
74 http://ocean.nationalgeographic.com/ocean/explore/pristine-seas/critical-issues-sea-temperature-rise/
75 Source: Global%20warming%20and%20sea%20levels.html
76 "A Climate Change Countdown for NASA," New York Times, April 5, 2016, pg. D1
77 http://earthobservatory.nasa.gov/Features/WorldOfChange/decadaltemp.php
78 http://climate.nasa.gov/400ppmquotes/
79 http://usatoday30.usatoday.com/weather/resources/coldscience/aiceshet.htm
80 http://news.nationalgeographic.com/news/2013/10/131031-climate-ocean-temperatures-years/
81 http://sealevel.climatecentral.org/news/floria-and-the-rising-sea
82 http://climate.nasa.gov/evidence/
83 http://usatoday30.usatoday.com/weather/resources/coldscience/aiceshet.htm
84 https://thinkprogress.org/were-aiming-at-200-feet-or-more-of-sea-level-rise-here-s-what-that-looks-like-5500c703671b
85 http://www.dailymail.co.uk/news/article-2945078/U-S-maps-major-cities-look-like-submerged-hundreds-feet-water.html
86 http://www.waterencyclopedia.com/Ge-Hy/Glaciers-Ice-Sheets-and-Climate-Change.html
87 http://www.rmcmi.org/education#.WE7FBBydzjQ
88 http://phys.org/news/2015-01-million-gallons-minute-oil-cheap.html
89 http://www.rmcmi.org/education#.WE7FBBydzjQ
90 http://www.greencarreports.com/news/1093560_1-2-billion-vehicles-on-worlds-roads-now-2-billion-by-2035-report
91 http://www.greencarreports.com/news/1093560_1-2-billion-vehicles-on-worlds-roads-now-2-billion-by-2035-report
92 https://www.reference.com/vehicles/many-airplanes-world-7e1c82a9521508ed
93 https://www.reference.com/vehicles/many-airplanes-world-7e1c82a9521508ed
94 http://climate.nasa.gov/400ppmquotes/
95 http://climate.nasa.gov/400ppmquotes/
96 http://climate.nasa.gov/400ppmquotes/
97 http://www.rmcmi.org/education#.WE7FBBydzjQ
98 http://www.rmcmi.org/education#.WE7FBBydzjQ
99 http://www.rmcmi.org/education#.WE7FBBydzjQ
100 http://www.rmcmi.org/education#.WE7FBBydzjQ
101 http://oceanservice.noaa.gov/facts/sealevel.html
102 http://climate.nasa.gov/evidence/
103 http://climate.nasa.gov/evidence/#footnote_2
104 http://climate.nasa.gov/400ppmquotes/
105 http://climate.nasa.gov/400ppmquotes/
106 http://climate.nasa.gov/400ppmquotes/
107 http://climate.nasa.gov/evidence/#footnote_3
108 http://climate.nasa.gov/evidence/#footnote_4
109 http://climate.nasa.gov/evidence/#footnote_9
110 http://climate.nasa.gov/evidence/#footnote_10
111 http://climate.nasa.gov/evidence/#footnote_11
112 http://climate.nasa.gov/evidence/#footnote_12
113 http://climate.nasa.gov/evidence/#footnote_13
114 http://climate.nasa.gov/evidence/#footnote_14
115 http://climate.nasa.gov/evidence/#footnote_15
116 http://www.universetoday.com/22577/venus-greenhouse-effect/
117 https://www.ncdc.noaa.gov/paleo/ctl/cliihis100.html
118 http://www.climatecentral.org/news/the-last-time-co2-was-this-high-humans-didnt-exist-15938
119 http://ircamera.as.arizona.edu/NatSci102/NatSci102/lectures/venus.htm
120 https://www.nasa.gov/content/goddard/antarctic-sea-ice-reaches-new-record-maximum/
121 https://www.nasa.gov/feature/goddard/2016/2016-arctic-sea-ice-wintertime-extent-hits-another-record-low

122 http://nsidc.org/arcticseaicenews/
123 http://www.livescience.com/39147-arctic-sea-ice-melting.html
124 http://www.realclimate.org/index.php/archives/2011/06/2000-years-of-sea-level/
125 https://www2.ucar.edu/climate/faq/how-much-has-global-temperature-risen-last-100-years
126 http://ocean.si.edu/sea-level-rise
127 http://nca2014.globalchange.gov/report/our-changing-climate/sea-level-rise
128 http://www.nytimes.com/2017/01/18/science/earth-highest-temperature-record.html?mwrsm=Email
129 https://www.ncdc.noaa.gov/sotc/global/201513
130 http://www.antarcticglaciers.org/question/ice-antarctica-melt-much-global-sea-level-rise-quickly-likely-happen/
131 http://www.businessinsider.com/5-terrifying-impacts-of-rising-sea-levels-2015-2
132 http://therealdeal.com/miami/2016/04/07/miami-beach-property-values-may-fall-as-sea-levels-rise-experts/
133 http://www.charlestoncitypaper.com/charleston/new-interactive-map-shows-effects-of-sea-level-rise-on-charleston/Content?oid=4972978
134 http://www.npr.org/templates/story/story.php?storyId=120498442
135 http://www.nytimes.com/interactive/2012/11/24/opinion/sunday/what-could-disappear.html?_r=0
136 http://www.climatecentral.org/news/us-with-10-feet-of-sea-level-rise-17428
137 http://www.climatecentral.org/news/us-with-10-feet-of-sea-level-rise-17428
138 https://nsidc.org/cryosphere/quickfacts/icesheets.html
139 http://www.oceanites.org/antarctica/
140 http://www.climatecentral.org/news/melt-of-key-antarctic-glaciers-unstoppable-studies-find-17426
141 http://news.nationalgeographic.com/news/2014/05/140512-thwaites-glacier-melting-collapse-west-antarctica-ice-warming/
142 http://www.livescience.com/42994-gulf-coast-sea-level-rise-extremes.html
143 http://www.nature.com/articles/nclimate1979.epdf?referrer_access_token=9Oz45XnDaBZp7ls_Jzvch
9RgN0jAjWel9jnR3ZoTv0N9E7c_E3-bmB5JRDBAJanymHn-
949fELJ8OgAj1_X9mfRfd6EPvTHhn7NkFI-
4k9scmL6uKylIWkymJl6IJgZCDt3mUtlRaADBWs1WpOSDmieYgeowKz5wlkLzbGq13G1ZGW
4bDgHExb43XEMY-
SdyYRf8654nKXK9DFHtppzo5fO5ovBftGwYch2kRdEsxD5OIjb8XLVmdo4UViyx7ngZKDQgR
K37NvjPuIHmmoJmQ23hMKoUlC22R1KCTE8DWe4%253D
144 https://www.epa.gov/climate-impacts/climate-impacts-alaska
145 https://www.epa.gov/climate-impacts/climate-impacts-alaska#Reference%203
146 https://www.epa.gov/climate-impacts/climate-impacts-alaska#Reference%203
147 http://www.nytimes.com/interactive/2016/11/29/science/100000004788791.mobile.html?_r=1

Chapter 6: From Oil to a Green Economy
148 New York Times, op ed, "Jihad's True Face," William Kristol, Dec. 1, 2008, A29
149 http://www.climatehotmap.org/global-warming-effects/drought.html
150 http://www.teslamotors.com/
151 Apteras, http://gas2.org/2008/03/12/apteras-26000-electric-car-and-300-mpg-hybrid-coming-soon/
152 http://archives.cnn.com/2001/TECH/space/05/25/kennedy.moon/
153 United States at War, Development and Administration of the War Program by the Federal Government, Prepared Under the Auspices of The Committee of Records of War Administration by the War Records Section, Bureau of the Budget, http://www.ibiblio.org/hyperwar/ATO/Admin/WarProgram/index.html
154 War Materials Source: Military%20production%20during%20World%20War%20II%20-%20Wikipedia,%20the%20free%20encyclopedia.html
155 FDR Fireside Chat #21. http://www.mhric.org/fdr/chat21.html
156 Energytommow.com, international energy agency, U.S. Department of Energy
157 Sources: Institute for the Analysis of Global Security and Apollo PAC
158 Sources: Department of Energy and Maryland Energy Administration and Apollo PAC
159 New York Times, "Idle Electronics, Busy Draining Power," May 10, 2016, pg. D3
160 http://www.teslamotors.com/
161 http://www.chevrolet.com/electriccar/

162 venturebeat.com/2008/01/10/27-electric-cars-companies-ready-to-take-over
163 http://gas2.org/2008/04/23/affordable-electric-cars
164 New York Times, Nov. 12, 2008, B9, "As Public Transit Grows, Cities Desire Streetcars," John Tabliabue
165 Energytommow.com, international energy agency, U.S. Department of Energy
166 www.chrisp.com.html
167 U.S. Primary Energy Consumption by Source and Sector, 2007," Energy Information Administration, http://www.eia.doe.gov/emeu/aer/pecss_diagram.html
167 www.chrisp.com.html
168 New York Times, "Idle Electronics, Busy Draining Power," May 10, 2016, pg. D3
169 Source: Energy Innovations report and Apollo PAC
170 New York Times, "Idle Electronics, Busy Draining Power," May 10, 2016, pg. D3
171 GAO Report, Energy Efficiency: Potential Fuel Savings Generated by a National Speed Limit Would Be Influenced by many Other Factors, pg.ß
172 New York Times, editorial, A32, Jan. 14, 2009, "Geothermal Future"
173 New York Times, op ed, "A Better Shade of Green," J. Wayne Leonard, A21, Jan. 24, 2009.
174 Space Studies Institute, www.Beaming%20Electricity.html
175 Fraser.stlousfed.org, download/114/section 13.
176 The American Prospect, "Obama's Economic Opportunity," Robert Kuttner, p. 13, Jan./Feb. 2009
177 The World Almanac and Book of Facts 2008, pgs. 54-55

Chapter 7: Solar America
178 http://www.businessinsider.com/map-shows-solar-panels-to-power-the-earth-2015-9
179 http://um.dk/en/news/newsdisplaypage/?newsid=25147b44-3dce-4647-8788-ad9243c22df2
180 https://www.theguardian.com/environment/2015/jul/10/denmark-wind-windfarm-power-exceed-electricity-demand
181 https://www.technologyreview.com/s/601514/germany-runs-up-against-the-limits-of-renewables/
182 http://useconomy.about.com/od/usdebtanddeficit/a/National-Debt-by-Year.htm
183 http://www.businessinsider.com/map-shows-solar-panels-to-power-the-earth-2015-9
184 http://engineering.mit.edu/ask/how-many-solar-panels-do-i-need-my-house-become-energy-independent
185 http://3s9h7h3y0i6u2n9j4h5vgkf1.wpengine.netdna-cdn.com/wp-content/uploads/2013/02/solar-infographic-1.jpg
186 http://consciouslifenews.com/solar-panels-every-familys-roof-infographic/1150012/
187 http://engineering.mit.edu/ask/how-many-solar-panels-do-i-need-my-house-become-energy-independent
188 http://www.cfr.org/united-states/implications-reduced-oil-imports-us-trade-deficit/p32245

Chapter 9: Electric Cars
189 The American Prospect, "Obama's Economic Opportunity," Robert Kuttner, p. 14, Jan./Feb. 2009
190 Fraser.stlousfed.org, download/114/section 13.
191 The American Prospect, "Obama's Economic Opportunity," Robert Kuttner, p. 13, Jan./Feb. 2009

Chapter 10: Toxic Politics
192 http://www.politicususa.com/2016/08/09/time-weeks-trump-campaign-threatened-kill-hillary-clinton.html

Chapter 10: Toxic Politics
193 http://www.politicususa.com/2016/08/09/time-weeks-trump-campaign-threatened-kill-hillary-clinton.html
194 http://www.oxfordlearnersdictionaries.com/us/definition/english/falsely-shouting-fire-in-a-crowded-theater
195 http://www.nytimes.com/2016/11/07/business/media/medias-next-challenge-overcoming-the-threat-of-fake-news.html
196 http://www.nytimes.com/2016/11/07/business/media/medias-next-challenge-overcoming-the-threat-of-fake-news.html

198 George H. W. Bush, Republican National Convention speech, 1988, August 18, 1988. Speechwriter: Peggy Noonan.

199 http://www.nytimes.com/2016/11/21/us/wisconsin-redistricting-found-to-unfairly-favor-republicans.html?_r=0

Chapter 11: Public Funding of Elections

200 https://www.techdirt.com/articles/20130313/02101422307/how-much-does-it-cost-to-win-election-to-congress.shtml

201 https://www.techdirt.com/articles/20130313/02101422307/how-much-does-it-cost-to-win-election-to-congress.shtml

202 New York Times, A1, Nov. 2008, "For Capital's Lobbyists, No Downturn, Just a Turnover"

203 New York Times, A1, Nov. 2008, "For Capital's Lobbyists, No Downturn, Just a Turnover"

204 The News Hour, 2006 posting.

205 http://www.opensecrets.org/527s/index.php

206 New York Times, A1, Dec. 22 2008, "In Steven's Fall, a Pipeline For Lobbyists Is Shut Off," A1

207 Broken Government, John Dean, pgs. 45-50

208 Broken Government, John Dean, pgs. 45-50

209 Broken Government, John Dean, pgs. 45-50

210 Clients' Rewards Keep K Street Lobbyists Thriving, Jeffrey H. Birnbaum, Washington Post

211 New York Times, "Firms That Got Bailout Money Keep Lobbying, "by David D. Kirkpatrick and Charlie Savage, p. 1, Jan. 24, 2009

212 Washingtonpost.com, "The Road to Riches is Called K Street." Jeffrey Birnbaum, June 22, 2006.

213 New York Times, In Transition Tangle of Ties to Lobbying, David Kirkpatrick, p. 1, Nov. 15, 2008

214 https://www.techdirt.com/articles/20130313/02101422307/how-much-does-it-cost-to-win-election-to-congress.shtml

215 New York Time, editorial, "An Even More Dysfunctional F.E.C." Jan. 20, 2009, A32

Chapter 12: Garbage

216 Oxford American Dictionary, Heald Colleges Edition

217 Sailing The Seas Of Trash, Vast Area Of Pacific Ocean Polluted With Plastic. REDONDO BEACH, Calif., Jan. 6, 2004, CBS News Report, Katie Couric, Jan. 6, 2008

218 U.S. Environmental Protection Agency website
   http://www.epa.gov/osw/nonhaz/municipal/index.htm

219 New York Times, A1-33, Nov. ?, In Mayor's Plan, The Plastic Bag Will Carry a Fee, David W. Chen (weekend)

220 The Center for Arms Control and Non-Proliferation,
   http://armscontrolcenter.org/policy/nonproliferation/

221 United Nations, Secretary-General SG/SM/10466, text of UN Secretary-General Kofi Annan's address at the University of Tokyo, May 18, 2006,
   http://www.un.org/News/Press/docs/2006/sgsm10466.doc.htm

222 The Heritage Foundation, March 23, 2006, Assessing "Rights" Under the Nuclear Non-Proliferation Treaty by Baker Spring, Heritage Lecture #930,
   http://www.heritage.org/Research/NationalSecurity/hl930.cfm

223 Congressional Research Service, CRS Report for Congress, Received through the CRS Web Order Code RL32857, "The Nuclear Nonproliferation Treaty Review, Conference: Issues for Congress," May 16, 2005, by Sharon Squassoni, Specialist in National Defense, Foreign Affairs, Defense, and Trade Division, Carl E. Behrens, Specialist in Energy Policy, Resources, Science, and Industry Division, The Nuclear Nonproliferation Treaty Review, Conference: Issues for Congress
   https://www.policyarchive.org/bitstream/handle/10207/2393/RL32857_20050516.pdf?sequence=2

224 https://www.armscontrol.org/factsheets/Nuclearweaponswhohaswhat

225 Congressional Research Service, The Library of Congress, CRS Report for Congress, Order Code RL32595, Nuclear Terrorism: A Brief Review of Threats and Responses, September 22, 2004, Jonathan Medalia, Specialist in National Defense Foreign Affairs, Defense, and Trade Division,

Nuclear Terrorism: A Brief Review of Threats and Responses
226 https://www.armscontrol.org/factsheets/Nuclearweaponswhohaswhat
227 Foreign Affair, "Stopping Nuclear Terrorism: The Dangerous Allure of a Perfect Defense," Michael Levi, Foreign%20Affairs%20-%20Stopping%20Nuclear%20Terrorism.html

Chapter 14: Government Debt

228 http://www.statista.com/statistics/216998/forecast-of-the-federal-debt-of-the-united-states/
229 http://www.wsj.com/articles/BL-REB-30486
230 http://useconomy.about.com/od/usdebtanddeficit/a/National-Debt-by-Year.htm
231 http://useconomy.about.com/od/usdebtanddeficit/a/National-Debt-by-Year.htm
232 http://www.usgovernmentdebt.us/debt_deficit_history
233 http://www.afcea.org/content/?q=price-life-united-states-1946-vs-2006,
234 http://www.afcea.org/content/?q=price-life-united-states-1946-vs-2006#sthash.ei4fhODw.dpuf
235 http://useconomy.about.com/od/usdebtanddeficit/a/National-Debt-by-Year.htm
236 https://www.thebalance.com/national-debt-by-year-compared-to-gdp-and-major-events-3306287
237 http://useconomy.about.com/od/usdebtanddeficit/a/National-Debt-by-Year.htm
238 http://www.usgovernmentspending.com/federal_budget_interest
239 https://www.cbo.gov/publication/45684
240 https://www.nationalpriorities.org/budget-basics/federal-budget-101/spending/
241 http://www.brookings.edu/research/opinions/2015/04/08-federal-debt-worse-than-you-think-haskins
242 http://www.justfacts.com/nationaldebt.asp#f45
243 http://www.brookings.edu/research/opinions/2015/04/08-federal-debt-worse-than-you-think-haskins
244 http://www.usnews.com/opinion/mzuckerman/articles/2013/12/13/its-time-to-deal-with-our-national-debt-and-budget-deficit
245 http://www.usnews.com/opinion/mzuckerman/articles/2013/12/13/its-time-to-deal-with-our-national-debt-and-budget-deficit
246 http://www.wsj.com/articles/BL-REB-30486
247 https://www.washingtonpost.com/opinions/robert-samuelson-the-true-national-debt/2013/02/24/1a133c78-7eac-11e2-a350-49866afab584_story.html
248 http://www.justfacts.com/nationaldebt.asp
249 http://www.justfacts.com/nationaldebt.asp

250 https://mobile.nytimes.com/2017/04/17/us/politics/tax-code-overhaul-trump.amp.html

Chapter 15: The Scourge of Drugs

251 https://www.drugabuse.gov/publications/drugfacts/nationwide-trends

http://humansarefree.com/2014/02/drugging-america-19-statistics-almost.html
252 https://www.drugabuse.gov/publications/drugfacts/marijuana

253 http://www.drugwarfacts.org/cms/Drug_Usage#sthash.MV9pFnsS.dpbs
254 (HHS Publication No. SMA 15-4927, NSDUH Series H-50), p. 1.)

255 (http://www.drugfreeworld.org/drugfacts/crystalmeth/a-worldwide-epidemic-of-addiction.html)
256 https://www.rt.com/news/169024-un-report-afghanistan-opium/

257 http://www.usnews.com/news/blogs/data-mine/2015/08/19/the-heroin-epidemic-in-9-graphs

258 http://www.usnews.com/news/blogs/data-mine/2015/08/19/the-heroin-epidemic-in-9-graphs
259 https://www.bop.gov/about/statistics/statistics_inmate_offenses.jsp
260 http://thinkprogress.org/justice/2013/01/02/1386251/almost-half-of-federal-prisoners-held-for-drug-crimes/,
http://www.bjs.gov/content/pub/pdf/p11.pdf
261 http://www.columbia.edu/cu/record/archives/vol20/vol20_iss10/record2010.24.html

Chapter 16: Education

262 New York Times editorial, A38, Oct. 29, 2008, "Numbers Game"
263 PBS New Hour, School In New Orleans Report, Feb. 3, 2009
264 Parentstv.org, http://www.parenstv.org/ptc/facts/mediafact.asp
265 SoundVision.com, http://www.soundvision.com/info/misc/tvturnoff.asp

266 Parentstv.org, http://www.parenstv.org/ptc/facts/mediafact.asp

267 A.C. Nielsen Co., http://www.csun.edu/science/health/docs/tv&health.html

268 http://www.simpletoremember.com/articles/a/television-awash-in-sex-study-says/

269 Teen Drug Abuse, http://www.teendrugabuse.us/teen_drug_use.html

270 Policy Study No. 234, January 1998, School Violence Prevention: Strategies to Keep Schools Safe (Unabridged) by Alexander Volokh with Lisa Snell, http://www.reason.org/ps234.html

271 http://www.nytimes.com/2013/08/24/nyregion/citys-annual-cost-per-inmate-is-nearly-168000-study-says.html, https://www.google.com/#q=average+cost+per+prisoner+in+united+states

272 http://www.nytimes.com/2013/08/24/nyregion/citys-annual-cost-per-inmate-is-nearly-168000-study-says.html, https://www.google.com/#q=average+cost+per+prisoner+in+united+states

273 http://www.northsidecenter.org/

274 http://www.smithsonianmag.com/innovation/why-are-finlands-schools-successful-49859555/

275 New York Times editorial, A38, Oct. 29, 2008, "Numbers Game"

Chapter 17: The Fine Arts

276 http://www.infoplease.com/askeds/number-us-public-schools.html, https://nces.ed.gov/ccd/pub_overview.asp

277 New York Times, "Study Finds Instruction in Art Lags in 8th Grade," Sam Dillon, A12, June 16, 2009

278 San Francisco Chronicle, http://www.sfgate.com/cgi-bin/article.cgi?f=/c/a/2002/05/15/DD200607.DTL

279 Wallace Foundation, Wallace,%20arts.html http://www.wallacefoundation.org/KnowledgeCenter/KnowledgeTopics/CurrentAreasofFocus/Arts Participation/Pages/cultivating-demand-for-the-arts.aspx?WT.mc_id=artslearningcampaign

280 Wallace Foundation, Wallace,%20arts.html

281 http://www.bos.frb.org/economic/nerr/rr2003/q2/requiem.htm

282 New York Times, Decline in Listeners Worries Orchestras, June 25, 2005 http://www.nytimes.com/2005/06/25/arts/music/25ravi.html

283 enewschannels.com

284 http://www.americansforthearts.org/public_awareness/artsed_facts/001.asp

285 http://www.americansforthearts.org/public_awareness/artsed_facts/001.asp

286 http://www.usgovernmentspending.com/year_spending_2015USbn_15bs2n#usgs302

287 http://www.unionps.org/youtharts/

288 http://www.geohive.com/earth/his_history3.aspx

Chapter 18: Population Growth

289 http://www.google.com/url?q=https://en.wikipedia.org/wiki/World_population&sa=U&ved=0ahUKE wiZsNXRlvbPAhXDQSYKHQmUATMQFggcMAI&sig2=4GIszYRUWLg4Ki17EyvJjg&usg=AF QjCNGVzoPI4n-tD8nINTKk_xejNIFxOQ

290 http://www.geohive.com/earth/his_history3.aspx

291 https://fusiontables.google.com/DataSource?dsrcid=225439#rows:id=1

292 http://www.worldometers.info/world-population/us-population/

293 http://www.census.gov/content/dam/Census/library/publications/2015/demo/p25-1143.pdf?

294 http://travel.cnn.com/shanghai/life/china-infographic-see-chinas-auto-demand-1980-2020-869635/

295 http://www.greenpeace.org/usa/forests/amazon-rainforest/

296 http://www.npg.org/library/press-releases/pr-10042016.html

297 http://blogs.wsj.com/economics/2016/04/07/the-new-magic-number-for-monthly-job-growth-145000/

298 http://cepr.net/blogs/beat-the-press/we-need-90000-jobs-per-month-to-keep-pace-with-the-growth-of-the-population

299 https://cleantechnica.com/2016/04/18/why-is-china-still-building-new-coal-plants/

300 https://www.populationinstitute.org/newsroom/press/view/20/

Chapter 19: The Bully Pulpit

301 Speech before Congress, JFK%20Man%20on%20the%20moon-.html

302 Presidential speech archives, AMERICA%20On%20The%20BRINK%2012-
13/XX%20RESEARCH%20FILE/xx%20DONE%20RESEARCH/fireside%20-ALL!.html
303 ADDRESS OF THE PRESIDENT RADIO FROM THE WHITE HOUSE, March 12, 1933,
AMERICA%20On%20The%20BRINK%201213/XX%20RESEARCH%20FILE/xx%20DONE%2
0RESEARCH/fireside%20Chat1%203-12-33.html
304 FDR Fireside Chat, "On Sacrifice," April 28, 1942
http://millercenter.org/scripps/archive/speeches/detail/3327

Chapter 20: Lotteries & Taxes

305 http://www.theatlantic.com/business/archive/2015/05/lotteries-americas-70-billion-shame/392870/
306 http://www.worldcasinodirectory.com/american-casinos.asp#CASINOLIST